Pieces of Me

A Life-in-Progress

RÓISÍN INGLE

HODDER
HEADLINE
IRELAND

Columns and articles reproduced with kind permission of *The Irish Times*

First published in book form in 2005 by
Hodder Headline Ireland
8 Ca[illegible] Castleknock, Dublin 15, Ireland

A CIP catal[illegible]tish Library.

ISBN 0340 83918 X

Typeset in MT Sabon by Hodder Headline Ireland
Printed and bound in Great Britain by Clays Ltd, St Ives plc
Hodder Headline's policy is to use papers that are natural, renewable and recyclable products and made from wood grown in sustainable forests. The logging and manufacturing processes are expected to conform to the environmental regulations of the country of origin.

Cover design by Anú Design, Tara
Inside illustrations by Amanda Brady
Author photography courtesy of Alan Betson/*The Irish Times*

Hodder Headline Ireland
A division of Hodder Headline
338 Euston Road, London NW1 3BH

www.hhireland.ie

For Ann and Peter Ingle

'The greatest thing you'll ever learn
is just to love and be loved in return'

(from 'Nature Boy' by Eden Ahbez)

Introduction

I didn't have to do this. I could have just typed "hope you enjoy this book" and gone back to lying on the sofa with my boyfriend and a hefty slice of his divine homemade walnut and banana loaf. This book is already packed with columns I wrote in *The Irish Times Magazine* over the past three years. It could quite reasonably have been argued that there wasn't room for anything else.

But after much consideration and wrestling with my inner lazy child, I decided now would be as good a chance as any to answer some of the questions readers regularly ask about my weekly outpourings and put my life, as glimpsed through these columns, in context.

One of the most frequently asked questions concerns whether my family are ever embarrassed because of the deeply personal nature of some of my writing. You'd have to ask them, but yes, I suspect they sometimes sigh deeply to themselves, shake their heads and ask, "Couldn't she just go to a counsellor like normal people do?"

Regular readers are also interested in whether my boyfriend, Jonny, is really the saint that I regularly make him out to be with his baking, cleaning and ironing fetishes. And he is, I suppose, but that doesn't mean his halo hasn't been known to slip.

They also want to know whether everything I write about is true. And, apart from those times when I try to protect the identity of certain acquaintances by altering a few facts, everything is true. Ask my mother if you don't believe me.

But the question I am asked more than any other is: "How did you end up writing the column?" I sometimes wonder about that myself.

It wasn't supposed to last three years. It wasn't even supposed to last three months. In May 2002 I was asked to write "a few columns" for *The Irish Times Magazine* while they found somebody suitable to replace the respected journalist and author Nuala O'Faolain. I agreed mainly because they said I'd only have to do a total of three. Three I could handle. We weren't talking about years you see. We were talking about weeks.

When they offered me the chance to become a regular columnist, I was a bit reluctant. The column I was to take over was called 'Regarding Ireland', a prime slot full of intelligent analysis and deep insight into the significant issues of the day. I am not ashamed to admit that the prospect of trying to attempt this task scared me witless. If they'd suddenly changed the title of the column to 'Regarding Reality Television' or 'Regarding Karaoke' I might have been slightly more enthusiastic – but only slightly.

As I considered the idea, I was gripped by the same kind of fear I felt on my first day in *The Irish Times*. Only a few years earlier I had been working on a local newspaper in Sandymount called *NewsFour*, writing exclusives about how I met The Hothouse Flowers at the ATM machine. The paper, which was part of a government-funded Community Employment Scheme, appeared four times a year and was a gentle introduction to the world of journalism. My friend Kim, who was then the photographer with *NewsFour*, wangled me a week of work experience in *The Sunday Tribune* and I kept turning up week after week until they eventually mistook me for a member of staff. After a couple of years in *The Sunday Tribune* (where I received journalism training from the best) and a brief spell in a new sports paper *The Title*, which is now *Ireland on Sunday*, I found myself in *The Irish Times* office needing to use the toilet very badly but scared to ask anyone where it was.

You know that feeling you sometimes get when you think this is the day you are going to be found out? I've had it nearly every day of my journalistic life. The prospect of being found out used to scare me silly but I got used to it, the way I imagine an actress gets used to her pre-performance nerves. Eventually you learn to make it work for you rather than against you. Some of my best work has been fuelled by the fear that it might turn out to be my worst.

You have to be realistic at the same time. After five years in the business, I knew my journalistic strengths but I was also intimate with my weaknesses. The latter list included, and still does, the grasping of complex political arguments, the analysing of historical events and the general ability to comment on society as a whole. "I don't know anything" I used to moan constantly to my best male friend Paul Howard, the eminently fanciable, award-winning sports journalist and bestselling author (he made me put all that in, obviously) who appears to have been born knowing an annoyingly large number of things.

It was obvious that even for three weeks 'Regarding Ireland' with me at the helm was never going to work. If I set myself up as a commentator on Irish affairs I'd be found out pretty quickly and probably never recover from the ignominy of mixing up tribunals, or some other inevitable gaffe. I needed another subject and I needed one yesterday. It took me about a millisecond to realise that if I was going to get away with it, my three columns would have to be all about me.

For the first few weeks, the editor left 'Regarding Ireland' at the top of the column but, in my mind, I am not ashamed to say that I replaced it with 'Regarding Róisín'. I sat down in my flat and I wrote about my attempt to train for the mini-marathon and the voluminous yellow Brazil jersey I had inexplicably purchased for the event. My mother was in America at the time and I remember emailing the finished column to her, sweating over every sentence, every carefully chosen word. "Is it OK, Mum? Is it OK?" A nervous refrain she would get used to over the next couple of weeks, the next couple of years.

I spent the following three Saturdays refusing to leave the house or answer the phone in case anybody mentioned the column to me. I should have been delighted for myself, chuffed that I'd been given a whole page in a national magazine. Instead I scolded myself for my self-indulgence. For my lack of a world, or even Irish, view that led me to take up valuable space in a magazine with personal trivia about cheap running socks and baggy football jerseys.

By week three ("Is it OK Mum? Is it OK?") all I could think was thank goodness it was nearly over so I could go back to being a reporter and occasional feature writer. But the people who decide these things decided to keep me on. I suppose I'm an accidental columnist .

It took a while for some readers to get used to the idea of me. I understand that, because it took a while for me to get used to it too.

There were people who didn't appreciate my weekly offerings at all. This e-mail sums up the view of some early critics: "Dear Editor, Please get rid of the flibbertigibbet on page three. Her plain, plump features and inane ramblings are driving me insane."

Little did he know I was the kind of person who never tires of *The Sound of Music* and as a result views flibbertigibbet as the best kind of compliment. I put it in a file named 'To Be Kept'. I knew it would come in handy one day.

The main reason I wanted to add some new writing to this book of columns is the knowledge of how irritated I'd be if I bought a book and it turned out every single word had been published in a newspaper before. The reader is therefore requested to view this section in the same way one regards the 'extras' on a DVD. They sometimes turn out to be a complete swizz but mostly they give you a bit more for your money, which is no bad thing especially in this Ireland of the hundred, thousand rip offs. Personally, I'm a big fan of bonus bits especially when you get a look behind the scenes and find out things like the blood in *Psycho* was really corn syrup. Fascinating stuff.

Speaking of what goes on behind the scenes, I was told recently about a sociological theory that suggests everyone has a front stage and a back stage. With apologies to the eminent academic who came up with it, I'd like to present my own understanding of this 'all the world's a stage' analogy.

As I see it, the front stage plays host to the smiling, charming, version of us. It's where we stand centre stage in front of life's footlights and give the best performance we possibly can. Meeting someone you haven't seen in ages, when you're looking as fabulous as it is possible to look without resorting to surgery, is a pretty memorable front-stage moment. You almost want to take a bow but you just smile instead.

Back stage is a different country and we do things differently there. This is where we let down our guard and relax the jaw that aches from too much smiling. It's where we loosen the belt, unplug the hair straighteners and set that frizzy cow's lick free. With only our neuroses and bad habits for company, we give vent to our worst personality traits. The beauty of behind-the-scenes life is that there is nobody else around to see what goes on. Most of the time anyway. When you are still wearing your pyjamas at 6 p.m. and have red wine stains around your mouth and you open the door to the nice woman who delivers your organic vegetables, it's only natural that you'll forget your lines and be struck by a bad case of stage fright. It's not something I'd recommend. When I was told about this theory, it struck me that what I have done with my column is brought my back-stage life to the front of the stage. Those parts that the theory dictates I should be hiding – the self-esteem issues, the laziness, the domestic ineptitude, the overeating, the reality-television addiction – I put all of that out there for inspection. In fairness, I had no choice if I was going to try and sustain a weekly column. I knew I couldn't set myself up as an expert commentator on economic issues, on the state of the nation, on politics or on poverty. But if there was one thing I could pontificate on with authority it was me.

Sometimes when you get close enough to someone to be given access to their back-stage area, you are so appalled at what goes on there that you exit stage left quicker than you can say 'what a dirty nose picker'. But sometimes it can be liberating and, like Dorothy in *The Wizard of Oz,* you are grateful for the chance to find out exactly who is lurking behind the curtain. Allow me to offer you a back-stage pass. It's Access (Almost) All Areas because, let's face it, there are some things you just do not want to know.

I grew up in Sandymount, Dublin across the road from a park, around the corner from the strand and two doors down from the best chipper in the world. We lived in a white house on the Green. The key was in the door all day and the dinner was on the table at exactly 6 p.m.

There were eight of us children and there was my mother, Ann, who made delicious meals with not very much money. She made, among other delights, meatloaf, chicken curry and rabbit pie. When I was three years old, my mother taught me to read using flashcards. Whatever else I would later loathe about school, I always loved reading and English. From an early age I could lose myself totally in the pages of a book. I still do.

As well as my brothers and sisters and my mother, there was my father too but my memories of him are hazy, like scenes from an old movie that nobody has yet bothered to digitally remaster. I know from stories my mother tells that my father loved gambling, drinking, socialising and singing. I grew up loving the same things. Unfortunately, my father and I never got a chance to talk about our shared hobbies because, when I was eight years old, he died.

My primary school was Scoil Mhuire, Lakelands, and was located a short walk from the house. Early school reports record how gloomy I was. But I do have some good memories. Singing 'A Frog Went A Courtin'' with Miss Price in infants. Learning joined-up writing with Miss Daly in sixth class. Why is Róisín so miserable? The head teacher Sr Dolores would write home to my mother. By all accounts I was a living nursery rhyme: when I was good, I was very, very good but when I was bad, I was horrid.

Like most of the schools in this country Lakelands was a Catholic institution but, for various reasons, I never had time for religion. I remember being outraged at the invasion of privacy masquerading as the sacrament of confession. I always questioned the automatic acceptance of the rules of the Catholic Church. Luckily at home, we had a brilliant relationship with the local Sisters of Charity. The living, loving saint Sister Agnes Philomena gave us money, second-hand toys and clothes. The family put on a play for her and the other sisters every Christmas. At home there was never any pressure to go to mass or pretend to care about religion when I so obviously did not.

In subsequent years, I would become outwardly hostile towards the Catholic Church, though I have mellowed slightly in recent years. I trace this hostility back to an experience I had in sixth class when the parish priest came on one of his regular visits. I can see him now, leaning on a desk, relishing the entertainment he was about to provide to a bunch of impressionable 11 year olds.

The priest told us all about the confessional and the kind of sins he had heard there. "But," he said smiling, "there is one sin I have never heard. I want you guess what that is."

I love quizzes. Still do. But this was one quiz the priest didn't want anybody to win. "Murder," said someone as we all gasped at her audacity. "I've heard that," he replied, cool as an ecclesiastical cucumber. The game continued for around ten minutes. Various pathetic sins were called out and each time our holy quizmaster shook his head. I was convinced I had the answer. I knew that, even if they were thinking it, none of the other girls would have had the guts to say what I was about to say. I raised my hand. "Yes?" said the priest. "Abortion," I said, colour flooding my cheeks. He paused and scrutinised me, head cocked to one side. "I have heard that too, child," he said. I sunk back in my chair defeated waiting for the answer to come.

There was a long and dramatic pause. "The only sin I have never heard is a really serious one, a mortal sin, and that is the sin of suicide, the taking of one's own life. For reasons that should be obvious to you, nobody has ever confessed that to me."

The priest was triumphant. I wanted to kill him, but I didn't, obviously. What I did was laugh nervously along with everyone else.

It is September 1980. I am eight years old. I sleep in a narrow room with chipboard walls next to my parents. You have to walk through their bedroom to get to mine where I share bunkbeds with my sister Rachael. I don't sleep that particular night. I can't seem to settle. I go into my mother's room thinking to snuggle up with her and Daddy, but he isn't there and my mother seems concerned. It is late. "When is Daddy coming home?" I ask her. She doesn't know.

I sleep. I am woken in the morning. One of my older sisters is telling me something has happened. "We mustn't look out of the window," I hear someone say. "Whatever you do, don't look out of the window." She wakes me, and I ask her to confirm something which sounds absurd even as I say it. "Daddy's dead. He's dead, isn't he?" It is more of a statement than a question. She says, "Who told you Daddy is dead?" and I say I just knew.

Downstairs is full of people. Nuns and neighbours and nosey parkers. There is one policeman who looks kindly at me and another one who can't meet my eye. The people all have red eyes and white faces and keep saying things like, "He is gone to heaven", as though it makes any kind of difference where he has gone. He's just gone. That's all. I am told I can miss school if I want. Normally this would be cause for celebration. There would be a race down the road to the chocolate factory to forage for defective seaside rock, the kind that has a misspelt seaside town running all the way through it. But today I go to school desperate to escape the abnormality at home. The tragic eyes of the sympathetic callers, the dead weight of their stooping shoulders. Normally I love a fuss, a dramatic occasion, but this one leaves me cold. I feel as though I am looking down on everyone, I can see them and hear them, but none of it is real. I pack my schoolbag and walk to Lakelands singing to myself all the way along Durham Road until I see the school gates. Usually a source of annoyance, today they represent sanctuary. Safe at last.

When I get there everything is normal. I feel relieved.

An assembly is called, another welcome distraction. I stand in the circle with the rest of the school grateful for the order that has descended, glad to be away from the disorder at home. Prayers are said. We pray for the departed soul of Peter Ingle, Róisín Ingle's father. We pray for Róisín and her family. Disorder now. Everyone looking. I feel anger bubble up inside me. Why didn't anyone ask if I wanted them to pray for my father? Why is this happening? Which one of you imagined that I would want your prayers?

Dozens of pitying eyes swivel in my direction. A teacher places a hand on my shoulder. A voice asks if I want to go home. "No," I say, not crying, not anything. After assembly a girl comes up to me and says she is sorry. "Why? Did you kill him?" I ask her. The hurt in her eyes is like a victory to me. Punishment for her invasion and for them not leaving me alone. I leave school early. Escaping again. Miss Roddy in the local shop gives me a free bag of penny sweets. People are nicer to me than usual. The house is packed with people I don't recognise saying things I don't understand. What I do understand immediately without it being said is that in this new post-Daddy climate, I can do anything I want. Nobody will give out to me. Nobody will mind. But all I want is the bit of peace and quiet that I know is not going to come. I can hear my little brother Michael crying in the front room. He is standing by the fireplace my Daddy built, stone by stone, before he got sick.

A sweet memory interrupts the sound of Michael's howling. One time when Daddy came back from the hospital he knocked on the front door and when I opened it I shouted, "Mammy, there is a man at the door." I didn't know who he was, this big bearded man offering me a fizzle stick. But he was my Daddy. Everyone laughed and told me he was my Daddy. I laughed then too and took his hand and led him into the front room. Now in the front room Michael is screaming and roaring. I think to myself that if Daddy was here he would shout, "Give over, Michael", and Michael would shut up straight away. But nobody tells him to shut up. He can do anything he wants now – we all can. Michael is gulping and sobbing so hard he can't breathe properly. After a while he calms down enough to ask me something. "Do you know how our Daddy died?" he asks, his red face all indignant. I tell him what I have been told and what I haven't been moved to question further. He was sick and then he died. "No," shouts Michael, defiant now, his little blond head shaking from side to side, "that's not true."

He spills it out. That ugly thing he has heard. He was outside when a boy his own age, a boy passing on a bike, taunted him with the news he is telling me now. He can't wait to get the words out. It's like he desperately needs someone else to know. "It's not true," I say to my mother who is sitting on the settee beside me. "Tell him it's not true." "It is," she says with a sadness that seems to crush her. "It's true."

The boy on the bike had the story right. My father had killed himself. He suffered for five years with Schizophrenia, a mental illness which, after it had been treated with electric-shock therapy and a cocktail of pills, robbed him of his personality. I didn't know him very well but I know this much: Peter Ingle was not born to sit in zombie mode in front of a television set or nurse a few quiet pints in Sandymount House before ambling home at closing time. Every single day for the last six months of his life, he would tell my mother that she and the rest of us would be better off without him. Without this version of him anyway. Every single day, loving him whether he was mad or sane or numb to everything, my mother told him not to be so silly. Of course we needed him. Of course we did.

He was a carouser. A crooner. A gambler. A charmer. His dedication to the above roles meant he wasn't always a good husband or a good father. Before he got sick, he was wildly irresponsible with finances to the point where he once stole my sister's confirmation money so he could go out drinking. He was also wildly irresponsible when it came to work, leaving his taxi illegally parked for a couple of days if one of his passengers told him there was a party going on. Call him irresponsible and he'd probably sing you a few bars of the song. Maybe you'd smile and maybe you wouldn't. It depended if he'd just found all the money you'd managed to hide from him under the lino in the kitchen leaving you with eight mouths to feed.

Before he got sick there were days my mother had to keep one of us away from school to make sure he went to collect and bring home the dole money. I remember one day, when it was my turn to be a mini-security guard, he took me for a towering knickerbocker glory ice-cream sundae. I remember the smell of hops from the pub as we walked home. I remember him on his way out the door smiling as he explained he was going to see a man about a dog, a euphemism for the Shelbourne Greyhound track over the Ringsend Bridge.

That's about as far as my memories stretch. He got sick and spent most of his last four years in various psychiatric units in Dublin. Then one night he wrote a note. He believed we'd be better off without him. And maybe we were.

I was taken to see my father laid out all in white in the funeral parlour. After his death, my mother had donated his eyes to medical science. I remember staring at his eyelids and wondering what the space where his eyes had been a few days ago would look like. I stood and stared and felt nothing for him, this stranger in a shroud.

At eight years old I didn't understand what he had done. I didn't understand anything. The best thing about the funeral was that we got to be minded by the Borzas in their sitting room at the back of their chip shop. They brought us huge plates of fish and chips and we could have as much as we liked.

The eldest of the eight of us children was 17 and the youngest barely two years old when my father died. People say to me, "Your mother must be a wonderful woman." I say, "Yes, she is", but that doesn't do her any kind of justice. She was 41, she had eight children and her husband had grown virtually unrecognisable from the handsome fellow with the sparkling smile she had fallen in love with. He once had a singing voice to charm birds from trees and other birds from certain London hostelries. He charmed my mother in Newquay, Cornwall, in the 1950s when she was pretending to be a beatnik and he was doing what he always did best, just being himself.

Last January I took my mother to stay in the Culloden Hotel just outside Belfast. I wanted to ask her more about Daddy and his illness and what life had been like for our family then. I felt I needed to know more. I felt I wanted to know. Before I began writing this introduction, it hadn't seemed important but as I began to frame in my mind what I wanted to say, it began to mean everything.

Sometimes during those hours of conversation beside the swimming pool, over dinner or lying exhausted on our twin beds she told me things so shocking and moving about my family history that I stared at her open mouthed. "Why have you never told me this before?" I asked her more than once. "You never asked," she replied. There was no answer to that.

Mother never hid anything from us about what happened to Daddy but that weekend away in Belfast was the first time I had actually asked any probing questions. She brought a suitcase of letters and documents with her to the hotel, taking me through her marriage in 1961 right up to those first months in the mid-1970s when he began to get ill. As a young girl I was oblivious to his illness but what she told me made me ache with sadness for her and for the older members of my family who had had to live with it all.

With the pure generosity of spirit that is probably the thing I love most about her, my mother presented her life to me in a suitcase and it was a privilege to go through it all. Among the love notes and personal memos were many medical documents and prescriptions along with letters to and from doctors. One small publication featured an explanation of Schizophrenia and pinpointed Daddy's symptoms. It is important for me and for the many people who suffer with Schizophrenia and their families that I include this explanation of the disease here.

SCHIZOPHRENIA

To find a suitable name for an illness with so many facets was naturally a difficult problem. The original name "dementia praecox" (early madness) has long been discarded. Schizophrenia (splitting of mind) is compounded of two Greek words. Unfortunately it can easily be misunderstood as pointing to the "split mind" or "double personality" which is a rare but well-known form of hysteria exemplified by Dr Jekyll and Mr Hyde; this has nothing to do with Schizophrenia. The term "schizophrenia" was nevertheless adopted because it does suggest the splitting or internal disturbances, distortions and cleavages which in various ways develop within the sufferer's thought processes, feelings and perceptions, drastically influence his conduct, cause him to make a kind of withdrawal from the outside world.

This withdrawal can take various forms which may be exhibited at different times by the same person over a long period. One classification is as follows:

"The Paranoid Type" comes on later than others

usually after thirty. It is characterised by unrealistic, illogical thinking and above all by the presence of major delusions. The sufferer may feel that he is being watched, talked about, plotted against, persecuted by specific or unknown persons. "Voices" are heard, hostile and tormenting. The patient's attitude, linked with his delusions, is frequently hostile and aggressive. There may also be delusions of grandeur; the sufferer is some great person such as the Shah of Persia, Napoleon or Einstein. Nevertheless, in paranoid schizophrenia the personality as a whole may remain relatively well preserved for a considerable time.

I was four when Daddy got sick. My mother told me that the doctors had thought he was an alcoholic at first. They only diagnosed Schizophrenia after the voices in his head grew more insistent and started telling him he was Jesus and that to save the world he had to kill himself, my mother and us children. Once when he was lashing out with a knife in the front room she, and two friends who had called around unexpectedly at a particularly opportune time, sat on a coffee table with him underneath until help arrived. My mother saved my father that day, knowing well she might not be able to save him all the other days of his life. And she was right.

He needed to die, he would tell her often, especially when his delusions were at their worst. "Don't be silly Peter," she'd say giving him the medication that would dull him, turn him into a blob in the armchair where he would doze off in front of the racing and shout "Don't touch that" if we tried to change the channel.

He left a note that night on one of those early-learning Ladybird books. It was one that featured Peter and Jane. He might not have noticed at the time but he wrote the note on the page where 'I like Peter' was printed in easy-to-read lettering. "I loved you the best, Ann. I can't stick it no more, forgive me. God Bless you and all the children, Peter." As he wrote his biro must have died and there is a doodle where he tried to resuscitate the pen. The doodle is in the shape of an eight and I like to think he saw that. A final goodbye written next to a frustrated eight, the number on the door of the house, the number of children he was leaving behind, the age I was when he decided to go.

My mother views his suicide as a gift from him to us. She says it was the only gift he had to give. Those who believe these things say Jesus died to save the world. She says Daddy died to save us too. I can't help wondering what our former parish priest would have made of that.

I've been thinking lately about how his death affected me. It may sound strange but it's not something I've thought much about before. For years I used his death only as a way to shock. I don't remember making a decision not to care that my father had killed himself but I must have because I derived genuine pleasure from the horrified look on people's faces when I told them how he had died. I delighted in their confusion when I would describe the tree in the back garden. The branch where we used to hang a tyre swing. The gnarled rope I found that day, resting innocently on the washing machine. These were just macabre details. They didn't move me at all.

I don't know how else to explain it. I never felt comfortable in my own skin. I walked around with this feeling, rarely articulated or really understood, that I was in the wrong body, in the wrong time, in the wrong place. I felt a lot of shame. It doesn't make sense now, when I can understand that a small child has nothing to be ashamed of. Whether I developed this sense of being a bad person, a different person, a strange person later or whether it was nurtured by life experience, I can't say. I just always felt like the odd one out.

The illness and eventual death of my father confirmed this feeling. Nobody else I knew had a father with a mental illness. Nobody else I knew had a father who would go away for weeks on end and come back a different person, a person I didn't even recognise, never mind love. Normal fathers didn't go out to the back garden and make sinister dead places out of an innocent apple tree. I was different. And not in a good way. This was established from an early age.

There was another incident that confirmed it. One summer a few years after my father died, my mother rented a caravan in Fanore in the West of Ireland. My brothers Michael and Peter and I filled our days playing swingball and swimming in the sea. There was one weekend when a family friend came down to spend a few days with us.

The sun was setting slowly as we all sat drinking tea and laughing in the caravan. I can still remember how I felt. The simple joy of it. Somehow it wasn't enough. I decided I wanted to go swimming. I wanted to be in the Atlantic Ocean, battling with giant waves, playing wargames with the jellyfish, just being free. Darkness was creeping in around us but that didn't deter me from my mission.

The family friend didn't want to go swimming that night. He said that he was tired after the long drive from Dublin. He said the sea would be too rough. He said that instead we'd go first thing in the morning. Finally, after my pleas grew louder and my whining voice had risen to a pitch that would set on edge the teeth of the most patient person, he presented a compromise to me. He said if I ran down to the water's edge and looked at the conditions, and if I saw it was calm enough then, and only then, would we go.

The beach was a few minutes away. I left the caravan and stood for five minutes behind it, crouched out of view of the adults, instead of wasting valuable swimming time going down to the shore. I didn't care whether the sea was rough.

It didn't matter. All I wanted was to top off this perfect evening with a water-based adventure. So I didn't do what I'd been asked to do. I waited five minutes and came back into the caravan and shouted in the door, "It's lovely. Let's go." And that is what we did.

My little brother Michael came too. By now it was cold and drizzling and the waves on the shore towered magnificently, the surf like an expensive bubble bath tempting all true adventurers to dive right in. Michael, at nine years old, examined the waves and decided he would just watch us instead. It was one of the wisest decisions he ever made.

But we went swimming. And it was fun at first. I always used to play this game with the waves where I would go right up to them, just at the point when they collapsed into themselves. Then I'd be sucked under and spat out again by the force of the water. It was exhilarating normally. But not this night.

This night, when I was sucked under, the waves were not so quick to spit me out. Our friend had swum out further than me and within a few minutes was just a black dot on the horizon. As I bobbed out of my depth I saw him waving and shouting at me. I see now that he was calling a warning.

I remember the feeling of going under and holding my breath until, it seemed like hours later, I surfaced again. I'd try to gulp in the air but before I could manage even half a breath I'd go under. I took in mouthfuls of water when what I needed was air. For the first time, the roar of the Atlantic seemed menacing. I believed then with certainty that I was going to die.

I still don't understand why or how I didn't. The terrible pattern repeated itself over and over and all I could do when I went under each time was stick my feet down as far as they would go and say to myself, if I feel the sand I will be all right. I will be safe then. I just need to feel the sand.

When I went down for what I believe would have been the final time I suddenly felt the salvation of wet ground between my toes. I scrambled then, desperate, scared, half dead already. I finally burst onto the shore gasping and sobbing and trying to breathe. When I opened my eyes Michael was shivering and pointing out to sea at the place where our friend should have been. The horizon was clear. He wasn't there.

There was a man on the shore who had seen everything. He said, "Don't you worry, he is probably back in the caravan having a cup of tea." I didn't believe him. Later people we didn't know came in and out of the caravan. A policeman. The man who ran the site. People from the other caravans. I sat there staring out of the window at the lashing rain, ignoring requests that I please drink a cup of sugar-laden tea. For the shock, they said, you'll feel better, they said. "He will come back," said a woman. "He's probably playing a little trick on you." But nobody would play a trick as mean as this one. It didn't make sense.

There was a Police song, 'Spread a Little Happiness', that was never off the radio at the time. I sat and sang it to myself all that night and all the way home on the train to Dublin.

Even when the darkest clouds are in the sky
You mustn't sigh and you mustn't cry
Spread a little happiness as you go by
Please try.

I didn't think the song would make any difference but for a while those words somehow held me together. A few days later when the body had been found crashed against rocks, the drowned man's mother called our house. She asked to speak to me. When I picked up the phone, she wanted to know why we had gone swimming. "I don't understand. It was late. The weather was not good," she said. I dropped the phone and called for my mother. I didn't want to tell the woman on the phone that her son had gone swimming, that her son had drowned, that her son had gone away forever because of me.

He was only 33 and I had killed him. At least that's the way I framed it in my 11-year-old head. Before it could consume me, I buried the familiar shame, swallowing it down like one of those nasty spoons of medicine my mother kept in the bathroom cabinet. A neighbour asked me to join the local swimming team after that. Said I must be a strong swimmer to have survived when my friend had not. Sometimes I wished it had been me that had been washed away. For a long time, the guilt of this experience bubbled away under the surface waters of my life.

I was a difficult child and I became a difficult teenager. Growing up I caused my mother more trouble than any of her other children. I was secretive. I rejected intimacy. I bullied my little brother Michael until he grew strong enough to physically overpower me. And I terrorised my family. After another meal I'd refused to eat preferring the delights of the chipper was splattered on the wall and one too many doors had been slammed until our old house shook, I was taken to a family counsellor. My mother and my brothers and sisters sat around in a circle talking about the disturbance I was causing in the home. But I was too far gone for their concern to make any noticeable difference.

At secondary school, while I had a deep respect for one or two teachers, I messed my way through classes on those days when I bothered to turn up. I used the fact that my father had killed himself as a way to distract attention from my rebellious behaviour. Or maybe my rebellious behaviour was some kind of reaction to the fact that my father killed himself. I don't know. I just know that there were times I would ask teachers for lunch money, begging I suppose is the technical term, knowing that their sympathy for me would have them reaching into their purses for coins before I had even finished the sentence.

A dead father guaranteed a sympathy vote. A dead father who committed suicide was like gold if you wanted to get away with things. I've never been very good with authority anyway. My report from religion class read: *Róisín contributes but always aggressively.* I didn't accept truths just because they were uttered by someone older than me. What does age have to do with it? Respect had to be earned in my world or respect would not be given.

I was convinced pitying glances followed me through school when, in truth, few people would have known there was a reason I should be pitied. When it suited me I would play the dead-daddy card. Or best of all the dead-daddy-who-killed-himself card. When it suited me. I never felt ashamed of the manner of my father's death. I was too busy being ashamed of myself.

I look back at photographs of myself now and I remember how much I hated that person. I looked in the mirror and saw an ugly, obese, boring, nothing girl. In reality, while I was never skinny or must-write-home-about pretty, I was far from obese or ugly. I had a lovely smile. I found fun in almost everything, I sang silly songs and made people laugh. My insides churn when I remember, despite all the outward signs of cheeriness, the self-hatred that oozed from every pore. I see now that I was normal. I was healthy. I was perfectly fine. I saw something else when I was younger though and what I saw just wasn't good enough.

As a result, I spent a lot of this time trying to be somebody else. If you have ever tried it you will know this type of activity can be a full-time job. As I made the transition from primary to secondary school I began spending most of my spare time with a girl who lived near me but went to a different school. A familiar pattern began. She was much more beautiful than me. She was much more popular. She had cooler clothes and boys wanted to be with her. We got on brilliantly because I was up for anything and didn't mind doing whatever she asked.

It was inevitable given the amount of vodka naggins and cider bottles involved in our adventures, that my efforts to somehow morph into a version of her would one day be thwarted. One embarrassing evening when I was 14, my mother walked from Sandymount to Ringsend to reef me out of a pub and tell me I could never talk to the girl again. This girl is a mother of two now and we laugh about it whenever we meet up. Barred from seeing my vodka buddy, at secondary school I gravitated towards troublemakers, misfits and rebels. There was one girl there – taller, trendier, wilder, skinnier – who I particularly revered. She got pregnant and we lost touch after that.

At various times during these years, I moved away from those friends who cared about me and treated me with respect. There were plenty of people around with whom I never felt that twisted desire to be anything other than myself. Looking back, these friendships must have seemed too wholesome for my taste. (I'm grateful that I can still call these people, particularly the magical Amanda, my friends.)

It was the same story with food. I have porridge for breakfast these days. I even sprinkle it with sunflower seeds, but back then foods such as porridge were the enemy. I have always taken refuge in food but it had to be the right kind. This started at home, when I was just a child, turning my nose up at the delicious and nutritious dishes my mother created. I'd refuse to eat the dinner but later rob money from her purse to buy chips or burgers. I see now I was anaesthetising myself, trying to dull the pain of self-loathing. Some people use drink or scratch their arms with razor blades. My form of self-harm came in a take-away box. In my late teens, when I was unknowingly emulating my father and going through a compulsive gambling stage, my self-harm came as I handed over money at the counter of the local bookies. Each fruitless transaction provided the numbness I wanted to feel. Win or lose – mostly lose – it always worked.

I met my friend Marie at Dublin Youth Theatre. She was, she still is, beautiful, talented, creative, unpredictable, original, generous and irresistible. If someone had given me a magic wand and said it could transform me into someone else, I'd have chosen her over every other famous person, living or dead. But I didn't have a magic wand. I did have a friend who was a hairdresser though. In fifth year he dyed my mousy brown hair platinum blond, almost the same shade as Marie's Marilyn Monroesque crowning glory. I was the original Single White Female. I excelled in the role.

I laughed longer and harder with Marie than I ever have with anyone else. I got into more exciting situations with her than with anyone else. To do our adventures justice would take a whole other book.

I cried a lot during this time too. Fat, jealous, hateful, self-pitying tears. It's not easy being in the company of somebody whom everyone finds more interesting, more attractive, more everything than you. Every time she was adored and I was ignored, every time she was put on a pedestal and I was made to feel surplus to requirements, it simply reinforced the things I wanted reinforced. I was nothing. I deserved nothing. I always would. Not surprisingly, given the foundations it was built on, our friendship was often fraught, difficult and intense – but never boring. You could never have said that.

In my early twenties Marie and I moved to London via Birmingham where we had been hanging out for a year. She had a clutch of self-penned and brilliantly powerful songs.

She played guitar and I was trying to learn the bass. In Dublin, a few years before, we had won a busking competition. In England, we were a band for a while but apart from a few decent harmonies and some truly awful bass playing, I didn't contribute much. The pop-star life was not for me. From the first night I met the man who would eventually become my husband, I had a new focus. I began to put all my energy into that.

Perhaps the only thing that could have stopped me leeching off someone else's life was finding someone who would marry me. I was just 22. Searching for a life partner was not what most of my friends were doing. They were having fun and flirting and getting their hearts broken and breaking hearts. They were planning summers away. They were being students. They were being themselves. Or at least they were having a good time finding out who that was.

I had never been successful in the boyfriend department. In retrospect it was probably my overly rigorous approach to the search which scared boys off. I was inclined to meet one and immediately latch on to him like one of the limpets we used to prise off the rocks on Sandymount Strand. Despite all this hard work, I had managed to get to the age of 22 without ever having a proper boyfriend. Sordid one night stands I had. Three-week obsessions I had. Boyfriends came there none.

Why was I so obsessed? The simple reason, I suppose, is that I hoped having someone else would fill in those missing pieces of me. It had always felt as though there were gaps, cracks in the wall of my life that needed to be filled. If a boyfriend loved me then surely I would love me, and I wouldn't need to turn myself into someone else, someone that I thought I might be better able to love. A boyfriend represented the ultimate polyfilla and that's why I so desperately wanted one.

Before I met Mladen, nobody had managed to last to the month mark without running scared in the opposite direction, terrified I was going to be down at Hickey's getting measured for a wedding dress. I can't blame them although, in my defence, I should point out that the second-hand store Eager Beaver in Temple Bar rather than Hickey's would have been my wedding dress emporium of choice.

Mladen had limited English, was a refugee from war-torn Bosnia and his worldly possessions amounted only to those bits and pieces he had managed to carry when he fled. In retrospect, it was fortunate for both him and me that I walked into that pub on the Finchley Road in London on that night in 1992. He was sitting with a gang of foreigners talking a funny language, wearing pale purple jeans and a morose expression I would soon come to recognise as his default mood. In fairness to him, if you'd been asked to become a fighting machine for the Serbian army or leave your family and home forever, you'd have been morose too. You could say I saved him. We saved each other in a way.

Once I'd spotted Mladen in the pub I used my usual pulling technique. It was a kind of 'stare for thirty seconds straight into their eyes and then look down in the lap for five seconds' combo. I'd been using it since I was a teenager without much success. Once a boy who I ended up kissing in a Dublin hostel told me that he almost didn't come over to me because I was giving him this scary stare and he thought I might have been mentally disturbed. That might have stopped a lesser girl using that technique again but not me.

So there I was, staring and looking away, looking away and staring – which is actually quite tiring if you think about it – until my brother Brian, who I was out drinking with, could bear it no more. "What's the story?" he said. "I think," I said with more prescience than I normally display, "this one is marriage material."

When Marie and I moved to London I spent a lot of time with Brian who was studying osteopathy near the Finchley Road. He'd cook me Thai dinners and we'd go out drinking together sometimes. He'd look after me if I got too drunk or tried to go off into the night with scary-looking Iranian men on motorbikes. This happened more often than you might imagine. There were no cultural barriers I wouldn't negotiate for love.

Brian was duly despatched to suss out where Mladen was from and collate general information, such as, did he have bad breath/dangerous looking scars/tattoos with women's names on? Not that any of that would have put me off necessarily, it's just good to be prepared. I watched him talking to Mladen who didn't seem to be saying much back. At one point Mladen raised his sad brown eyes and his pint of Guinness to me but I was in the middle of my 'look away for five seconds' manoeuvre so sadly I couldn't quite acknowledge the gesture.

Brian came back from his reconnaissance mission with a big grin on his face. "He is Bosnian," he said cracking up. "He is a bloody Bosnian refugee." Now for many people this might have been the end of it. Brian certainly thought it was. But where others might have seen only cultural conflict, I saw a possible blending of two people from troubled countries. Where some might have seen a language barrier, I saw an opportunity to experience a love that was beyond words. While some people might have seen those washed out purple Levis and ran screaming for the fashion police, I looked forward to throwing his clothes in the bin and getting him a whole set of new ones. It's called optimism I think. "You are off your head, Ró", was how Brian assessed the situation.

Soon Mladen was staring back at me in a purposeful fashion. Then a few minutes later he was by my side doing the universal mime for "Can I buy you a drink?" I pointed first at the cider tap behind the bar and then at his pint, just in case he tried to fob me off with a mere half pint of the stuff. Brian thought I was messing around just trying to get a few free drinks, which was normally what we did on a night out, but I had never been more serious in my life.

I don't think we had a conversation as such. I just stood around chatting to Brian and giving Mladen flirty looks every five minutes in case he thought I'd lost interest. When the bell rang for closing time, Brian suggested we call it a night. I, in turn, suggested that he call it a night and head off home without me. "I'm going back with the Bosnian," I hissed under my breath in case Mladen could understand us. Knowing there was no arguing with me when I was in that condition and comforted by the knowledge that Mladen didn't own a motorbike, Brian went home while I put the rest of my plan into action. Mladen lived around the corner in West Hampstead in a flat that had become something of a ghetto for exiled ex-Yugoslavians. For the purposes of getting to know him better, I had told him that I only lived down the road from him. In reality I lived around ten tube stops away in downtown Willesden Green. I knew we didn't have much time, so I asked him if I could come up and hang out for a while. His Slavic features contorted in fear. Jesus, I thought, don't tell me I've scared him off before we've even had a snog.

Later it transpired he liked me so much he didn't want me to see the veritable refugee camp he was living in. The place was packed with Bosnians, Serbs, Croatians and the odd Cypriot or Swedish straggler, all of them camping out in too few rooms and re-enacting the war among themselves as they watched the news from the former Yugoslavia every night.

But I didn't know any of this. All I knew was that I needed to get in that door so Mladen could fall in love with me and ask me to marry him. I pulled the toilet trick. When you tell a boy you like that you are going to have to relieve yourself on his doorstep if he doesn't let you in they generally open the door I find. With Mladen by my side, albeit looking as though he was going to be sick, I walked up the five flights of stairs to the apartment where it appeared there was some kind of Eastern European party going on.

With 12 people staying in the flat the toilet was permanently occupied. I had to pretend the lack of bathroom facilities was a source of great discomfort for me. I hopped around on one foot for a while until I forgot about my bathroom ruse and he did too. The kitchen was too packed so we sat together on a ledge in the hall. The smell of *cevapcici*, a delicious Yugoslavian sausage dish, being cooked in the kitchen added to the cosy atmosphere. As beautiful fiery women screamed at each other and stormed out slamming doors, he looked at me with that sad expression I would grow to love. It said: "They may come from my country but these are not my people." I gave him a look which said: "I know." And then he kissed me.

I was fascinated with how Mladen had ended up in London. I'd watch the news bulletins from Sarajevo and Mostar and his hometown Banja Luka and try to understand the complicated animosities that had built up between the warring factions after Tito died.

I wanted to take care of him, I suppose. He was far away from his comfortable home, separated from his mum and dad and his sister. He didn't understand the language. He couldn't go home because the Serbian army viewed him as a traitor after he had fled the country rather than take up arms. The call had come shortly after he'd returned home from a year spent on national service, the final weeks of which dovetailed with the beginning of the conflict. He never liked to talk about that time. When the soldier came to his door and told him to report for duty or get out of the country, his parents agreed that the best thing he could do was pack a small bag and leave for good.

He'd gone first to relations in Croatia where they wouldn't let him go outside, even for a walk, during the day in case neighbours saw that they were harbouring the son of a Serb. Eventually they asked him to leave and he went to his uncle in Germany. His most recent girlfriend in Banja Luka had gone to London so he decided to follow her there. The relationship ended. This was a new and vulnerable phase in his life.

Mladen's English improved every day and gradually I began to understand how he had ended up in London. It reminded me of Anne Frank's diary when he talked about how one day you had friends of all different backgrounds and your parent's religion was not an issue. Then the next day a lifelong friend who was a Serb might cross the road to avoid you because of your 'mixed' parentage. At home, he'd been an independent person who didn't follow the crowd. In London, he was dependent on that crowd for everything from information about social-security entitlements to English translations of the instructions on a ready meal. The privacy he had cherished at home disappeared. Everyone in the flat had an opinion on the minutia of his life even when one wasn't asked for.

It appalled him, he would tell me, that these people who had only the clothes they stood up in were so obsessed with speculating about the money they could earn. How much they had now and how much they hoped to accumulate one day was the endless topic of conversation that went on over coffee and cheap cigarettes late into the night. He appraised his compatriots through compassionless eyes and saw that they had been like him at home. Middle class, comfortable and reliant on their parents for clothes and cars and accommodation. Now they sat drinking bitter coffee and having bitter conversations in kitchens all over London, unable to adjust to their new situation. Dreaming of ways to claw themselves back to where they had been. That was Mladen's take on it anyway.

Not being from that country myself, I didn't share Mladen's disdain and, unlike him, I had compassion for this dislocated crew. It was about survival and Mladen just had a different notion of exactly what that meant. I became absorbed in their culture. I loved their food. Their language. My party trick was learning the most graphic swear words and expressions and then showing off my linguistic talents to the next Bosnian I met.

I asked Mladen recently what it was about me apart from my dodgy dyed black hair, falling apart Doc Martens and excellent English-teaching skills that attracted him to me. He said it was my can-do outlook on life and the fact that I didn't seem to care about money. When we were together, it felt like anything was possible. I know what he meant. I felt it too.

Mladen knew from the start that I wasn't normal. He swallowed his apprehension well used, as he was, to taking risks. From the first night I slept over in his flat, I kept my boots and everything else on because I was terrified of anything sexual developing. If so much as a stray arm wandered near me during the night, I'd wake up with a jolt. I think he found it amusing rather than an early-warning sign. In retrospect, I don't think there was a massive physical attraction on either side at the start. I think that developed as our bond grew stronger, as our 'us against the world' mentality took shape and we began to operate as a team.

I'd taken to spending all my time with him and increasingly less time with Marie. I'd found another focus now and the dream of stardom evaporated as I chased the security of a long-term relationship.

Mladen and I would make an adventure of going to the cheapest supermarkets in London to buy industrial size cartons of coleslaw for 20p and bread Mladen thought tasted like cotton wool – there was no such thing as processed sliced pans where he came from – and spending the rest of our dole on tube tickets and gifts for each other. When it was my birthday, he hid my present under my duvet in my Willesden Green flat, which was located above a greasy spoon and smelt of fried eggs. Mladen had spent two weeks' dole money on a pair of new Doc Martens. It was around this time I asked one of his flatmates to tell me the Serbo Croat for I love you. "*Volim te Mladen*," I told him as we ate a dinner of packet noodles on toast together one night. I was officially in love.

It wasn't long before Mladen and I decided to move in together. I had done a flit from the Willesden Green grease-pit and lined up something much better in Maida Vale. But there wasn't room for all of us, so I decided to move in with Mladen in a flat in Golders Green, peopled by a few of the ex-West Hampstead flatmates. We lived there quite happily for the best part of a year before moving out on our own.

Mladen did any odd-jobs he could find and, after one particularly heated row about money, I stormed out of the flat and arrived home victorious with a waitressing job in Garfunkel's, an unremarkable chain restaurant with an all-you-can-eat salad bar. I loved that job. It was the first time I actually earned money in London and it felt good to be working for a living. I also made friends with a host of incredibly well-groomed waitresses who came from Portugal, Turkey, Egypt and the former Yugoslavia. Away from home, they became my family. We were like dysfunctional sisters united by a desire for large tips. They despaired of my unkempt uniform and gave me regular fashion hints which I ignored. I had a perverse fondness for the place. Every dodgy art print on the wall. Every awful salad component – radishes and crabsticks anyone? Every tightfisted customer who thought they were doing you a favour by leaving 10p on the table. I loved it so much that, after the civil ceremony in Burnt Oak, I had my wedding reception there.

I'd been talking about marriage to Mladen since a few weeks after we met. It made perfect sense. I felt we'd be doing it sooner or later anyway, thereby regularising Mladen's increasingly fragile position in Britain. It was logical the way I saw it. Mladen had never been keen on the idea, worried that we'd be rushing things but, over the following two years, I wore him down. I wanted to move back to Dublin and it would make life easier for him there if we were married. Thinking about it now, I can understand how this might be perceived as a slightly unromantic approach to marriage but I felt very different at the time. Marriage would give him, and by extension our relationship, more security so I reckoned the ceremony would mean even more to us than it did for most couples.

Understandably it took a while to persuade my mother of this. I rang my best friend Amanda. "You know the way I always wanted a boyfriend?" I said. "Well I'm getting married so that means I'll have a boyfriend for life."

I couldn't wait to go home to Dublin with my new husband and start our new life.

At first we moved into the house in Sandymount Green with my mother. A few days after we arrived we went to the dole office on Marlborough Street to fill in all the forms. While we waited to find out how much I was entitled to, we went for a coffee. I remember emptying my purse and being delighted we had exactly enough for a hot drink each. That was how it always was between us. It didn't matter what we had as long as we had enough.

We got jobs in a nightclub on the quays. My new job in

Dublin saw me in the cloakroom, taking coats and handing out tickets. I wasn't as good a cloakroom attendant as I was a waitress. At the end of the night there were always spare coats that didn't match the tickets people produced. Mladen was collecting glasses. We'd missed out on a lot living a fairly frugal life in London. We didn't understand why people were massaging each other and only drinking water and smiling all the time. Then someone told us about a drug called Ecstasy and the set up became as clear as Evian. I was taken off the cloakroom because of my incompetence and put in charge of the 'chill-out zone' downstairs where I sold coffee and tea and water.

We came to Dublin with nothing. Within a few years we had everything we ever dreamed of. Despite his lack of qualifications, Mladen had landed a job in a computer company. I remember standing in my mother's house and us marvelling that he was going to be earning £9,000 a year in his new job. It seemed like a fortune. Most of what he knew about the industry he'd learnt from magazines and books bought while on the dole in London. He'd be working with people who studied this stuff in college. I was dizzy with pride.

As for me, I was getting steady journalism work. Writing had been the career I'd longed for since I was small, an unworkable dream, or so I thought thanks to my lack of academic ambition. But when I came home from London I got a place on *NewsFour*. It was the start I needed and the articles I wrote enabled me to get an NUJ card. Eventually I landed the work experience in the *Tribune* which led, in time, to an actual job. The impossible had somehow happened. I was being paid to interview people and write about their lives.

Suddenly, all our life's boxes were being ticked. Thanks to a loan from my Uncle Ron, we managed to buy a two-bedroom apartment on the quays. We even did the green card interview and Mladen became the proud owner of an Irish passport. It was us against the world and it seemed we had won. Maybe that's why it all started to go wrong.

How can I explain? We grew apart. We weren't compatible. Mladen fell out of love with me. It was simple really when I think about it. But when I got around to writing about the details I found I had to call and ask him for more information. We are still on good terms even if I haven't seen him since Millennium Eve when I begged him to let me come home with him to his new flat and he walked away from me for the very last time.

"What happened to us?" I asked him, phoning from a writing retreat in the wilds of West Cork. "Why did it go so wrong?" It wasn't long into the conversation before I was wishing I hadn't bothered. What he had to say was extremely hard to hear. I suppose that's when you know you have to listen.

The more he talked, the more I had to face up to how I had packed away our relationship in a few neat little boxes without properly examining what was inside. According to the contents of the box marked 'The End', our break-up was a straightforward tale of love and love's capacity to fade. A romantic disintegration that could not have been avoided, only prolonged. A descent from passion to ambivalence. Sure it happens all the time.

I wrote about our divorce in a column once. About how I didn't regret our relationship and how so much good had come from it. It was all true. But now here he was talking about things I appeared to have completely blanked out. The picture he painted of our relationship wasn't pretty. In his view, I was an alien hurtling towards planet self-destruct. He described how, as he saw it, my inner-saboteur went into overdrive during the Dublin years of our relationship. While I began to achieve professionally what I never thought possible, I seemed to be intent on making sure my personal life became a disaster zone.

I stayed out all night. I drank too much. I didn't care what kind of a pigsty I lived in or what kind of food I ate or how much of it I ate or how I treated him. We had blazing, violent rows about all of these issues. I grew fatter and more depressed than ever and then ate more to ease the pain.

I wasn't happy. When confronted with my behaviour by my husband, all I could say was that I wasn't happy. I would regularly ring my mother in tears, begging her to fix things, while Mladen looked on coldly and shook his head. In response, he grew hard and cruel. There were comments about my weight, words that fed my insecurity and led me to lash out more. There were nights when I'd block out the unhappiness by going off with any man who showed me a bit of attention. I convinced myself that this was because Mladen didn't love me. The truth was, as Oprah Winfrey would happily conclude, I didn't love myself. One night, after a particularly nasty row, I rang him – I have only a vague recollection of this – and said that I was standing by the Liffey and was going to throw myself in. That was the moment he decided to leave. In all this time, he had never told me that before.

I felt sick. Too sick to respond. But no response was necessary. It seemed Mladen could have talked all night about what drove him away from me. He could have walked forever down this murky memory lane. Maybe he needed to. But I had heard enough. "I see the problem," I said, irritated and sore. "You've made it clear. I was impossible to be around. *I get it*," I told him. "You just couldn't bear to live with me anymore."

There was a beat on the line as Mladen considered this last statement. "It wasn't that," he said as gently as he could. "You just couldn't bear to live with yourself."

*

The day Mladen told me he was leaving was bright and hot. I was due to go to a Schizophrenia conference in Jurys Hotel in Ballsbridge for a feature I was researching. Looking back, I suppose I could have got out of it but I was propelled there by something I couldn't have explained.

I see myself now, getting a taxi from our flat, sitting in the back row of the conference. I don't hear anything, I don't care. Not anymore.

I can't concentrate. It's like I'm not really here. I leave before the conference is over and I walk home. To 8 Sandymount Green. I sleepwalk all the way to the door. I might be eight years old and trudging up to the school gate. I climb the stairs to my old bedroom. My old bed. I lie down and howl like I am trying to physically expel the pain through my vocal chords. It is primeval and frightening and it finishes as quickly as it begins.

On Monday morning I go into work in *The Irish Times.* Over the next few days, I help Mladen find a flat and pack his things. I tell him to call if he needs anything. And when he leaves I make a decision not to care about the fact that my husband has left me. And I carry on not caring. Mostly about myself.

Left alone the cracks in my life grow wider. I am sleepwalking through the working day, eating pizza, Chinese takeaways, microwave burgers through the night. Food, always a loyal ally, now becomes my best friend. Food is the only one who understands. I don't give anyone else the chance. The deep despair that has always been bubbling away under the surface begins to consume me. I can see no good in anything. Least of all in me.

The gambling problem that surfaced as a teenager, a problem I thought I had kicked, re-emerges. I spend hours sticking money into slot machines in an arcade on

O'Connell Street. As the coins go down and I press those flashing buttons, I am transported somewhere else. A place where I don't have to think about my life. For those hours I don't exist. I like that feeling. I like it too much.

Curled up in my back-stage area I fall slowly apart. Front of house, I give a first-class impression of someone who is soldiering on because becoming a victim, pitied by colleagues and friends, is not something that appeals. But back stage I am sliding into a well-oiled pit of misery from where I think I will never return.

One miserable day I reach a conclusion that I am amazed didn't occur to me years ago. It is like a light bulb going off over my head. Life is nothing but misery. Life is only suffering. It seems as though no one else in the world had copped on to this and it is up to me to cope with my disturbing and, what I consider, profound revelation. But I can't cope. I don't want to cope. I can see no point in the constant suffering. I just want it to end.

It's funny, the things that change the course of your life. The corners you turn. The roads you take. In my case it was a phone call to my brother Brian in work one day. He was far away in New Zealand and maybe that's why I called him, knowing he wouldn't be able to put his arms around me and tell me it would be OK.

Since leaving London, Brian had travelled the world searching for 'the meaning of life' or 'a higher truth' – or both these things when he was feeling particularly industrious. He had been a guru's devotee. He had worshipped a mountain. He'd even tried yogic flying which, incidentally, looks as painful as it sounds.

So I picked up the phone and, when I heard his voice on the other end, I cried. Trying to remain out of earshot of the news editor, I told him my conclusion: life, all life, was meaningless and empty and hellish and I didn't want to be part of this great charade anymore. His reply shocked me with its callousness. He said, "Good." And he said, "I'm glad." Far from talking me down from the edge, he was confirming all my darkest thoughts. Before I had a chance to slam the phone down, he explained exactly why he was so happy that I was so unhappy. Something shifted in me that day.

Brian and I have had our moments but, as he spoke, I found myself calm for the first time in years. He said I was right. He said life was full of suffering. He said that now I had realised what he considered a universal truth, I could take the first steps to help me cope with the vicissitudes of this earthly existence. He told me about an ancient Buddhist meditation technique taught over an intense ten days during which you could neither talk, drink alcohol, smoke or read. "Vipassana," he said, "might save your life."

I was grateful that he did no more than tell me about this meditation technique. He left it up to me to trawl the internet and discover that there was a course taking place in Portumna, Co. Galway, in a few weeks' time.

That's how I found myself at the top of O'Connell Street laden down with a colourful blanket, some cushions and other meditation accessories. I had never done anything like a meditation course before. I had always been first in line to slag Brian whenever he found a new guru, had another enlightenment experience or insisted on lighting incense everywhere on those rare occasions when he came home.

A few days before, the organisers of the Vipassana course had sent me the Code of Discipline for the course. The check list of things not to bring – books, phones, cigarettes, music systems, writing materials – was daunting. I had to agree not to leave the course boundaries and to subscribe to five precepts: to abstain from killing, stealing, sexual activity, telling lies and taking intoxicants. It would be just endless meditation each day with a group of what I reasoned must be hippy weirdoes without access to a McDonald's quarter pounder with cheese and not a sniff of a double gin and tonic, my painkillers of choice at the time.

There would be no talking. No reading. No writing. No smoking. I would be out of bed at 4 a.m. every morning, eating only wholesome vegetarian meals the last of which would be served at 11 a.m. I look back on all this and I realise how desperate I must really have been not least because I had a totally unfair and unfounded hatred of vegetarians at the time.

I took ten days leave from work. I told only a few people what I was doing. "Yeah, of course, Róisín, you are really going to last ten days without speaking, smoking or drinking," was the typical response. I had asked Brian for some advice because he was the only other person I knew who had completed the course. He said, "Surrender yourself to the technique." I made a decision that I would see it through. I knew it couldn't make me feel any worse than the way I was feeling already.

The first three days were a nightmare, only serving to confirm my new insight that life was hell on earth. I was not able to meditate. I could not sit still cross-legged. As I tried to clear my mind, every horrible thing I had ever done to Mladen, to my mother and to myself clogged up my brain until I would wander, in a fog, back to my room and fall into a tormented sleep. On Day Three, I escaped from the meditation hall to do some washing. It was just an excuse not to sit. One of the volunteers who cooked our meals came into the bathroom and whispered that I should be in the hall. That's when I decided to escape past the police-style tape that indicated the course boundaries and take my chances in the miserable world outside. But as I went into my room to pack my bag, I heard Brian's voice. "Surrender," he whispered. I am glad that I did.

That afternoon, the Vipassana technique itself was taught. Up to then we had just been observing our breath and trying to clear our minds. Despite my turmoil, as I sat down I realised that my mind was not as full of rubbish as it had been three days before. I was ready to learn the real technique.

Vipassana is an ancient form of meditation that was taught by the Buddha two thousand years ago. After being largely forgotten, it was revived in the last few decades by SN Goenka, a former businessman from Burma. His teachings were relayed on tapes during meditation and videos at the end of each evening session. Surrender, I said to myself, as Goenka began to talk.

As we were directed to observe the subtle sensations in our bodies, starting with the top of the head and working down to the tips of our toes, a very strange thing happened. I began to feel pins and needles on my head and, as I moved down my body, a million different sensations, most of them deeply unpleasant, manifested themselves on my body. Goenka was telling me to observe them, not to react to them, but to remain equanimous whether the feelings were nasty or nice. And in an instant it all made sense.

This old man had been talking up to now about how all misery stems from craving or aversion and our resulting blind reactions to these two feelings. When something we don't want happens, we react with sadness or with anger. When we crave something but we don't get it – a feeling of fitting in, a happy-ever-after marriage – we tie ourselves up in knots inside. Knots that never go away.

The key, according to Vipassana, is merely to observe the sensations that crop up in the body whenever the unwanted happens or when something we want remains elusive. Observing the sensations in my body over the next six days, I came to realise the impermanence of everything and the futility of reacting when the reality is that everything eventually passes away.

By Day Eight, the intense pain in my legs from sitting cross-legged for hours at a time became sensations to observe, instead of annoyances to eradicate by changing position. By Day Nine, I was experiencing a subtle but blissful tingling all over my body, which, understanding the technique completely now, I did not react to.

At the end of the course I was elated. My eyes were shining. My heart was light. It was like a mountain that had been pressing down on me for years had lifted. I came home and my mother said I was like a different person to the one who had left, shoulders slumped under the weight of her sleeping bag. After a while the initial elation wore off. But it was a new beginning. A new start.

I wrote an article about my experience afterwards, apologising in the introduction for the fact that the piece was an unashamed bit of what is dubbed 'confessional journalism' – a bit rich given the personal nature of the column I would begin to write for the magazine just two years later.

"Ideally you are supposed to continue meditating even when you leave," I wrote. "I didn't, but my whole approach to life had changed. Instead of wallowing in misery and spreading it to others I had learnt to be aware of it, aware that everything arises only to pass. I did not become a flawlessly happy person but I had taken the first baby steps on the path to such a state."

My first Vipassana course was one baby step. There have been others. I went to a counsellor who helped me to see the importance of being more gentle with myself. I was open to anything now. I attended another Vipassana course, this time with my new boyfriend and my brother Brian. I explored meditation further with the Open Dharma group on a two-month visit to India. With each step, I grew. I still have a long way to grow.

In the months following the Vipassana course I became calmer and more contented than I had ever been. This coincided with a decision to move to Belfast where my sister Rachael lived at the time. I was grateful that *The Irish Times* allowed me to leave the Dublin office because those two years in Belfast were like a new beginning for me. I was doing different work in a new environment and spending quality time with my sister and her new baby, my godchild Hannah. I was eating healthy meals and felt happier because the need to punish myself with food appeared to be dissipating. And, as a bonus, an unexpected extra, I met a boy.

People are always asking me about Jonny. Some people even think he is a figment of my imagination. He's not, although a boyfriend who does all the housework and hardly ever complains does sound like a bit of a dream. I met him during one of those hot Julys when the Orangemen were gathered around Drumcree Hill in Portadown, trying to walk down the Catholic Garvaghy Road when the streets were being taken over by protesting Protestants, clashing with the army and the RUC.

It was love at first riot, really. Jonny was out for what he would call a dander in the sunshine to have a look at the protest that had gathered around the estate where his sister lived.

He was tall and thin. He had an elegant nose. He needed a haircut. In a bobbing crowd, half carnival, half chaos, he caught my eye. And then he was gone.

I know it's a little hard to take. A riot is brewing, the army are mobilising, RUC men in riot gear are gathering and meanwhile the *Irish Times* representative charged with documenting the event for future historians is busy checking out the local talent.

I was just getting a quotation from some scary-looking man with tattoos when a voice in my ear told me that I had taken down what the man said wrongly. In fairness, scary man's Portadown accent might as well have been Mandarin for all I understood but I wasn't about to let some yokel look over my shoulder and tell me my job. I turned around ready to throw whoever it was a filthy look and there he was. "Thank you so much for your help" is what I said to him before moving in for the kill.

I looked at him and a plan formed in my head. It wasn't ethical. It wasn't professional. It wasn't even moral. Apart from that, it was a pretty good plan. I argued with myself. I needed a good story, didn't I? If I happened to fancy him as well that couldn't be helped. I asked this boy if he would help with this article I had to write. And this boy, he told me his name was Jonny, said he would be glad to help.

The next hour or so was a happy blur. My new friend, my new *source*, and I wandered around talking about life in Portadown. I remember one particularly memorable moment when he took my arm to help me down a grass verge so that I could get a better look at the car that was in flames on the railway track. The romance of it all was overwhelming.

What I did next was merely good journalistic groundwork. I told him, truthfully, that I had to file a story about the protest in an hour and that, again truthfully, I wasn't sure how I would get back to the hotel. Did he have a computer? Would he mind if I borrowed it? Could I have his number? I should win some sort of award for my intrepid information gathering. It didn't take much to worm the relevant digits out of him.

I had his number but I knew time was ticking away and that he was quite possibly one of the most laid-back, least-likely-to-make-a-move people I had ever met. Drastic action was required.

I told him about this story I wanted to write. About how I wanted to spend time with him and his friends to get into the heart and the minds of the Portadown Protestant. Would he help me? He would, he said but he wasn't sure whether he knew the kind of people I needed to speak to. And that's when the rioting started.

It couldn't have come at a more inconvenient time. The armoured vehicles started to move towards us from one side and a line of RUC men carrying batons and plastic shields closed in on the other. The locals had started attacking the police, aiming sticks and stones and whatever missiles they could find at the men in bullet-proof masks. Extremely thoughtless of them in the circumstances, but then the course of true love never ran smooth. I, on the other hand, ran as smoothly as I could at that point. Into some bushes where tiny pebbles began to rain down on my head.

I like to think I recovered well from my first riot. I was given a lift back to my hotel room where I wrote up my news story with one eye on the clock. There were two deadlines looming. I had told the office my news story on the riot would be in by 5.30 p.m. I had told Jonny that I would call him to discuss how he could help my important research by 6 p.m. After sending in my story I called him. It was two minutes to six.

Jonny sounded uncertain and shocked to hear from me. I pitched my idea to him again. Hearts and minds. The untold story. I should say at this point that it actually was a feature I was interested in researching but, at the same time, my motives were not exactly pure. I had this idea that if Jonny and I got to know each other against the backdrop of petrol bombs and general social upheaval, something powerful could happen between us. And if I won a media award along the way that was just a cross I would have to bear.

I was singing Spandau Ballet's seminal song on relationships which flourish in conflict as I skipped down the corridor to the hotel lobby where I had arranged to meet Jonny. "*And we made our love on wasteland, through the barricades*," I sung. I could only pray it would be true.

I know at this stage I might sound a tad irresponsible, hightailing it over to the potentially dangerous Protestant side for mainly romantic purposes. Let me counter this by saying my next move was to inform my colleague Patsy McGarry, currently the religious affairs correspondent of *The Irish Times*, of my professional, if not my personal, intentions.

Patsy and I have always had a great working relationship and in Drumcree I always felt safe when in his company. But his collegial concern and loyalty worked against me that night. In fact his big-brother routine was threatening to ruin everything.

I told him straight about my plans for the evening. "Patsy," I said, "I met this young man today called Jonny, a fine upstanding Protestant with no tattoos, earrings or other outward signs of terrorist activity. He has kindly agreed to accompany me to the other side of the hill and facilitate me talking to young people of his own cultural tradition about life over there. He is coming to pick me up in five minutes. I will have the mobile turned on if you need to contact me."

Patsy looked worried. He said he understood my journalistic passion – I had the decency to feel a slight thud of guilt at that point – and told me that he didn't think it was such a good idea. What if something should happen? How did I know I could trust this man? I felt sick.

Jonny was due through the hotel doors any minute. Patsy said he would check to see what another colleague thought about my proposal and they were talking with worried looks on their faces when I realised I had left my mobile phone in the hotel room. There was only a minute to go, and

Jonny seemed like such a punctual person. I legged it back to the hotel room, got the phone and made it to the lobby in time to see Patsy in close conversation with a terrified-looking Jonny.

This was not part of the plan. I spent a few minutes trying to persuade Patsy to let me go before he decided it would be OK, as long as he and another journalist came too. In fairness they didn't know that, in my eyes, this was more a date than a work assignment, but it still felt like I was being chaperoned. What was worse, though, was that Jonny looked a lot less enthusiastic than he had been when we spoke earlier. Bringing one journalist up to the hill was going to be hard enough to explain to the brethren – but three?

As I sat in the front of his car, I realised that however much I fancied him, it wasn't worth putting him in this position. I told him I didn't think it was a good idea anymore and opened the door to go. He leaned over, shut the door and turned the key in the ignition. And that's how it all started.

I managed to lose our chaperones on the hill and, despite Patsy's best efforts to escort me back to the hotel, I went without him to Jonny's house where I drank two bottles of Smirnoff Ice, the only alcohol in the house, and Jonny had some class of cream bun and a nice cup of tea. He drove me back to the hotel and we talked in his car until 4 a.m. A year later, I was chatting to Patsy at our Christmas Party and I asked him did he remember that nice Protestant boy who helped me out on Drumcree Hill last year. Patsy nearly choked on his chorizo – it was an Italian restaurant – when I told him he was now my boyfriend. Five years after the incident, Patsy still refers to himself as the Fool on the Hill. And I still call Jonny my boyfriend.

It's different with Jonny. Ever since we met, we have been

growing together and trying to use our many differences as a way to strengthen our relationship. Going on the Vipassana course together and meditating in India were beautiful experiences. When I first met his sister Caroline she said, "The girl who ends up with Jonny will be treated like gold." And I am. Most of the time. Regular readers will recall the coat hooks he gave me one Christmas. I have it on good authority that with that gift he lowered the bar for the entire male present-buying population. Something he can always be proud of I'm sure.

While Jonny and I are open to spiritual stuff, it's important that I don't give the wrong impression. It isn't all incense and meditation around our house. Jonny may be a yoga boy in the making with self-discipline to burn but I am lucky if I manage ten minutes to meditate each day.

I am really grateful that Jonny is on this journey with me and that he did not disappear through a trapdoor the minute I gave him a back-stage pass. He has seen me at my worst and still claims to love me. I have lashed out at him the same way I did with Mladen and there have been times when I thought he might leave. But he has impressive staying power. And I hope I help him with his demons as much as he helps me.

The echo from the years of overeating and self-abuse still linger. As I sit here writing, I weigh more than I ever have in my whole life. I used to imagine myself clinically obese when I wasn't. And now – I think it's what you call a self-fulfilling prophecy – I most definitely am. I still eat to reward myself. I still eat to punish myself. The difference now is that my actions are more like a bad habit which I know I will one day break rather than a mechanism I use to survive. I gave up smoking almost overnight three years ago and I feel I am closer than ever to saying goodbye to my eating problem.

In the past, overeating was a method of self-protection

from the feeling I had that I was an alien alone in a strange world. I don't feel quite so alien anymore. Still, the part of me that is used to needing that protection, that buffer between the world and me, will sometimes propel me down the road to Fairview for a sausage burger and chips that I don't want or need. And then I will come home and make a big dinner for Jonny and I will eat that too. It happened just the other day. It will happen again. Like I said, I weigh more now than ever. At the same time I like myself more than I ever have in my whole life. Now I just need to get fitter. For myself. Because my body, while it may not be a temple, is not a rubbish tip either.

The column has helped. It's been three years of free therapy really. I see myself differently now and that's why remarks that used to wound me don't go half as deep as they used to. In the past I would have used the "plain, plump" part of the comment from a reader, which I referred to earlier, to fuel my self-loathing which I saw then as something precious. Something that needed to be fed and watered every day with whatever substances came to hand. It was not half as precious as I imagined it to be.

These days I know the truth. I look around and I see that a sprawling back-stage area leads to alcoholism, drug addiction, gambling, self-harm, overeating, undereating. The spiralling suicide levels, especially among young men in this country, are testament to a section of our community that don't feel able to share their deep-rooted feelings of inadequacy, of sorrow and of shame. So they die before they realise that there is no shame in not being perfect. The shame comes only in the constant raging about the fact that we are not.

When I started the column, a colleague confided she was worried about me. She was concerned that some of my writing appeared to be a cry for help. I think in a way some of the columns were exactly that. And while it was never my intention this has turned out to be an unexpected blessing. Letting go in my writing was excruciating at first but it wasn't long before the very act of setting down my feelings as honestly, openly and as viscerally as possible began to feel like a pardon. And when readers began to respond in a way which suggested they understood exactly what I was doing, the absolution seemed complete.

The column I wrote about bullying, written from the perspective of a former bully, is probably the one that got most reaction in the three years I have been doing the job. In the piece I examined my cruel streak and spoke about the shameful way I had treated someone weaker than me from my past. It was though another dark cloud lifted from my head even as I typed the final paragraph. Poof. One minute it was there, the next it was not.

That article brought many people sidling up to me, the nicest people you could ever meet, admitting that they had bullied once. In e-mails and letters, people unburdened themselves, grateful for the chance to be honest about things they had done that had made them feel ashamed. My columns have often made my mother cry, especially when I wrote about the most painful times in my life. But she has always supported me because she believes, as I do, that the pure honest expression of our deepest thoughts and feelings can only be good for the soul.

It has taken me years to forgive myself for what happened at Fanore. And even longer to realise all I was ever guilty of was childish exuberance. I can now allow myself to feel sad about not having a father and, as a result, I am more loving with memories of him these days. More protective. Less matter of fact.

I close my eyes and smell the hops from the pub and see him walking across the road, stopping the traffic with one wave of his hand just like the policeman in 'The Mountains of Mourne', the Percy French song he used to sing. I see us sitting in an ice-cream place near the dole office – just me, him and a knickerbocker glory. I hear him shouting "give over" in his Bath Avenue accent when we got too rowdy. Shouting "go on ye daisy" at the horses on the television. I see him at the door with lollipops and fizzle sticks. A stranger in a beard. A stranger in a shroud. But I am kinder to him now just as I am kinder to myself.

I've been asking myself some hard questions lately. What am I striving for? What am I trying to achieve?

It's simple really. I want to be able to look at myself in my internal mirror and accept, without terms or conditions, the person who is reflected back at me. I want to live secure in the knowledge that how I am now is exactly how I am meant to be. I am lucky to be related to people and to have friends who I believe possess this kind of unconditional self-love. Being with them feels like coming home, it's a precious gift. More than anything else I wish that for myself.

What I have set down here are the darker pieces of me and I was worried, for a while, that I hadn't let in enough of the light. But this is just what came out when I sat down to write this introduction and I've learnt, over the years, to trust that voice. I hope there is enough sparkle in the columns that follow to make up for the gloom.

Before I finish, I want to make it clear that I didn't get into journalism to write about my life. Of course I wanted to move people with what I wrote, but not through stories about my divorce or my lack of housekeeping skills or my woeful performance at the Irish Monopoly Championships.

The most satisfying piece of journalism I'd written up until the column started was about an elderly traveller in a broken down caravan near Tallaght who was living in his own waste, the flies buzzing around as he pulled up his trousers tied low on scrawny hips with string. A couple of days after the article was published, a cheque for £500 was sent in to *The Irish Times* by a barrister who wanted to remain anonymous. A man was no longer living in his own excrement because of an article I had written. If I never did anything else in my life, at least I could feel proud of that.

And I've come to be proud of these columns too. Three weeks turned into six and the weeks turned into months and before I knew it I was a columnist in *The Irish Times*.

I feel privileged to be able to share these journeys with readers and glad the issues I write about sometimes touch people. A reader sent me a letter once praising me, on the one hand, for writing an entertaining column but dismissing me, on the other, as no literary genius. Far from being insulted, I would have to agree with that. A lot of the time, my columns are concerned with the heart, not the head and I don't believe genius of any kind comes into it. The ones where there is no head and all heart are my own particular favourites.

"No literary genius" is fine by me. All I have ever tried to do in the columns is be myself, even when that is not a pretty sight. I spent so long as a teenager and in my twenties trying to be somebody else that the column became a way for me to move towards accepting myself, to try and shake off the past and appreciate who I am now.

Thanks to the column, my back-stage area has shrunk in size, but that doesn't mean there aren't still demons lurking in the darkness, scared to move into the spotlight, scared of being exposed. It's been a cathartic few years. If you feel you know me through these columns, then you probably do. Pieces of me. Underneath the expertly applied greasepaint, the word-perfect scripts and the designer costumes we are all the same anyway. It's just taken me a while to figure that out.

Róisín Ingle
Dublin, 2005

Significant Others

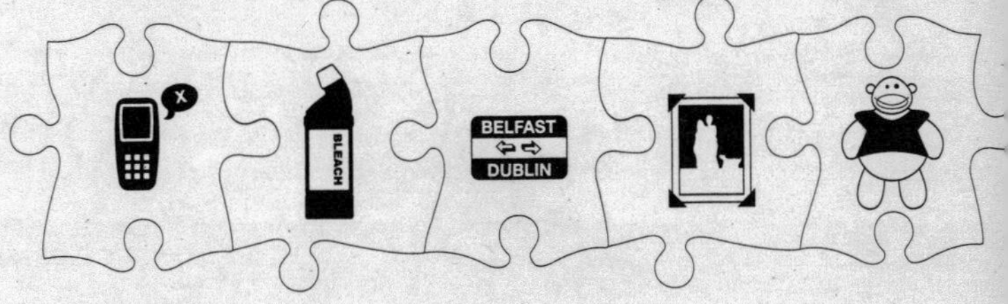

Motherly Love

The things you learn when your boyfriend's mother comes to call. A good homemaker can never have too much bleach. Or too much tomato soup. Or toilet roll. The way to a man's heart is through apple pancakes and chocolate fingers and endless cups of tea. And, lest we forget, one can never have too much bleach.

She has been stockpiling it underneath our sink when she thinks we are looking the other way. Bottles of own-brand bleach which, she declares, with all the authority of someone who has thoroughly investigated the issue, are just as good as the posher products.

It turns out there was some kind of special offer on in Rice's of Keady, Co. Armagh, a bargain-filled grocery store. There, goods such as bleach are given the prominence that people like my boyfriend's mother think they deserve, and not stuck down the bottom shelf like they are in most supermarkets.

Her own mother, Sarah, who lives in Keady, gave her the nod about the bleach bargain. So, of course, my boyfriend's mother bought 20. Just in case. "Because," she says patiently, "you never know who might knock on the door and want to use the bathroom." I tell her that actually I do, because nobody I know goes visiting without texting or phoning ahead. "You never know," she insists, squirting half a bottle underneath the rim with relish.

My boyfriend's mother, Iris, lives in Portadown with her husband, John. When we told them we were buying a house in Dublin, she said, "Ach now, would you not prefer to have a little house in Portadown?" And then refused to believe us when we said no.

We have given them a key to the house and every so often Iris comes down to Dublin, gets out the mop, and when she is finished bleaching the floorboards she says: "Now then, that's more Protestant looking", before clamping her hand guiltily to her mouth. "No offence," she says, laughing. "None taken," I say, shaking my head.

When Iris comes to visit she takes down the ugly net curtains, sticks them in the washing machine and requests a needle and thread to darn a hole that I can barely see. I don't have a sewing kit, I tell her. She hangs them anyway. You realise then that the net curtains weren't ugly, they were just filthy. "Look at the difference," she says. And you have to agree it's amazing.

Iris never stops talking. She can even talk with pegs in her mouth. I found this out one afternoon when I came home from work to find her hanging our underwear out on the line. She says that you could do a hundred things to an old house, important fiddly things, and nobody would ever know how much you had done. She says that we should take our time, that it will all come together in the end. My boyfriend comes home from work to the smell of his mother's cooking mixed with the all-pervasive odour of bargain-basement cleaning products.

"Ah," he says, "it's good to come home to a clean house for a change." Translation: "Ma, my girlfriend doesn't know how to scrub pots like you, she cleans the kitchen but it still looks dirty, Ma. I love you. Ma, don't leave me." Iris, to her credit, tries not to look too pleased.

Meanwhile, her husband goes quietly, methodically around the house. Screwing on vents. Adjusting toilet roll holders. Fixing towel rails. He only stops for a fairy cake or three and a cup of strong tea supplied by Iris. After *Emmerdale* he is off again. Hammering in nails. Fixing holes where the rain gets in. "Ah, dear," he says, "ah, dear." He left his stick behind this time, it's hanging on the edge of the sofa. So we know he'll be back. We hope he comes back.

One day Iris scooted down the new bypass with half of Tesco in the boot of the car. "Just a few essentials," she said. Like an eight-pack of tomato soup. Like shortbread. And the buns and the brown bread that she calls wheaten. Then there's the exquisite ham and cheese that tastes like nothing I've ever had, even when I've spent three times the price in one of those sun-dried delicatessens.

Iris doesn't say it, but it's clear she thinks I don't give her boy enough treats. She stuffs the cupboards full of crisps, chocolate, peanuts and Madeira cake. I can hardly close the door for the bumper supply of Kit-Kats and Rocky bars. I don't want to nag, I tell him when she is gone, but can't you hide them so I am not tempted to have one every time I go into the kitchen? I hassle him so much about it that he goes one better. He brings the whole lot back to her the next time he is in Portadown. "Oooh," she says, on the phone. "Did I offend you with my confectionery?" She brings twice as much the next time. I don't mind, really. The kettle is on, there are buns in the oven and my U-bend sparkles like no other.

Forgetting to Forgive

I'm waiting for someone to say sorry. I know I will be hanging around in apology limbo for a while because at the moment this person is still pretending she doesn't know what she has done. Normally I find it impossible to maintain this cold, clinical expression on my face. The one that says "I'm not talking to you so don't even try it." I almost always crack.

It would be so much easier to forgive, forget and go back to talking about the weather or whether Madonna is really pregnant again. But not this time. For some people, sorry really is the hardest word, and so I will wait until a guilty conscience sends her to my open door, begging for forgiveness.

The reason we fell out is not really important. The point is, I know my grievance is worth a giant apology. And so I am nursing my hurt feelings like a mother hen protecting her eggs. Every so often, I check to make sure the sore spot hasn't healed. If I sense the pain is fading, I rehearse the incident in my head. She said this. She did that. She betrayed my trust. She lied. She disrespected me. By the way, this ritual is the emotional equivalent of wolfing down a mega-hot curry to check if you still have an ulcer. Please don't try this at home.

There is a theory that apologies are unnecessary. The best people don't look for them while the worst people take advantage of the situation when forgiveness is sought. Some people don't think it is worth saying sorry unless you also make an effort to right the wrong – that you should not seek forgiveness unless you plan to make amends for whatever offence has led to your remorse.

I have a friend who loves saying sorry, sometimes when he hasn't even done anything wrong. He says he got into the habit as a seven-year-old when he started making confession. The vast majority of seven-year-olds are too young to have anything to apologise for and so make up their sins.

My friend's favourite was "Father forgive me, I said f-off to my mother", when in reality if he had said any such thing to his mother he would have been in no fit state to attend confession. He also confessed to having broken a series of fictional windows over a period of five years. In fact, if you think about it, some of the first sins we ever committed were probably the lies we were forced to invent in the darkness of the confession box.

Some people say sorry when they really mean something else. When my father died, I remember a classmate coming up to me all red eyes and shaking hands telling me she was sorry. I will never forget the look on her face when I replied, "Why are you sorry? Did you kill him?" She was sorry for my troubles I know now, but as a child I didn't understand.

Buses and queues and busy streets all over this country are full of people bumping into and pushing roughly past each other while mouthing the all-purpose "sorry" mantra. What they really mean to say is: get out of my way or excuse me. Or, get a move on, can't you see I'm in a hurry?

Sometimes no matter how many times a person tells you they are sorry, it can't take away the pain. And sometimes sorry comes too late.

Anyway, I was out at an Italian restaurant making a face at the person who was heartlessly demolishing a chocolate bread-and-butter pudding when I realised I was actually forgetting crucial details of the recent betrayal.

Another night, watching Leo smooth-talk his way across

the world in *Catch Me If You Can*, a fragment of the offence returned and then disappeared again when the credits rolled. In the taxi home, I tried to concentrate. She said ... it will come to me in a minute. She did ... something. She lied, but there was some truth in her words. There was disrespect, but the lines of communication were blurred and maybe, just maybe, something I had said or done to her another day lay at the heart of it all.

I was taking dying lilies from the vase, pouring fetid water into the sink, when I noticed the hurt had left me altogether. It was three o'clock in the morning. Outside, a boy and a girl were screaming at each other. A barrage of alcohol-fuelled expletives flooded the air before she ran crying along the quays, leaving him standing nonplussed by the river's edge. I wondered how long this girl and this boy would nurse the hurt. How long it would take them to say sorry. Or how long it would be before both of them realised what I just had – it really doesn't matter which one of us says it first. I'm sorry.

The Skinderella Saga

I have a friend who is so obsessed with looks-preserving lotions and potions that I have taken to calling her Skinderella. She is the kind of girl who could talk for hours about how a little pot of magic can make you look at least five years younger, or how another miracle cream does wonders for thread veins and stretch marks. For her birthday, she treated herself to a newly engineered face cream. She said the secret ingredient was some class of collagen which, yes, all right, smells of cow's hooves but had the effect on the wearer of a mini face-lift. When I protested that the smell might put me off using such a cream, she just sighed and looked meaningfully at my more pronounced laughter lines.

I admit that I have a lot to learn when it comes to skin products. I tend to change my moisturiser only when it's getting a little gloopy and the bottle is so empty I have to stick a teaspoon inside to get the stuff out. Skinderella on the other hand is the kind of woman who needed reinforced bathroom shelves built to take the weight of her stash of skin lubricants. Because she's worth it, OK?

But the path to beautiful skin does not always run smooth. Skinderella's husband has started to complain about how getting close to her is like trying to catch hold of a goldfish, what with all the creams and oils she ritually slathers on herself at bedtime. There was an occasion, a few weeks back, when he managed to get her in a clinch but it didn't last long. He reckons he would have been more successful had he tried to climb a greasy pole.

These days it is not unusual for him to wake up in sheets that are soaked with fragrant smelling face cream. At work, Skinderella's colleagues know within seconds when she has been sitting at their desks or using their phones. Like a snail, Skinderella leaves a glistening trail wherever she goes but the payoff – and it's some payoff – is that her skin has a texture not dissimilar to a perfectly ripe peach.

Skinderella's cosmetic addiction was manageable, even endearing, until a few months ago, when she discovered that when it comes to skin care, the world wide web was the ultimate apothecary. She started small: ordering a pot of eternal youth here, a jar of life-prolonging elixir there. Her graduation from skin products to other purchases was inevitable and it happened almost overnight. A moisturiser company sent her a link to a perfume retailer which in turn suggested that a discerning shopper such as Skinderella might be interested in sites that sold other gifts For Her and For Him.

A whole new world opened up to her – a world of pen-knives and pocket torches, egg-timer cufflinks and giant garden Jenga. I think you will understand the scale of the problem when I tell you that Skinderella has had all her Christmas presents bought since July. CD players that you can use in the shower. Cameras the size of a matchbox. A special device which locks the cork on a half-finished bottle of wine to thwart drinks-cabinet-raiding teenagers. A remote-controlled helicopter, to go with the rollerskates. And the two-way radios. All of them bought in bulk by tapping her credit card number into her keyboard.

In the beginning she found that internet shopping provided that it's-my-birthday feeling every day. The carefully wrapped packages arrived into her office most mornings and, even though she was the one who ordered the items, she still got a little thrill when she held them in her thoroughly moisturised mitts. She suspected if she had them delivered to their house, her husband might not appreciate the volume of internet booty she had been accumulating. But he won't mind when he sees what she got him for Christmas. Or so she hopes.

But lately, the constant clicking on that little electronic cart had started to make her feel nauseous. Sometimes she found the products inside were more like the novelties you find inside a Christmas cracker than the gift which looked so enticing on the computer screen. We were nibbling olives and having the would you/would you not Botox discussion when she blurted out to me that her credit card bill had reached €3,000. What started out as a harmless search for Audrey Hepburn's complexion had led to serious credit card debt.

Luckily Skinderella doesn't just have great skin, she also has great friends. She was glad when one of them took away her credit card and relieved when another gave her an interest-free loan. The last time I saw her, she revealed that she had given up on her more expensive potions and was rediscovering the delights of her first teenage skin cream which does a similar job and costs considerably less. She's learnt a couple of things over the past six months, she told me. Beauty can't be bought online. And it smells divine, not bovine.

Bends of Brother

Yoga boy is back from India. He was only in the country five minutes when he had me bobbing about in the sea at the Half Moon swimming club in Ringsend. Embarrassingly, the boyfriend insisted on swimming in his full Liverpool strip although, dressed in baggy and hastily borrowed 1950s-style flowery togs, I couldn't really complain. Sun, sea, stillness, silliness. There will be more days like this before my brother Brian takes off again.

After a quick dip, he strutted about in his Speedos with the men who have been swimming there for 40 years. Then, in the hot afternoon sunshine, he decided, as you do, to strike some inverted yoga poses.

"The world looks better upside down," he said from a headstand. At times like this I am half mortified, half proud. That's my brother with the six pack, the tan and the straggly blond hair. That's my brother who doesn't care who is looking at him. Upside down or right way up, he welcomes the stares.

Close by, a family from Central Asia were eating sandwiches and taking pictures. I looked up and the father was balancing his baby on one hand. It could have been a Michael Jackson moment except the baby was clearly enjoying herself. She had done this before with her father. She knew no fear.

Yoga boy reminisced about coming here with my other brothers and sisters as a child, racing them down the pier to the red lighthouse. Still balancing on his head, legs in the lotus position, he asked one of the Half Moon men about our father who, before he died, was a regular down here. The man said he saw him once, laughing and diving fearlessly into the water with the late Luke Kelly from The Dubliners. A scrap of information uttered with care by a stranger who knew that, to us, it was diamond precious.

The last time Brian came home, he tried to teach me yoga with mixed results. I possess a mat but I confess it hasn't seen much action since that first day when he introduced me to the downward dog pose and other yoga delights.

To his credit, he tried with me again the other morning and I'm beginning to think it is worth the effort. It has certainly worked for him. He has been going through a rough time and without yoga and meditation he said it would have been an awful lot rougher. It has helped ease the pain in his chest that he says is heartache – even yogis have girl problems – and that yoga is like therapy, a healing from within.

He said that yoga works for everyone, even if your name is not Geri or Madonna or Gwyneth. I wanted to believe him but my legs wouldn't do what I asked. Then I stopped trying so hard and afterwards, just like he said, the world looked a little better.

Yoga boy's evangelism can be off-putting but he genuinely wants to share what he has learnt. For example, in between his osteopathic clinics at the Harvest Moon centre, he is holding a free yoga class in St Stephen's Green in Dublin. I'm furiously texting my yoga-friendly friends and hoping they will give it as much support as the flash mobs have been getting recently in New York.

Everyone is welcome to yoga in the park. Beginners, experts and the just plain curious. You don't need to bring anything except an open mind. Personally, I'm kicking myself that I am going to miss it, as I will be away for the weekend. At the very least, it will be a diverting hour; at the most, it could change your life.

Because he's my brother and I love him, I am hoping this experiment will turn out to be a unique mass yoga experience but it could just as easily end with him standing in the rain in the park with a mat and a smile. Either way I know he will laugh about it afterwards.

Yoga boy is no saint, and at times he can be as irritating as he can be edifying, but I believe there's a simple choice with people like my brother – you can look at them and laugh or you can listen and learn. I'm listening. I have to. Because he'll be gone again before I know it.

Henless Chickens

I have never been a fan of that premarital ritual known as the hen party. I'd rather stick baby hedgehogs in my eyes than sit through an evening where a normally dignified friend agrees to suck beer through a straw that resembles a part of the male anatomy. My mother didn't have a hen and neither did I, so it's obviously hereditary. Perhaps we are both missing some vital girly gene.

My abhorrence of the so-called "last night of freedom" nonsense is the reason that, back in Temple Bar's hen-filled heyday, I avoided the cultural quarter of Dublin on Friday and Saturday nights. I am allergic to the eardrum-splitting laughter caused by a learner sign being hung around a nearly married neck, indicating that the bride-to-be – that's her in the tasteful veil-and-horns combo – is a tad inexperienced in the bedroom. Caroline was well aware of my feelings on this matter when she called me from Belfast last November. That is almost six months ago, you will note. "I know you don't know her very well," she offered, "but I am organising a hen party for Clare."

This is Clare, who Caroline at least had the decency to admit, I hardly know. The same Clare who brought her fiancé John round to my old flat in Belfast once, when everyone was engrossed in a competitive game of poker, and proceeded to show said fiancé her cards. "Clare, you aren't supposed to show your cards to anyone," I said in my best, I'm-not-really-annoyed-but-you-better-watch-your-step hostess voice. The woman just ignored me and whispered loudly in her fiancé's ear, "I love you so much I don't care about winning or losing." Eurrrgggh.

"Please," said Caroline. "I'm rounding up a good gang of people and we're going to come down to Dublin for the weekend. It will be a laugh." Hmmmm. I hadn't seen Caroline for a while and, despite my reservations, I agreed. I even said I'd organise a restaurant and host a game of pool in the afternoon. I was feeling quite magnanimous about Clare and her hen party when Caroline called again. "Just checking you're all right for the weekend," she said. "Yes, quite looking forward to it actually," I replied, surprising myself. "Great," she said. "Just one thing. Clare isn't actually coming. See you tomorrow."

What madness was this? I called Caroline straight back. Apparently some kind of family emergency had caused Clare to back out of her own hen night. I pressed Caroline for more details. Turns out, the family emergency line was just a really bad excuse on the hen's part. Clare had simply decided she didn't want to participate in the event, so terrified was she at the prospect of strippers and suspenders and oddly-shaped edibles. The hen, it turned out, was too chicken to come to her own party.

We went ahead anyway and if you have never been to a henless party, I highly recommend that you go out and organise one immediately. Nobody is actually getting married, so there is none of that forced sexual innuendo that can turn the most timid of ladies into a character from *Viz.*

On our henless night, flame-haired Aisling (who is not engaged) wore the veil and the L plates and don't ask me why but it was actually quite funny. I confess I even shrieked with high-decibel laughter once or twice. The ten of us, most of whom had never met, went to see a brilliant two-piece guitar act in the Chancery Inn on the quays called, brilliantly, Mel and Collie. We bonded with Mel because like Clare, Collie hadn't turned up to do the gig. A lively pensioner did a girdle-flashing dance, a group of Scottish women on a real hen night turned up and Aisling was the belle of the ball. Clare, love, you would have hated it.

I'm convinced the henless night could catch on because anecdotal evidence suggests hen and stag parties, as we know them, are on their last, admittedly already fairly wobbly legs. It's all pampering weekends with the girls these days and hiking in the Burren with the boys, with barely a genital-shaped chocolate bar in sight.

"I don't think hen parties were in vogue when I got married," my mother told me the other night as I turned on the tele-vision to watch coverage of the war in Iraq. "Don't talk to me about the war," she said, suddenly going all Uncle Albert from *Only Fools and Horses.* "I already went through one, I was born ten days before the Second World War started. London 1939, I remember it well, I was evacuated you know." She was muttering something about never having seen a banana until she was eight, thanks to Mr Hitler, when I distracted her with the question of whether my Dad had enjoyed a traditional stag do. "Well if by stag you mean was your father poured out of a taxi on the morning of the wedding, drunk as skunk, accompanied by a man I had never laid eyes on, then, yes," she said. Sorry I asked.

A Message for Us All

When I lost my phone recently I suffered a bout of mobile anxiety. Gone, all gone, the numbers I had stored up in the phone instead of writing them down in a notebook like I always promised myself I would. I wouldn't mind but I had just hunted down Louis Walsh's contact details after losing them the last time, and every self-respecting journalist knows those precious digits are the very lifeblood of our profession. But it wasn't the missing numbers that grieved me so, rather the lost text messages.

Gone, all gone, my messages, I moaned to my terminally unsympathetic little sister.

"Oh really", said she, "Who do you think you are, Rebecca Bloody Loos?" Actually for her information there were a couple of explicitly romantic texts in among the treasure trove of messages. The kind you keep because sometimes you need reminding. "I xxxx you." "You said you'd be xxxx by xxx." "Don't forget to put the xxxx out." That kind of thing.

The other ones I miss are from friends. Messages containing things that probably wouldn't mean anything to anyone else. One of them, for example, read "To ourselves! For ourselves!" I can't remember what prompted that particular Sauvignon Blanc-fuelled bout of independence (it could, of course, have been the Sauvignon Blanc) but it always used to make me smile.

I have another friend who texts entire sentences from *The Office* or quotes from the ancient yet still classic comedy sketch show *A Bit of Fry and Laurie*. He is never short of something to say, type or text. The last few days I haven't heard much from him though. Our texting has been a one-way street. Then he phoned from the hospital lift saying that she only had a few days left. I was standing beside a dress shop on Grafton Street and it suddenly didn't seem so depressing that the hot pink skirt I was lusting after wouldn't go past my thighs.

I couldn't do her justice in this small space. Like her son, she is one in a trillion. If Santa came around to her house at Christmas time, even he'd be shocked by the amount of Yuletide paraphernalia decorating every surface of every room. "Do you like my new reindeer," she'd ask, pointing to two overgrown Rudolphs on either side of the mantelpiece. "Yes," I would say and, when I cracked up laughing at the over-the-topness of it all, she didn't mind a bit. Friends sent her boxes of the stuff from America or she would go browsing in charity shops looking for the best bargain pieces. When one of her sons left home, she afforded herself the luxury of her latest creation, a Teddy Bear room. An entire bedroom full of teddies, sitting on a tedspread, with teddy pillows, light streaming in when she opened teddy curtains. She liked her bears. She loved her family.

Text messaging took on new meaning over those days, when Laura was slipping away. You stopped worrying about the right thing to say and as the days went by, you wrote: "I'm here for you, xx" or "I love you" or "I'm thinking of you all, x". Somehow it didn't feel corny, it just felt right. "You don't have to reply" I'd write and he wouldn't. But one time he replied with a simple "x" and I cried just looking at the screen.

Last night he phoned me with the news. His voice was calm, he was telling me to take care of myself, to have a brandy, to remember her the way she was when she had cooked a chicken curry for me a few weeks before. Amazing, it was, the way he was trying to comfort me. He said to tell people not to send flowers but to give blood in her memory instead. He said this a few times. Over those days, he had seen the hope blood could create when everything was hopeless, the hope that the cells in what he called this "magical elixir" might kick-start her system again, the hope that she would be given a bit more time. Never mind the shortage of beds, nurses told him during those difficult days. What we really need is blood.

We are so fond in this country of giving out yards about the health service and yet only six per cent of us donate blood to help the health service we profess to care so much about. Some of us are afraid of the needles. Some of us think, wrongly, we might catch something. Some of us are certain that enough other are people doing it already. But enough people simply are not doing it. Not nearly enough.

When I put the phone down I sat looking for a while at the small candle I had lit on top of the widescreen TV. A strange kind of altar. The snooker was on. O'Sullivan beating Hendry. A glass of brandy. Cheap chocolate. Three remote controls. No control. A deathly silence, intones the commentator, in the Crucible. And on my phone an eloquent x for lovely Laura Howard, a message that I never want to erase.

Monkeh Planet

I have always thought those fake babies given to young teenagers in the UK to put them off pregnancy were a great idea. What generally happened was the teenager would take the baby home and after a couple of days get utterly fed up waking through the night to feed and change the baby. It provided a real taste of parental responsibility and made them think twice about whether they really wanted a baby in their young lives.

I was given a cuddly toy recently. And all right, so it doesn't wake up in the night with a soggy backside (thank the cuddly toy Lord) but we've found looking after it an onerous responsibility all the same. The person who gave it to us is one of those adults who still has soft toys inhabiting her bed. She has names for them. They have personalities. I think you'll understand when I tell you that one of them, the lovely Wendy, was a bridesmaid at her wedding.

We, meanwhile, were never a cuddly toy sort of family. I don't remember one soft character in our house, except the ones we brought back from Funderland, which never lasted long. We didn't have blankies or any of those comforting items that are trailed around by small children and smell faintly of egg sandwiches.

The closest I have come to the phenomenon is watching my fairy godchild Hannah, who shares her bed with Duck. He appears to have healing properties because, when her nanny broke her arm, she let Duck sit beside her. She's generous like that.

Anyway, my very first cuddly toy will be known to readers as the ITV monkey. It is a knitted creature that was used to advertise a new digital television service a couple of years ago. The service was soon defunct, but the monkey, known to fans simply as Monkeh, became a cult hit adorning offices (even *The Office*) all over the UK. He has long arms and a kind of sock puppet mouth. There are patterns on the internet showing you how to knit your own Monkeh, should you be interested in that kind of thing.

Our Monkeh is the seventh such toy my friend has liberated from the Gadget Shop, where she has become known affectionately as The Monkeh Lady (TML). She matches Monkehs up to their intended owners according to their personality. Our Monkeh, for example, is tougher and more independent than most. He has to be, reasoned my friend, because apart from the boyfriend's brief childhood fling with an overgrown Rupert Bear, we are just not used to looking after toys.

The main point of Monkeh, say both TML and the others who have received one from her, is that the more love he is given, the more he returns. But for us, fostering a cuddly toy feels quite strange. I'm just not convinced that hugging inanimate objects – if not encouraged at an early age – is something you can come to in later life. But I am trying, and so far Monkeh hasn't attempted escape. Sometimes, though, I look at him and he seems to be wearing a neglected expression that I couldn't dare tell my friend about.

Equally unsure of how to behave with a knitted monkey, the boyfriend has started to do laddish things with it, such as making Monkeh scratch a rude itch. When I told my friend about this, she was appalled, and sent us some guidelines which are so, er, unique I feel they should be shared.

1. The Monkeh must be placed in a room where the Monkeh owner/owners spend a lot of time, i.e. bed-

room or living room. This is to ensure that the Monkeh is involved in their everyday lives.

2. The Monkeh must be hugged AT LEAST ONCE A DAY by Monkeh owner/owners.
3. The Monkeh may not be brought to places where he may be lost or subjected to Monkeh abuse – verbal or otherwise. Not everyone understands how important it is to treat a Monkeh with the respect he so rightly deserves, hence the strict selection process and guidelines. Visits to pool halls and discos are strictly forbidden.
4. The Monkeh is a civilised member of our community. He is not like his wilder relatives, gibbon and human, and therefore does not scratch/rub his rude bits. Head and feet scratching allowed.

You get the picture. Thing is, the boyfriend's involvement is now limited to manoeuvring Monkeh into various yoga postures, while I recently went a whole day without hugging him (the Monkeh, not my boyfriend) and didn't even notice. We seem to lack the imagination required to look after Monkeh according to the guidelines.

This makes me sad. And it could be my underdeveloped imagination, but Monkeh doesn't look as happy as he did when he first arrived. It's as though he knows his stay has provided us with a real taste of parental responsibility. And that he's made us think twice about whether we really want a baby, I mean a cuddly toy, in our youngish lives.

A Girl's Best Friend

There are no ordinary mothers. And she is certainly not ordinary. She doesn't do Mother's Day. Doesn't need cards. Doesn't want chocolates. There are no rushed, guilty trips to the newsagent. No buying overpriced bunches of carnations that still bear the sticker from the convenience store. No fussing over which restaurant to take her to. Happy Mother's Day? No way.

A daughter wants to give her something anyway. This daughter has not always been kind to the mother. She has stolen coins from the drawer in the kitchen. She has stolen notes from the purse with the sticky clasp. She has lied so brazenly about where she was until, one night, the mother had to go searching the neighbourhood in a frenzy until she found her and dragged her out of the pub. The daughter hated her mother that night. But she appreciated the gesture when she realised exactly what and more precisely who the mother had saved her from.

One day the daughter decided to run away. She had been given too much maths homework and anyway there was this boy she liked who wore white make-up on his face and had black hair identical to Robert Smith from The Cure. He lived in Co. Wicklow, so she took a DART to the end of the line and then a bus and somehow arrived at the right house on the dark country lane.

The boy had seemed full of encouragement on the phone but now just looked embarrassed. And she thought he didn't look that cool any more, in just his posh school uniform, with no white face and no blood-red lipstick. Reluctantly, he agreed that the girl could live for a while in his garden shed. They ran across the lawn, bent double so his parents wouldn't spot them from the living room window, and down to the shed at the side of the house.

After a while she got bored and he got worried, so he told his parents who told her mother who had to get a friend to drive her the 20 miles to the house late on that rainy school night.

The daughter was impossible to live with. She was full of anger, she lashed out at everyone. When she was good, they said, she was very, very good, but when she was bad she was horrid. The mother tried counselling but that didn't help. The horrid daughter just sat there looking sullen while the rest of the children told the woman with the understanding expression how their sister made their lives a misery. She slammed doors until they fell off their hinges and pretended to be a witch to scare her younger brother.

All this time the daughter knew she didn't deserve the mother who would make beautiful meals: meatloaf and mashed potatoes, chicken pie and beans, a fry-up on Saturday morning, Bubble and Squeak with the leftovers of her perfect Sunday dinners. Sometimes the daughter would turn her nose up and buy chips instead. Knowing she didn't deserve her sometimes made things worse. She wanted to be good. But it just didn't work out like that.

The daughter was always saying sorry. Sorry for bunking off school. Sorry for letting boys into the empty house. Sorry they then wrecked the house and stole the special bottle of Martini and broke her sister's guitar. Sorry she got sacked from her Saturday job for liberating a packet of mouth fresheners from the shelf. She meant to pay for it. She forgot. Sorry for throwing a plate of Spaghetti Bolognese at the wall. "Sorry," she said.

The mother was always saying, I forgive you. I forgive you for worrying me to death. I forgive you for being selfish. I forgive you this. I forgive you that. It seemed to both of them as though the cycle would never end.

But if mothers and daughters are lucky, the cycle does come to an end. If they are lucky, one of them grows up. Eventually the daughter counts the mother among the people she can talk to most honestly and laugh with the hardest. The small encounters of their lives, the ones other people might be bored with, are discussed in detail. The daughter loves to listen to the mother's stories from her work. The tiny triumphs. The dramas and the politics. A perfect afternoon will be spent drinking coffee and eating cream cakes while rain pours down outside. There will be no slamming doors. There will be no crying over spilt spaghetti sauce.

Because this mother is not ordinary. She has superhuman strength. A heart that's always ready to give. Eyes that see through you, right into the beauty and the beast of you. And still this mother manages to love you, no matter what demons are discovered inside.

The daughter still says sorry and she is still forgiven. So, no flowers. Only friendship. Happy UnMother's Day.

Guest and Gestapo

Coming home from work after a hard day there are a few things you just do not want to find on your dining room table. A used cotton bud, fresh from the ear of your long-term house guest, has to score very high in this department. But there it was. An unappetising combination of cotton wool, plastic and earwax resting innocently on the table. You should have thought about this before you agreed to let him stay for five months, it seemed to mock.

I know I am not easy to live with. Everyone who has ever lived with me knows I am not easy to live with. That includes an ex-husband, a family, a mother and a boyfriend who every day has to bite his lip and marvel at how difficult I am to live with. However, even I never left used cotton buds on the table. Half-empty flagons of cider maybe. The odd dirty sock. I like to think I have some standards.

It all seemed like such a good idea at the time. "Can I stay in your house when I come over," my brother Brian asked. "Course you can," I said. We planned his visit. He would bring all his Indian spices and cooking instruments and herbal toothpaste and pictures of the holy mountain. We got a room ready for him, a chest of drawers, a table and a chair. I looked forward to us meditating together, cooking sumptuous Indian banquets, enjoying deep conversations deep into the night. Five months? Why not make it 12? He'd bring a little bit of India to Dublin 3 and all I had to give him was a roof over his head.

It's not quite working out like that. Forget Cottonbudgate,

it was Carpetgate that really made me question my decision to let him stay.

You see, he likes his baths. And the fact that I had asked him to please make sure and let the man in when he came to lay the carpet didn't deter him from his daily ablutions. The boyfriend and I were up at six that morning clearing out the room for the carpet. All my long-term house guest needed to do was let him in.

I rang him at 11 a.m. And at noon. "No sign of the carpet man," said he. So I rang the carpet people, who told me their man had been banging on my door for 15 minutes, calling through an open window if you wouldn't be minding. But answer came there none. The houseguest was in the bath with the radio blaring. The carpet men moved on to another house. Two weeks later I'm still getting over it.

There have been a million other incidents that may sound insignificant to you but have rocked my otherwise steady domestic life. These include: him not turning off the hot water switch after he has a shower. Him dumping all his stuff (anything from Zen Cards to incense) on the table instead of putting them away. Him putting coffee grounds down the plughole and questioning me about it when I ask him not to. Him using the tumble dryer without asking. Him breathing. Himmmmm.

I'm beginning to feel like the Gestapo in my own home. Snooping around for signs that he has been breaking the rules. Ve haf vays of making you put ze tea bags in ze bin instead of ze sink. That kind of thing.

Then there are the lectures. Since his arrival, our domestic habits have come under scrutiny. He is, after all, a doctor and knows a thing or three about health. He won't use our cheap saucepans, for example, because he says the aluminium on them will give him Alzheimer's. He thinks we are mad using regular toothpaste because, hellooo, fluoride is mega-toxic. Friends are jealous because my houseguest is also a yoga teacher who happens to be extremely generous with his time but, with all the inner turmoil I'm experiencing, I just can't bring myself to get on the mat.

Worst of all, if I'm really honest, I don't think any of this is actually his fault – except perhaps the bit about the carpet and the used cotton bud. His stay has turned me into a bit of a monster, and I'm constantly on high alert for his next dodgy move.

It has got to the stage where if he just sat meekly in his room, listening to gentle water music and praying for world peace, I'd be up there ranting at him like a woman possessed.

There have been chinks of light in this dark tale. The other night I had a dinner party, during which he played the guitar and sang and read his Zen Cards for the guests. It was a joyful night that reminded me why I wanted him in my house in the first place. The next day I got home from work, cleared his stuff from the table, turned off the shower switch and fished out a teabag from the sink. He ain't heavy, he's my brother. I just have to keep telling myself that.

The Youth of Today

It's brilliant when you have nephews, because you get to attend weekend functions that might otherwise remain at the periphery of your life's experience. You get, for example, to go to the Irish Beyblading Championships, even though you don't really know what a Beyblade is. You get to stand in a toyshop and discover just how baggy are the baggy trousers worn by boys these days. You are afforded unwanted glimpses of boxer shorts peeking brazenly from waistbands worn half-mast. It's a whole new, not entirely attractive, world.

Fionn and I went for lunch after the games. This took some time because we chose to go to the Epicurean Food Hall in Dublin and you have to walk around a few times before you decide what country you want to eat in. We finally settled on Mexico, and over lunch we talked about winning and losing and taking part.

He hadn't had a particularly satisfying tournament. First Fionn was accused by the referee of modifying his Beyblade – it's a kind of spinning top, that's all you need to know – when he absolutely hadn't. Then his equipment fell apart almost as soon as battle commenced. The whole thing smelt to Beyblade heaven as far as I was concerned, and I would have called for some kind of inquiry, but Fionn distracted me by pointing at the aisle full of Barbies.

"I don't mind, anyway," he said. "It's not about winning, I had good fun taking part." This is not what you expect from a healthy child of ten years old, not in this competitive age of points races and *Pop Idol.* Later, wandering around one of those new Asian supermarkets, I felt the need for some Auntie intervention.

This win-some/lose-some attitude is all very well, I told him, but, winning is not to be sneezed at. I know this probably sounds mad to you, but take it from me, winning can be even better than losing sometimes.

The little blader didn't bite. He said he had great fun taking part and changed the subject by pointing out a Durian fruit and telling me that while it smelt like rotten fish, it apparently tasted simply delicious. I was momentarily disarmed by his knowledge of exotic fruits until I remembered that he is the proud owner of a subscription to *National Geographic.* What is it with the young folk these days?

It's brilliant when your boyfriend has nephews because in the same weekend that you make your Beyblading debut, you get to take seven-year-old Stefan on the Viking Splash and watch him roar in a demented fashion at passing Celts.

It's not so great when, afterwards, he demands to go bowling, but he was down from the North and it was his first time in Dublin, so it was off with us to the Stillorgan Bowl.

Stefan, it soon transpired, doesn't share quite the same view of winning and losing as Fionn. Whether or not he managed to hit any of the pins with his bowling ball wasn't a matter of life or death – it was more important than that. He kicked, he cried, he shouted at his mother. I wouldn't have fancied Fionn's chances trying to explain to Stefan the joys of, you know, er, taking part? It could have got very messy.

The next day we brought Stefan to Dublin Zoo. It was one of those rare days when every animal seemed happy to be on show – as though the keepers had gone around the African plains geeing them up. "Now look, fellas, it's a sunny day, we're expecting a big crowd, just make a bit of effort. No squawking at the back."

Having nieces or nephews, niblings if you will, is just brilliant. You get to stare at gorillas for half an hour and watch as the biggest one puts his hand to his head in a very good impression of someone chatting on his mobile phone. When we visited, the chimpanzees were having an afternoon apple, eating party, the elephants were trumpeting away and, best of all, the seals were being fed.

Waiting for the keepers and their buckets of fish, we watched hungry herons until we were distracted by a screaming child. Stefan rolled his eyes in annoyance. "Can't concentrate," he said, "not with that one shouting." Then we were both distracted by another small child snuggling in the arms of her father. She was in hysterics, chuckling in that throaty way you do when someone close to you is pretending to eat you all up.

The both of us watched the scene until Stefan said in a small voice, "I wish I had a Daddy like that." He does have a Daddy, it's just that he hasn't lived with him for quite a while. "You do have a Daddy," I told him. "If I have a Daddy then what's his name?" he asked me without missing a beat.

The thing was, I didn't know. But in the end it was OK because quick as anything he had moved on asking me, "So, which do you like best of all, the sea lions or the gorillas?" I thought for a moment and said, "Neither, I just like Stefans." And the cheekiest monkey in the zoo threw back his head and laughed. Brilliant.

Emergency Nursing

I am one of the most squeamish people I know when it comes to hospitals. I hate the smells. The unexpected sights. A surgeon's blood-splattered slip-on shoes. Nappies piled neatly on a table beside an older person's bed.

It's as though I resent being reminded of what actually goes on there and I find this resentment hard to hide. If I needed to go to hospital and wanted a friendly face to gaze on, I would be the last person I'd call.

So take pity on my mother. Over the past few years, every time she ended up in hospital it's her hospital-phobic decidedly non-nursey daughter who for some reason has been the one to accompany her. I was with her when she went to the doctors for a routine checkup and it was decided that she needed a heart scan. I sat petrified and resentful in St Vincent's for an afternoon trying to think of soothing things to say. Mostly, "You'll be grand", if I'm honest, although I didn't know if she would be grand. She was, as it turned out. I, on the other hand, needed a couple of days to recover.

Not long afterwards she had come up to Belfast to visit me and we decided to go to the cinema to watch *A Beautiful Mind*. We were walking up the steps in the cinema and, when I turned around in the dark to ask her which row she fancied, she was gone. I followed a muffled groan to discover her lying on the plush carpet mumbling something about her left arm. I can see us now, both whispering in case we disturbed the other patrons' enjoyment of the trailers. "Are you OK?" I whispered. "No, I think it's broken," she whispered back. Embarrassed, I managed to get her up from the floor and lead her out of the cinema, whispering about whether we should get an ambulance to the Royal Hospital. We took a taxi instead.

The first thing I did when we got there was ring my sister. "Rach," I said. "I'm in the hospital with Mother. I think you better come here." The fact that my mother had said she didn't want to bother anyone else was immaterial. I was not about to start playing nurse when there was someone much more qualified at the other end of the phone. I don't think I relaxed until my sister came with her child and her husband and my mother was so full of morphine and we were all making so much noise there was no way she could possibly notice that I was No Florence Nightingale. We got *A Beautiful Mind* out on video a few months later. She cried.

The phone rang at around 9 a.m. one morning. "Róisín," she said, "I fell down the stairs at work and . . ." She had broken her other arm. This hospital visit was made slightly more bearable by the fact that, as she lay at the bottom of the stairs, she experienced some kind of paranormal event. She had been willing her right arm to move and it couldn't oblige because it was fractured but wanting to grant this fervent wish, her beautiful mind had presented her with a picture of a right arm moving, even as the broken right arm stayed where it was.

My mother rubbed her eyes in disbelief and did the same thing again, with the phantom arm humouring her with a repeat performance. At the hospital she was so obsessed with this story, that she kept retelling it to anyone who would listen and before I knew it, I was putting her gingerly into a taxi, safe in the knowledge that other nurses would take over when she got home.

Four months later, the right arm has not healed. An operation is called for. In an operating theatre in St

Vincent's, a portion of bone will be taken from her hip and grafted on to her broken arm. Everyone else is at work and, though I have deadlines looming, I'm moved to action by the thought of her waking up from the anaesthetic all disoriented and frightened.

So against my will, against every unbroken bone in my body, I am there, stomach squirming, as she emerges, an oxygen mask on her face and a drip coming from her arm, looking as confused as a child.

"Am I OK?" she asks and I tell her that she is. And she asks me to kiss her, so I do on the forehead. I stroke her hair like I remember her doing to me when I was young. I listen to the nurses in the ward sympathising with this lady about her frail hips and that young girl about her accident. Smiling and joking and cajoling even as they empty out bedpans and listen to pain and wipe away blood. I think they are some of the most incredible people I've ever seen. And I think I am one of the most cowardly.

But, I tell myself, I am here. And I don't believe her, but my mother smiles over from her hospital bed and she tells me that is enough.

Undying Friendship

We think about him every day. A railway bridge straddles our road and the trains wouldn't let us forget him, even if we wanted to. He loved them, knew everything about them, had been there and worn the anorak while never quite turning into one. David Boyd. Irish Railway enthusiast – you called him a trainspotter at your peril – extraordinaire. The trains rattle by on their way to Belfast, and we think of him still.

I remember the first time I met him. At the railway station in Portadown, on a train to Scarva for the annual outing of the Royal Black Preceptory. My brand-new boyfriend's oldest friend. He made me laugh all the way to Scarva. Me a reporter from the South terrified of saying the wrong thing on a train full of Orangemen; him an irreverent young guy with a wicked sense of humour. He was carrying the banner of the Portadown Orange Lodge, not out of loyalty, but because the 50 quid they paid would make a tiny dent in his student loan. I knew from that first train journey that he was special.

That night, Jonny and I were to have our first official date in my hotel. He rang half-an-hour after he was supposed to arrive and asked, "Do you mind if I bring my friend?" Of course I do, you scaredy cat, I thought. "Not at all," I said.

So they arrived. We drank the hotel out of Smirnoff Ice. I started kissing Jonny until he got so embarrassed that he ran away to give Boyd a lift home. On our second date he asked me to go to a party and arrived, late again, to pick me up with Boyd in tow. I almost gave up when Boyd turned up with him a few nights later at the cinema.

I soon found out why they seemed joined at the hip during those early days. Jonny's last girlfriend was jealous of their close friendship. He spent less time with Boyd as a result and, when the relationship ended, he felt terrible about the months when he had relegated his snooker pal, his football friend to the second division. A girl was never going to get in the way again.

And, despite wanting to be centre of his universe, I was oddly moved by this. Boyd was my text-obsessed mate, my sometimes annoying little brother and the platonic love of my boyfriend's life all rolled into one.

Boyd didn't just know about trains. He had a near photographic memory and a talent for lots of disparate things. One day he wanted to be a journalist, the next a DJ or an international playboy.

Once he helped me with an article that involved riding trains all over the six counties. We ended up on the Dublin-bound Enterprise. I wanted to impress him with first-class tickets but you couldn't see well enough from first-class windows for his liking so he dragged me into economy. When we got to my apartment in Dublin, I slept on the sofa and let him sleep in the spare room. He fell out of bed that night. In the morning, dazed and with a bloody nose, he told me he thought this type of thing might have happened before and was perhaps the result of a head injury sustained during part-time work the previous summer. Six months afterwards, he was diagnosed with grand mal epilepsy, but neither he nor his parents were warned just how potentially lethal the condition could be.

Jonny's sister made the call to our flat in Belfast late one night when we were just about to go to bed. Is Jonny with you? Something's happened. "What?" "It's Boyd. He's dead." I turn to Jonny in panic and I say – what do I say? I take a breath and say, "Jonny, you have to be calm", and he says "What is it?", and starts to cry. He is crying before he even knows And I say, I say, "It's Boyd, he's dead." And that's when my boyfriend collapses like a wet tissue and curls up in a ball on the floor.

And then we are at Boyd's funeral and it's too real for tears. I can't help wishing the stern-looking minister would say more about who that brilliant boy was in this world instead of telling us to take comfort in the idea that he is on his way to the next.

Another victim of sudden unexpected death from epilepsy (SUDEP). Boyd was just 21 when he died from this much misunderstood illness. On our last journey together, I remember looking out at the *Coronation Street*-style houses with him as the train approached Connolly Station and Boyd pointing and saying that is where he would live if he lived in Dublin. We live there now. And it hurts too much to say it out loud but we miss David Boyd every time the Belfast train goes by.

Just Don't Needle Me

Make sure you have finished your cornflakes/porridge/croissant/fry before reading on, and don't say you weren't warned. My good friend, I will call her Diana after the late princess, didn't have the decency to let me finish my bangers and mash before telling me about her recent experience with colonic irrigation.

The fork was halfway to my mouth as she began to wax lyrical about the benefits of a procedure where every undigested morsel is sucked out of you – look Nurse Reilly, a ten-year-old mushroom! – through a tube. I haven't been able to look at a sausage since.

I expected this to happen, but not for a while. I thought it would be at least ten years before friends would start availing of plastic surgery or colonic irrigation, ten years before these visits would be deemed about as shockworthy as a trip to the dentist. But that time is now, apparently, and in a development reminiscent of the days when everyone else in school had a pair of black pointy suede shoes with buckles on from Simon Hart except me, I am starting to feel left out.

My friend Diana is feeling much better since her colonic experience, which I was glad to hear when I rang her the other day. She said she felt cleaner and fresher but she couldn't talk for long. She had work to finish if she was going to make her next appointment, a date with a lady and a needle as it happened. She was having, she told me, her second Botox session.

When I calmed down, she explained that she'd had the first treatment just before being interviewed for her current job. She had started to notice these lines on her forehead, especially when she smiled, and she didn't want to look ancient when she was being given the once-over by the panel. It was quick and painless – the interview and the Botox – and none of her friends had noticed any difference. But she did. She felt much more confident and could now wear her hair back off her face in the style she is normally too self-conscious to attempt.

So what? That was the response of another friend when I called to tell her about Diana's colonic escapades and her €250-a-pop Botox habit. She said that she herself swore by this thing called micro dermabrasion, which costs €120 a session. "Listen," she said, "people are going into Brown Thomas and buying pots of face cream for €200 when they would be far better off getting more invasive treatment that actually works, for the same price." She used the word invasive as though it were a good thing, and then told me about a 26-year-old colleague who gets Botox injected under her arms to stop her chronic sweating.

Yet another friend thinks I am being hypercritical in my mild disapproval of this carry-on. She pointed out that everyone, including me, tries to enhance their natural assets, whether it's with a kohl stick or the latest laser treatment. Some people go further than me in their quest to look their best. What, she wanted to know, was my problem?

So I thought about it and I realised that my problem was that it made me sad. I looked into the future and saw a time when I will be meeting my friends and even though they know I'm coming, their latest procedures will mean they look unnaturally surprised to see me. If I don't succumb myself, people will say things behind my back like that one – and I am thinking of starting a campaign to ban this phrase – has "really let herself go". They will then discuss whether I was too far gone for the latest acid facial to make any real difference. Casual conversations will take place, in restaurants, in coffee shops, about the fabulous man who flies in twice a month from Harley Street. Casual conversations are already taking place.

I know a woman in her sixties who gets electrolysis because otherwise she would have a well-developed beard by this stage, just like her late mother. Somehow that is acceptable to me. She dyes her hair from light grey to brown, which I also can understand. She has her eyebrows plucked, her nails trimmed and gets regular reflexology. All of these things make her feel better in herself. None of these things make me uneasy.

Bring a needle or a toxic chemical into the equation and I waver. Something in me says medical procedures should make an ill person feel better, not an ageing person look better. But then, if having a medical procedure to make you look better actually makes you feel better in the process, where's the harm? I don't know. Where is the harm?

The day before Diana told me about her Botox sessions, I was walking down the road to work, and it struck me that she looks better now than at any stage in the ten years since I have known her. She is beautiful. With or without Botox. I think I'll tell her that more often from now on.

Casing the Joint

We've just got back from old Amsterdam, where we called on the Blings, the enchanting couple who became godfathers to my niece a couple of months ago. Mr and Mr Bling – so-called for their love of jewelled cufflinks and rings the size of children's fists – are friends of my sister. The boyfriend and I bonded with them over beers in the small English village where my niece was christened, quickly deciding they were well worth stealing from her. So, as you do, we did.

They live around the corner from the Anne Frank House, a place I have wanted to visit since reading her diary umpteen times as a teenager and a few more times as an adult. We had put it and the Van Gogh Museum at the top of our not very long must-see list. The Anne Frank House was as moving as I had imagined, but, it being Amsterdam, we kind of got diverted as we cycled towards the Van Gogh Museum. One out of two isn't bad.

The Blings' apartment was, as anticipated, a work of art, and we found it easily enough. After landing at Schiphol airport, which turns seamlessly into a beautifully designed railway station, we took a double-decker train and a tram, then walked through cobbled lanes, past shops selling magic mushrooms and marijuana, to Keizersgracht, one of the pretty canals that dominate the city.

Their dog, Nicholas – named after the tsar, of course – rushed down the marble staircase to greet us. Then Mr Bling led us into their apartment. It was a couple of hours, and a few glasses of the finest champagne, later by the time we managed to scrape our jaws off the floor.

We didn't know where to look on our tour of their three-storey apartment. At the massive signed Andy Warhol prints of Queen Elizabeth on the red walls of the kitchen? At the downstairs bathroom lined with black rubber? At the stunning antique furniture – "that chair was made by Napoleon's brother" one of the Blings blithely informed us – in the formal canary-yellow dining room? At the pillars imported from an English bank? At the art-deco chandeliers? After all that, we needed a lie down. The guest suite, on the top floor, was better than that of any five-star hotel with a sauna in the bathroom and a tanning machine near the bed for those pale-skin emergencies.

It was inevitable, when we eventually ventured out, that our walk took us past a coffee shop where one of the Blings purchased for us some delicious chocolates laced with the kind of herbs that don't grow in Darina Allen's garden.

The way drugs affect people is always interesting. Drugs such as alcohol, for example, can make some people merry and others depressed, while turning usually entertaining folk into intolerable bores. Marijuana is no different. I tend to forget everything I have just said, everything I am saying and everything I wanted to say, which leads me to talk even more nonsense than I normally do. Then I eat vast and eclectic amounts of food – crisps, scrambled eggs, brioche, blood sausage on toast – and fall into a deep, snore-filled sleep.

It turns out that the boyfriend, not previously experienced in the way of the weed, becomes more alert than usual, spouting profundities and adopting an expression that suggests he has just discovered the meaning of life. He grows even more fanciable under the influence. Unfortunately, he confessed to not being able to say the same about me, after

I'd repeated once too often my regret at spending our Van Gogh time in a coffee shop.

I didn't know there was such a thing as a hash hangover. I do now. The morning after I got back to Dublin I took to cycling around in a muggy haze, wearing my new floaty aquamarine skirt, thinking I looked all bohemian and arty, like all those Amsterdammers who cycle around in kitten heels and other inappropriate clobber.

The reality was a little different from the art-house movie playing in my head. I was whizzing past Trinity College when the pedals stopped turning. I looked back to see the floaty skirt twisted into the back spokes. I tried to yank it out discreetly, but the skirt just got more entwined. Naturally, a small crowd gathered to watch. It took six people 20 minutes to hoist the bike up and cut my pride and joy out of the wheel. Thankfully, I was wearing an underskirt, so my modesty was protected, but my new skirt was now covered in oil and ragged and torn at the seams.

The lesson for today is: when in Amsterdam, think carefully before you do what Amsterdammers do. The high may be fun, but a messy comedown can leave you red faced and in rag order.

In the Blink of an Eye

Life can change in an instant. That's what it says on the jacket of a book I'm reading. One minute you're eating a Chinese takeaway in front of *The Apprentice*, the next the phone rings and the voice at the other end is saying something that simply doesn't compute.

Suddenly the sweet-and-sour prawn balls that you shouldn't be eating anyway – they're so far off the glycaemic index it's not even funny – taste even more like plastic than they did when you started eating them. As Alan Sugar decides which of his protégés to fire, the voice tries to convince you that a close relative has gone missing. Bizarre and unbelievable but, apparently, true.

I will spare the blushes of all involved by not naming the main characters in this story. The missing person had been due to meet his wife and a colleague in a city-centre hotel that night for dinner. By the time I got the call, his wife and colleague had been waiting there for an hour and a half. Our missing person couldn't be contacted on his mobile and, because not turning up without an explanation was totally out of character, the man on the phone with the bad news – also a relative – had called the gardaí, who had contacted the hospitals. Would I please go to the hotel to comfort my relative's wife, who was in the throes of imagining the worst? Is the Pope German? Oh, ja.

It would hardly have been polite to refuse, although as well as suffering from acute indigestion I was, by this stage, utterly confused. The confusion swiftly became panic, which in turn morphed seamlessly into fear. When was the last time I saw him? What were the last words I had said to him? Why had I forgotten to text him on his birthday? I confess that, with a deadline looming, I also reflected on whether this family emergency was a good enough excuse for not delivering an article on time. I'm a tiny bit ashamed of that now.

By the time we had driven to the hotel I was up to ninety, thinking of all the horrible things that might have befallen the missper, as they call them on those cop shows. In the lobby, his distraught wife and I hugged and cried, then scurried back to the car, saying we would check her home for signs of our missper before deciding what to do next. We spent the ten-minute journey retracing his steps that day and trying to convince ourselves, unsuccessfully, that he was safe. Our voices were strange and strained and speeded up. We were waiting for everything to change.

For a few moments I know we were thinking the same thing. We were imagining a world without him. I thought of my mother enjoying Ibsen at the Abbey, unaware that the life she had left outside the theatre doors was not the same one into which she would emerge. I wondered if she had already sensed something was wrong as the characters moved across the stage. I wondered how we would tell her what that something was.

It was while retracing his steps in our head that a spark of hope lit up the gloom. One of us hit on the notion that, after a heavy week, he could have gone for a pre-dinner nap that turned into a sleep so deep that he couldn't hear his phone. Knowing the missper as we do, the snooze factor seemed a plausible reason for the unexpected events of the evening. Suddenly, I realised my breath wasn't coming in short puffs any more. It was as if a cloud had lifted. Sure enough, when we reached the house, we discovered that our missper was just a sleepy young man with a bad case of snoring. Embarrassed but relieved, I told the gardaí to call off the search, went home to congealed prawn balls and took painkillers for my headache.

Last December we didn't get the chance to imagine a world without my brother Brian. By the time we heard about the tsunami, he had already phoned to tell us that, despite the fact that he was bodysurfing when the wave hit, he was, incredibly, alive. We were spared that frantic, fearful time when nothing is certain and everything – everything bad, anyway – is possible.

The book I'm reading is called *Moments*. It's a collection of short stories by 39 Irish women based around those moments in life when something shifts inside us and we glimpse a light in the darkness or come face to face with the monster under the bed. Everyone involved, from the editors to the writers, has worked for free. The full cover price of the book will go to Goal, to help victims of the tsunami, who know more than most how quickly our world can change. In the time it takes to walk into a book shop and buy it, we can change somebody's world. That is in no time at all. A moment.

Stepford Boys and One-Night Stands

Heartbreak Highs

The job of a journalist carries with it many privileges, none more sacred than the occasional access to prominent people you hold in high esteem.

I'm quite predictable in my celebrity crushes. I go for obvious targets with the occasional foray into the realm of aged popstar. I don't normally do bad boys – I favour the Brad Pitts over the Colin Farrells. And I know some might think this weird, but if I ever get to sit in a room with Paul McCartney (on my own, obviously, Heather Mills being miles away digging up landmines or something), then, well, I can't even type straight thinking about it.

A few years ago I developed quite an unhealthy obsession with Ronan Keating. It was around the time his mother died and he ran off and got married that I first noticed I was becoming fiercely protective of him, too-tight crocodile skin trousers and all. I would almost become violent when anyone tried to slag him, which happened too often for my liking.

He stirred up feelings in me that I hadn't experienced since I cried all the way home from a Wham concert, because, "Waaah, sniff; waaah, George and me are meant to be together." (You fooled me if no-one else, Mr Michael.)

By the time I finally got my chance, Ronan's first child was a toddler. In the interests of research, I had a word with Yvonne Keating in the foyer of a Dublin hotel before my interview with her husband began. She was down-to-earth, witty and generous, so I wasn't in the best form as I took the lift to the penthouse suite to make my move, by which I mean to ask probing and deeply incisive questions of Ronan.

He was everything I could have hoped for, except for being a father, madly in love with the mother of his child. "Hi, I'm Ronan," he said, slightly unnecessarily, before leading me from the noisy lounge full of music-industry types into the bedroom where it would be quieter. It was at this point that the line between fantasy and reality became horribly blurred.

Ronan motioned with his hand and said, "Let's sit here, God bless, God willing" or something to that effect. To this day I don't know why I proceeded to walk in the direction of the huge double bed complete with silk sheets and leopard skin throw. In hindsight, I suspect Paula Yates and Michael Hutchence were not too far from my thoughts. Anyway, Ronan looked straight at me and said, "I mean here, at the table." It's difficult to recall anything else after that.

I gave up on celebrity crushes. Meanwhile, friends have crushed on regardless with no thought for the inevitable humiliation that results. One went as far as telling her five-year-old son that David Beckham was her boyfriend, to which he rolled his eyes and snorted, "David Beckham doesn't even know you exist." I also feel quite sorry for a guy I know who met and fell a little in love with a stunning girl, not realising that the object of his affections also happened to be a singer-songwriter adored by millions. There aren't plenty more of those fish in the sea.

The send-off for the Ireland soccer team at Dublin airport was the last gig at which I ever expected to develop a new crush. It was one of the all-too-frequent times when I have found myself interviewing people I didn't even recognise, a situation which forced me to seek the help of teenage boys. (Me: "Who was that I was just talking to?" Disgusted teenager: "Duh, Steve Staunton, you fool.")

That's when I met him. For all I know, Roy could have been confiding in me about the "personal problems" which led to him leaving Saipan, but the only thing I noticed were the butterflies in my stomach as he eyed some passing giant leprechauns with cool disdain. That was it. I spent the next couple of hours watching Keano watch everyone else and totally reviewing my no-bad-boys policy. I know I am not the only one who felt it: after his interview on RTÉ, there were intense discussions between women in the office about his allure. One male colleague made the point that, if he was talking about a female celeb the same way, he'd be lynched. Them's the breaks, is all I can say.

Sometimes celebrities don't live up to the expectations of the crusher. In a nightclub recently, myself and a male friend sat watching Andrea Corr shake her stuff on the dancefloor. While I was busy convincing myself she couldn't possibly be happy deep down despite that face and that figure, he shook his head and swore blind he had seen better-looking girls in his home town. If he's even remotely telling the truth (which I seriously doubt), all I can say is boys, get down to Nenagh, Co. Tipperary. Meanwhile, I'm off to Old Trafford. In my dreams.

A Case of Broken Hearts

I'm still not finished moving. It has been months now and there are boxes in the bedroom still unpacked. These are marked in black felt tip with enlightening phrases that I felt would be helpful when the time came to identify their contents. 'Miscellaneous Stuff' sits beside 'Things I Need' and the one I really dread opening, 'Bit and Pieces'. It's like I wanted to write 'Can't Be Bothered Sorting Through This Crap' but there wasn't room on the cardboard crisp box. So they sit there in anonymous piles, growing scarier by the day. Then there is a battered suitcase that has followed me everywhere. From Dublin, to Birmingham, to London, to Dublin, to Belfast and back to Dublin again. It doesn't need announcing because its contents spill out the sides. But if I did mark it, I would call it simply 'Letters' and probably never go near it again. At least until I'm advancing in years and want to remember that I had a life once. I wonder how impressed I'll be as an old timer when reminded I used to hang out at the roller disco an ever-so-slightly excessive three times a week.

This suitcase is filled with pages and pages scrawled from friends, missives about everything and about nothing, all stuck in pink envelopes and posted in the days before e-mail and text messages. I rarely send or receive letters anymore. When I do get them, they tend to be the nasty kind written in green ink that I'm more inclined to file in my dustbin then in the suitcase.

Along with the letters, the case is filled with out-of-focus photographs, ticket stubs for events I can't remember attending and birthday cards from people I wouldn't recognise. But at the bottom, wrapped in black tissue paper and pink ribbon, is a little bundle of memories I'll probably always carry around.

Every time I move house, that perfect package leers at me. As I moved from Belfast to Dublin I really thought I would do it . . . I thought I might open the ribbon and face the contents. But I didn't. These are letters 21-year-old me sent to 17-year-old Sam who broke my heart into a thousand pieces despite not having an ounce of cruelty in his bones. We met at a gig in Birmingham where he was pressing buttons on the sound desk. "I'm having a party," I said. "Would you like to come?" "All right then," he said. He was beautiful. Inside, outside, every way.

There followed three weeks of exquisite kisses because when things are this pure, anything else would just spoil it. Wouldn't it? Three weeks of feeding ducks and exchanging meaningful glances. Reading about the Kray twins in the rain. Eating space dust that exploded in your mouth.

Then one day he didn't call. And the letters began. Long and winding missives full of anguish and recriminations and vaguely psychotic ramblings. In hindsight, I can see I was coming on a little too strong. The letters were wrapped up in black tissue paper (the misery! the drama!) and never sent. But being me, I made the fatal mistake of showing him one of these rants, probably more for a critical analysis of my Emily Dickinson-style poetry than anything else, and the next day he met me in a coffee shop with a letter of his own. The gist of it was, "I'm sorry. I think you need a husband, not a boyfriend. I don't want to stand in your way." He walked me to the bus stop and I used up a whole packet of paper hankies on the way.

Two years later, I got married. Five years later, I was

crying again. And I wanted to find Sam. He was in Gran Canaria working as the Spanish equivalent of a red coat, which made me feel a little better because I thought he might be an underground film director or something equally cool. We spoke briefly and blandly, I have to admit I fantasised about me turning up at his hotel on a package holiday and us living happily ever after. But the thought of him in that uniform made me cringe.

And then I fell in love. Properly this time. With a gorgeous man who likes the fact that I come on far too strong and is learning to love any vaguely psychotic tendencies. For the first time in ten years, I realise that this particular bundle of memories doesn't matter anymore. In a box marked Revelations, I pack the painfully corny but truthful notion that romantic wounds, no matter how deep, eventually fade.

Just like the ink on an unsent letter. And these ancient infatuations, no matter how well they are packaged, just can't compete with the real thing. I think about this but don't quite have the courage to pull gently at the pink ribbon, peel back the black tissue paper and take a match to the contents. It wouldn't be fair. I think old-timer me might like to remember how it felt.

Seeking Mr Right

A friend in her early twenties has a problem with men. Or rather with the lack of them. Molly has no shortage of what I consider fanciable male admirers but can't seem to find a guy whom she actually wants to go out with. She will spend 2006 the same way she spent 2005: trawling bars and clubs and ticking off essential characteristics on a boyfriend shopping list that is almost as long as her flowing black hair. For a start, they have to be in the right sort of profession, which is either (a) publishing, (b) film, (c) art or (d) all of the above. Molly is a multimedia kind of girl. She doesn't think she is asking too much.

Some of her requirements are reasonable. Boys who wear white socks and black shoes simultaneously will not be considered, for example. And they don't need to be drop-dead gorgeous but they do have to be dead, dead cool. "I'm looking for that Moby vibe," she explained as she tried on her latest vintage purchase, and – while trying to look like I understood exactly what she meant – I asked her to elaborate.

"You know, neurotic but sexy and deep, with the wit of Woody Allen and the originality of Samuel Beckett."

She doesn't want to be taken to the pub or the cinema on a first date. "Would you like to go and see the bats in Dublin Zoo?" is her chat up line of choice. She doesn't just want a hero, she wants a superhero. "Spider-Man," she says enigmatically when pressed for specific details. Solvency is also important. He has to have his own home and live within scooter distance of Dublin city centre. A car would be a bonus but the lack of a motor will not lead to instant disqualification. In fact, a bicycle – painted purple with old-fashioned handlebars, a bell and a basket at the front – would be a definite bonus. She can see herself perched on the crossbar, going to the latest art opening, making sarcastic comments about fashion victims and wannabes with the superhero of her dreams.

I want to tell her this is never going to happen but I can't because sooner or later she will find that out for herself. I want to tell her that you can't invent somebody and then go around trying to find him, wasting a lifetime in search of a perfectly formed needle in a global haystack of eligible bachelors. But if I speak up, she will just look at me with pity. "I would prefer to be alone," she will say, "than with just anybody."

A few years ago, I remember being exasperated by another acquaintance who declared she didn't want just anybody. Amy, who spent most of the last decade trawling trendy bars in Manhattan, was worth more than that, or so she thought. She ended up with the kind of men she thought she deserved. And one morning she woke up and wondered if she was worth anything or anybody any more.

Eventually she found love, and he was nothing like the ones (dominant, attention-seeking, rude, arrogant) she had spent all those years chasing. And in best Mills & Boon fashion, she found the right person under her nose in a place she had never bothered to look.

This shopping list syndrome is not just a girl thing. One of the most excruciating examples of reality TV recently was the Mr Right series. Thousands of women applied for the chance to impress a wealthy, wifeless toff and around a dozen lucky ladies were chosen. They all lived together in the same house, going on dates with him on different days. As the programme progressed he ditched the ones he didn't like with a flippant if embarrassed “we just didn’t click”. Eventually he had to choose between two gorgeous blondes. When crunch time came, the one he wanted, the one who fitted all criteria, the one he clicked most loudly with, decided that she didn’t want him after all.

Molly thought she found Him a while ago, but then it turned out he was married with a young baby. His wife didn’t appreciate that Molly was more deserving of the purple bicycle and Woody Allen insecurities of her husband than she was. This brief encounter was as encouraging for Molly as it was disappointing. If one prime candidate existed, she reasoned, then there might be another floating around in the romantic ether.

For me the excitement of the relationship rollercoaster has always been in the not knowing, in the making of mistakes, in the taking of chances. Molly sniffs and says I lack standards. She quite correctly, if a little unkindly, points out that my open, transparent, take-’em-as-they-come approach led, in my case, to divorce but I still think that if Molly doesn’t modify her shopping list just a little, it can end only in tears.

Having loved and lost and loved again, I’d take the rollercoaster every time.

Treacherous Liaisons

Think back, through the mists of hangovers and turkey and New Year's kisses, to the office Christmas Party. Remember how newly married Jane from Accounts seemed to be laughing a little too loudly at the unfunny jokes cracked by Giles from Corporate Communications? Admit it, you wondered why the boss was talking so intently to the new woman in Human Resources. And what was very married Carol up to, slipping away before the dancing had even started and followed at haste by the very drunk but very cute techie Tim. A friend at this particular party said their premature exit had every single woman present silently seething into their sparkling wine.

It is possible, of course, that the above scenarios could all be viewed as innocent snapshots from the annual festivities but it is a truth universally acknowledged that Christmas parties across the land positively fizz with the potential for dangerous liaisons. Nicola O'Callaghan from Besom Productions wanted to talk to the increasing numbers of you who simply can't resist temptation.

Surprise, surprise, it turns out, you didn't want to talk. And I can't say I blame you. While researching the True Lives documentary *Unfaithful* for RTÉ, Nicola has been inundated with victims of infidelity anxious to spill the beans on the philandering ways of their loved ones. Getting the stories of the unfaithful has proved a little more difficult.

No doubt, if the programme was being made in the UK, there would be a queue of love cheats as long as their

Pinocchio noses clamouring to explain why they did the dirt. Ireland is too small and too full of squinting windows for that, but only a tiny number of individuals have got in touch.

When you think about it, infidelity is one of the last taboos in a society which discusses most things with impunity. I have been asking around, and the question "Have you ever been unfaithful?" is invariably met with silence and then laughter and then a forceful No. "And if I had," friends and relatives have said smiling, "do you think I would be telling you?" Well, not really, no.

Teenagers can get away with it on the grounds of immaturity, but it is rare to hear people confiding in even close friends about this kind of deception the way they might about pulling a fast one on the tax man or not owning up when they get too much change in a restaurant. Because unfaithfulness makes them feel rotten to the core; even when it can be justified, and perhaps sometimes it is.

For example, can you be unfaithful in a relationship where one party has already lost the faith? A friend of mine, who looked appalled when I suggested she might tell the nation her story, sought solace in a series of soul-destroying one-night stands when she knew that her boyfriend of several years had fallen out of love with her, but wasn't ready to admit it.

There was a brief dalliance with a guy at work who was also in a relationship. And an encounter with an old friend she met in the pub that resulted in awful sex. Another time, she and a married male friend went for a drink and ended up crying on each other's shoulders and eventually much more in a dark corner of a nightclub.

The split with the boyfriend happened only when she found a charge for a night in a Dublin hotel on their joint Visa bill. She dumped him for his stupidity as much as his infidelity.

The unfaithful fall into two main camps. The ones, like my friend, who are looking for the kind of affirmation of their desirability that they don't get at home. The others are people who may be perfectly happy in their relationships but find it difficult to square their genuine intention to stay monogamous with their rampant animal instincts.

A male friend who used to be unfaithful but has since seen the error of his ways felt terrible about his behaviour, but was tortured by the fact that he would never again experience those internal butterflies that occur when every love affair begins.

"You know when your insides are churning and your temperature rises when you see that person," he explained.

Although happy in every other way, he missed that feeling and tried to recreate it with illicit affairs. He was never caught out and lives in fear that his past might catch up with him. Or, even worse, that it will be revealed on national TV.

Fools for Love

My live-in lover/cleaner/personal assistant says if I ask him once more about his Valentine's Day plans he is going to hit me over the head with a box of overpriced chocolates. I don't think he actually means it, but my desire to be on the receiving end of a romantic surprise has him rapidly losing that loving feeling.

"How on earth," he mused, while giving the living room carpet a quick seeing-to with the Hoover, "can one surprise a person who is already pathetically wide-eyed in anticipation of a surprise?" While polishing the television, he complained loudly that I always put an unreasonable amount of pressure on him at this time of the year and that anti-warmongers aren't nagging George Bush even half as much.

As he and his calculator got to grips with the shocking document that is my Visa statement he demanded to know whether I remembered what we did last year on V-Day. Off the top of my head I hadn't a clue. But I am certain it was memorable at the time.

He is less enthusiastic about the occasion since enduring a series of heart-shaped disasters during his late teens.

Cyndi was his first love. She looked like Barbie (I've seen the photos) and by all accounts was just as demanding as the real thing. My then impoverished arts student would spend weeks concocting romantic evenings on a shoestring budget with the proceeds of his jobs in a video shop and a meat-packing factory.

He bought her tons of gold-effect jewellery from his

much-thumbed Argos catalogue only to see her turn her perky nose up at these offerings. One year he even brought her for a meal in a restaurant with real tablecloths but that didn't work out because she got sick during the first course after eating a mussel.

As thin as a whippet and just as much of a pest I like to think, Cyndi was always moaning about the size of her thighs. So, being a thoughtful kind of chap, her lothario saved up for months to buy a deluxe Thigh Buster. That was the last Valentine's Day he spent in the company of Cyndi and her never expanding thighs.

My still-impoverished mate knows better now. If I try really, really hard I can remember back to the meal he cooked where all the ingredients were red or reddish. Gallons of red wine were accompanied by very rare fillet steak, red onion confit and the whole thing was topped off with a raspberry crumble he made from scratch himself.

Another year he brought me to a bowling alley in Belfast. It was during those early days when even the way he tied his shoelaces was appealing, so while it seems a peculiar idea for a romantic date now, his originality knocked me for six at the time.

But still I am not satisfied. Perhaps some kind of rogue Barbara Cartland gene has me pining to be whisked away at a moment's notice in a helicopter to a castle with secret passages where we can sleep until lunchtime the following Saturday in a four-poster bed. In real life this is unthinkable because (a) I wouldn't get into a helicopter if you paid me and (b) I'd much prefer if he paid off my Visa bill than waste money on such an extravagance. A too-posh-for-peasants restaurant is another fantasy. I want a gastronomic evening where a violinist circles the table and I emit a ladylike gasp at the discovery of an exquisite piece of sparkling jewellery nestling in my dessert. The thing is, I would only lose it by the time I got home, and ten cheap and cheerful items from an accessory shop would thrill me just as much.

So, in an incredible U-turn, an attempt to distract him from the fact that I have done no housework or domestic accounting since that day he was ill six months ago, I have asked him not to plan anything for this Friday. No too-expensive flowers or too-fattening chocolates. No teddy bears, no cards – especially not ones with satin padding – and absolutely, positively no surprises.

I don't want to play a bit part in this annual romantic B-movie any more. Let other couples sit self-consciously over stubby candles eating meals that cost twice as much, and taste twice as bad, as every other day of the year.

Love is not just an emotion to be displayed on February 14th, no matter how hard the zillionaires at Hallmark try to convince us. Let us wear black and watch the *St Valentine's Day Massacre* on video. Or we could baby-sit for my fairy godchild Hannah B and watch *Snow White* instead.

I mean it, I told him as he toiled over the ironing board, don't go planning any surprises or soppiness or unfunny Valentines. I'm just terrified he will actually take me at my word.

A Game of *Mr & Mrs*

Although I lobbied more shamelessly than an Oscar-seeking actress, St Valentine refused to give me the nod this year. The weekend of lurve began promisingly enough with my heart doing a little jig at the sight of a candlelit card on the table on the morning in question but that, I'm afraid, was the extent of the drama.

The boyfriend had taken me literally when I insisted again and again that I didn't want him to plan any romantic surprises. He failed to realise this was actually an award-winning performance in the fine art of protesting too much. At least that is what he now claims.

I, on the other hand, presented him with a voucher entitling the bearer to a week without dish-washing and maxed out the credit card on a dozen red roses to be delivered to his office in a swirl of red crepe paper and gypsophila.

By 3 p.m. he still hadn't rung to say thanks, so I called him. "Anything strange or startling?" I enquired hopefully. "Nope," he said. By 6 p.m. I was cursing the blooming flower company for its callousness and myself for breaking a long-held vow never to order anything perishable from the internet.

We had dinner that night at the home of my brother and his wife. We drank cocktails and talked at length about the war in Iraq. One of the party was planning to march for peace with a placard reading: "The only Bush I trust is my own."

When we had sorted out global terrorism and those

interfering Americans, the five couples present played a kind of modern-day *Mr & Mrs*. Obviously we lacked some crucial ingredients such as presenter Nicholas Parsons and a soundproof booth, but it was fun anyway. For a while.

I was delighted to discover that I knew my boyfriend's favourite eircom league football team (Bohemians) but less pleased when he didn't know either the name of my secondary school or the university I attended briefly many moons ago. He redeemed himself by later revealing he knew exactly where I stood on the issue of the *You're a Star* twins from Glanmire, Co. Cork. (I thought they would have been the perfect ambassadors for Ireland in the *Eurovision*, a kind of TaTu without the tongues.)

The next day, we followed the 'Love Trail' that had been set up at Dublin Zoo. As though reading from the final scenes in the script of a Meg Ryan romantic comedy, the lion chose the exact moment we passed to begin licking his lioness's back. Sadly, that display turned out to be the romantic highlight of the weekend.

St Valentine might not have honoured me this year but St Nicholas had been more generous, sticking a couple of tickets to see Juliet Turner at the Helix in Dublin City University in my Christmas stocking last December. So that night we went to see the songsmith from Omagh and listen to her new songs which are more startling/insightful/powerful than anything she has written before. She mentioned the war but not St Valentine's Day and sang instead about one-night stands, pheasants crashing into windscreens and seasons of the hurricane.

When Turner performs in a theatre space such as this one, there is usually a pin-drop silence which sees the audience aching to catch every word and intonation. The man sitting beside me had different ideas. All through the gig he sighed as though the world was ending, complained loudly to his embarrassed girlfriend and took out his mobile phone every five minutes to check the time.

I could tell he wouldn't take criticism well, so when I could bear it no more I pretended to sympathise with him. "Don't worry it will all be over soon," I said. "No, it's not her, she is great, it's the audience; they're dead, there's more life in a morgue," he said.

The audience were not cheering enough, not engaging enough, not behaving the way people should be behaving at a rock 'n' roll gig. Man. He didn't like the audience and in his mind that was a good enough reason to sabotage the performance. An irate woman challenged him as we filed out of the theatre.

"I'm surprised you heard any of that," she said. "You talked the whole way through it." To paraphrase Mr Noisy, he said he could foorkin well do what he liked. He could scream and shout and dance around because he had paid as much as everybody else with their expressionless faces and polite clapping. "That is what people do at gigs," he said in a menacing tone, his girlfriend squirming red-faced beside him.

No amount of chocolates or flowers or mini-breaks in Paris could make up for having to put up with such an ignorant, bullying, insensitive boor. On Monday, the boyfriend came home carrying two dozen dead red roses which it turned out had been delivered to the wrong office on Friday. "They are the most beautiful flowers I have ever seen," he smiled.

And the Oscar goes to . . .

That First Kiss

Some five years in a row, I took the train from Heuston Station in Dublin to Scoil na nÓg in Glanmire, Co. Cork, like the thousands of students heading off to Gaeltacht areas across the country this month. If my experiences are anything to go by, they will learn a lot more than Irish at Irish college.

I remember every special thing that happened during those summers and yet I can't remember his name. Just that he came from Togher and that he pronounced his provenance like a curse. "I'm from Togher," he growled, dirty blond hair falling over dangerous blue eyes. As though Togher were a foreign country instead of a suburb located a short bus ride away from the college.

I don't know his name but I remember the two teeth on each side of his mouth, jagged and imperfectly shaped. Two teeth longer than the others so that when he smiled he looked like snooker legend Ray Reardon. We played table tennis for hours and he never tried to let me win. If I did manage to, and on rare occasions I did, he skulked off out of the gym hall into the sunshine with his sidekicks smirking beside him. (Less pretty Togher boys, who seemed to worship him even more than I did.) I would call after him to come back. I would pretend I had got the score wrong. Sometimes I had to wait a whole day before he sidled up to me again, "Do you want a game, or what?" All right then. If you like.

Sometimes he would just disappear. In the *bialann*, I

pushed potatoes around my plate and scanned the room for his small, sturdy frame. I don't know where he went on those days, because we weren't allowed outside the walls of Scoil na nÓg. One summer I climbed over the wall myself with a few other hapless adventurers. We were caught and it wasn't worth the scraped knees. The rest of us could always be located at all times, but he seemed to vanish when it suited him. Taking or leaving things, according to his mood.

On the days that I couldn't find my Togher boy, I exchanged table tennis for an outdoor pursuit. I was the Swingball queen that summer. There is a satisfying pop sound that only comes when you hit a Swingball ball square and true with your plastic bat. Then the string and the ball spin around and around, perplexing your opponent. I watched the ball, all the time keeping another eye on the tennis courts, the swimming pool, the snack shop where you could buy Wham bars so chewy they took all day to eat. I spent whole afternoons with one eye on the game and another looking out for him.

One day he asked me to go into the woods. We weren't allowed in there either and I knew exactly what this meant. He was going to ditch his posse for a while and grant me a private audience. We walked separately through the bramble and trees until we pushed through to a small clearing. I sat on a log and waited for him. The birds were singing somewhere to my left, I heard his footsteps from the right. He sat beside me, this tough boy from Togher, and put his arm around my shoulder. Then he clamped his mouth on mine. His incisors crushed my lips. His head never moved, he never adjusted his limpet lips. "You are doing it wrong," I told him disappointed beyond belief, that's not what it's like in the films. He laughed and ran back to his friends who I realised had followed him after all.

First kisses are crucial: too good, and you spend the rest

of your life comparing every kiss to that one; too poor, and every other kiss feels like an improvement, but you are cheated by the absence of that first, sweet memory.

I was still mad about the boy despite his brutal kissing technique. So at the ceilí on the last night, after the dance of the statues was over, I walked over and handed him my silver table-tennis medal. I had done well in the tournament, thanks to all our practise. He took it and smiled, those teeth bared, his eyes glinting under the strip lighting. He stared over as though he was thinking deeply about something, and then broke into loud laughter when his friend whispered in his ear.

I wonder when that Togher boy turned into a Togher man. And if he learnt to be a little more gentle. Not to open his mouth so wide. And to move his head a little. You learn much more than Irish at Irish college. I can't remember his name but I wonder has he realised that sometimes a heart can be shaped like a medal you win for table tennis. And that even if you are 13 and have no use for it, it's rude to get your friend to hand it straight back.

Regrets, I've Had a Few

The other night I was on my way to a dinner party, waiting for the man behind the counter in the off licence to locate a chilled bottle of something fizzy when a voice behind me said, "Oooh, living the high life these days are we?" This man was buying six cans of the cheapest beer in the place. He smelt. He swore. He was a one-night stand come back to haunt me.

He was older now, and looked like somebody's down-at-heel dad. "Ha, ha," I agreed. "Yes, the high life," I babbled. For some reason I was desperate to point out that my fizzy stuff wasn't half as expensive as the real thing. But he just slurred his words and asked me whether I wanted to join him in his bedsit – he was still in that bedsit? – for a joint.

When I declined his attractive offer, he tried another tack. I was looking well, he said. And I was, relatively speaking. I left him there, fishing five cent coins out of his dirty jeans pocket to pay for the beer. I rushed out into the rain afraid he might ask me again, repulsed by the thought of spending one more second in his company. I needed to escape an image of me standing in his room, looking through tobacco-stained net curtains, making yet another decision I knew I would regret.

These are the kinds of social encounters we don't think about when we have one-night stands. If we did, we would never have them. I am not, by the way, talking about the kind of one-night stands Carrie and Co. dissected gleefully over brunch in the coffee shop. I'm talking about the ones you wish never happened. The ones you didn't enjoy no matter how much you tried to convince yourself otherwise at the time. These are the encounters you will never tell your friends about over crostini and eggs benedict because there is no punchline. No playing it for laughs.

This town, this country, is too small for these hauntings not to happen and it's hard not to freeze in the face of those burnt-out flames. I have been on the other side of course. Bumping into a man with whom I had shared what had seemed in my memory like a not entirely unsatisfactory evening in a city-centre hotel a few months previously only to realise, as he turned green and rushed out of the pub, that he was – how should I put this? – repulsed by the thought of spending one more second in my company. I remember feeling sorry about this more than embarrassed, thinking we might otherwise have been friends. Oh, the platonic bridges we have burnt in the name of not going home alone.

I don't care what anyone says about no-strings fun and cheap thrills and sexual liberation. Mostly it's the fear of going home alone that drives people to those strange hotel rooms, those unkempt bedsits, those worn floors in other people's sitting rooms. Bringing a bottle or three along for courage, hoping it will get them through the early hours of what they know will be another meaningless morning.

I can honestly say that I have never fully enjoyed a one-night stand. Not the business end of one anyway. The flirting is fabulous. The anticipation is delicious. The moment of truth when it's just you and him, or you and her, and both of you know exactly where it's heading. It's all fun and games when his foot is getting to know yours underneath the table, but to my mind it's all downhill from there. Sharing the taxi fare. Sneaking in. Not wanting to wake his flatmates or (oh, Jesus what have I done?) his mother. And in the morning, lying there scared to move in case he wakes and you have to talk to him. Or waking to find that you don't have to talk to him because actually he legged it at first light leaving you to pay the bill for the grotty B&B.

I am jealous of friends who have only had the odd one-night stand or no one-night stands at all. There is a dignity in this that I once interpreted as being square. They weren't taken over by that dull panic at the end of a night out, a panic which led them to places they didn't want to be.

It's a shame I'm otherwise engaged because I think I'd be more ready for the Carrie style, no regrets and guess-what-he-did-then one-night stands now. I have a little bit more confidence and a lot more self-respect. I think I'd do it because I wanted to, because it felt right. And if it didn't turn out the way I expected, I think I would have the courage to walk away from the tobacco-stained net curtains and close the door firmly behind me.

It's a Jungle Out There

When I worked for another newspaper, many years ago, we had what we thought were very clever rhymes about everybody who worked there. If your name was, say, John Carty and you were known to be fond of socialising, the rhyme would be: "John Carty, he likes to party."

If your name was Pauline Fleming, and you had slavish fashion sense, it would be: "Pauline Fleming, she dresses like a lemming." I was married at the time, but let's just say that sometimes I didn't act that way. My rhyme, as a result, was: "Róisín Ingle, she thinks she's still single." Or, more obliquely: "Róisín Ingle, she likes her malt single." After a weekend chaperoning a younger friend out on the pull, all I can say is thank the love gods I'm not single any more.

Because I'm exhausted. And my feet, shod for the entire venture in my new silver clogs, are killing me. To put my expedition deep into the mating jungle in context, I haven't been out three weekend nights in a row since the days when Boyzone were just a twinkle in Louis Walsh's eye. Normally, a weekend is hectic if I've gone from work to a restaurant on Friday night and ended up playing pool at Renard's nightclub (which doesn't happen often enough for my liking any more). I spend the rest of the weekend in recovery mode, pottering around organic markets, going for six-minute jogs, having lunch with my family and watching my boyfriend make Mars Bar Rice Krispie buns. (What? I like to lick the bowl.)

But my very attractive friend, who lives outside Dublin

and is fed up with the men in her area, who never text when they say they will, was on a mission. So on Friday night we went to one of those ginormous pubs on Dawson Street, where the punters look as if they have walked out of an ad for hair straighteners – and that's only buachaillí na hÉireann.

The three of us – my boyfriend had reluctantly come, too – had barely taken our first sip when four likely lads arrived and asked to share our table. My friend had gone to powder her nose, so I wasted no time telling the lads that, of course they could share the table, as there was more than enough space for the very slender and pretty young woman who would be back at any moment. I'm good at this, I thought to myself.

And, sure enough, when she came back it was to the attentions of at least two of the men, one of whom she fancied. As the night ended and we made our way outside, my friend took one look at the horse and trap at the door and said: "I want to go in one of those." Like Cinderella, she was whisked off to drink champagne with her new friends, while the boyfriend and I walked home through crowds of freezing, miniskirted women who hadn't been as lucky as my friend.

Saturday night wasn't quite so successful. I chose a pub where the music was to my taste – The Smiths, New Order, The Clash, Joy Division – but it turned out that the men were not to hers. We got chatting about what it was she was looking for. She said there had to be "spark", which you would know was there – or wasn't – within two minutes of talking to somebody. And there had to be "potential". "I'm past the stage of looking for one-night stands. I don't want to waste my time with someone if I don't feel there is a realistic chance of developing a relationship," she said.

There was only one thing for it. Lillies Bordello. Oh dear

God. People actually wear hot pants in Dublin. By 1 a.m. my nerves were frazzled. I was treating this night out like a military operation. I couldn't relax and enjoy myself, because finding a man for my friend had become a reason for being out. The reason for standing squashed beside people busy having a good time, feeling about a hundred years old. I thought that shuffling my clogged feet occasionally in time with the music might make it look as if I was also having a good time, but I'm not the actress I thought I was.

"Let's get our coats," said my friend. "No offence, but I'm not that desperate that I have to stand and look at you pretending to enjoy yourself." Something clicked. "Let's have a dance," I said. I put my hands in the air – I even made woo-woo sounds when the dance music reached a crescendo – we had a laugh and then we caught the Nitelink home, which is another crazy jungle experience.

On Sunday night I played it safe and brought her to Songs of Praise, the brilliant rock 'n' roll karaoke night at The Village. I sang 'Brass in Pocket' and 'Borderline' while she applauded and scanned the place for spark and potential. Róisín Ingle, she's glad she's not single. Because she would never survive. Not in those clogs.

My Stepford Boyfriend

They have remade *The Stepford Wives*, that creepy 1970s movie about the men who turn their women into cupcake-making, flowery dress-wearing, starch spray-wielding, husband-pleasing robots. Of course, the film didn't actually need a makeover, just as *Psycho* didn't and *Willy Wonka* certainly doesn't, but these days film execs don't seem to give an everlasting gobstopper about what we think, preferring to shout "action" and hope for the best.

Boyfriend had never seen the movie. Until I mentioned it to him recently, he had never heard of the expression Stepford Wife. I explained that in the lexicon of life it had come to mean a woman who was compliant, made a concerted effort to look nice when her husband came home, always had the dinner on the table and was up for anything the husband desired 24 hours a day.

"You are the exact opposite of a Stepford Girlfriend," he observed, and before I had a chance to pretend to be offended there was a whirring noise that appeared to be coming from inside his head as something else sunk in. "Do you think I am a Stepford Boyfriend?" he asked. "Don't be silly," I said, polishing off the last bit of his divine spaghetti carbonara and admiring the view as he loaded the dishwasher.

In truth there is more than a hint of Stepford in my boyfriend. Until I had seen him in action I thought the Protestant work ethic was just a myth. But while I come home from work and flop directly onto the sofa, he starts a manic round of chores that are exhausting even to write about.

Filling the washing machine. Turning it on. Emptying it. Hanging out the clothes. Taking them in. Ironing them. Sweeping the floor. Wiping the worktops. Cleaning the cooker. Cooking the dinner. Opening wine. Lighting candles. Calling me from my supine position in the sitting room to join him for pork chops and pesto *à la* Jamie set out carefully in the dining room.

After dinner, it all starts again. "Relax, can't you?" I entreat, barely moving my eyes from the live *Big Brother* stream. "Look, Michelle is trying to get Stu to snog her again." "Can't stop, no time, bathroom needs cleaning," he replies in a worryingly mechanical manner.

Those female readers who in addition to going out to work all day are chained to the cooker/washing machine/ Hoover when they come home might imagine it's great fun and even quite relaxing to live with Stepford Partner. But in case they are thinking of trading theirs in for a more productive model, they should be warned about the perils of Stepford Guilt. The problem with this seemingly flawless setup is that these Stepfordish men are not actually robots; they have feelings and can only take so much before they start complaining and demanding parity of esteem, when it comes to housework.

My argument – that I am just not good at it, that it's not part of my personality, that he does it so much better than I do – only works up to that point where I fear he might short-circuit if I don't at least take out the bins. When I suggest that perhaps he should experiment by just refusing to do any chores, he looks at me appalled. "But then we would live in a tip," he says. It's even more appalling for him to discover that living in a tip doesn't scare me half as much as it does him.

Incidentally, Stepford Males appear to be multiplying

faster than you can say, "have a nice day at work, dear". One friend with a Stepford Husband says the secret is to accept their strange ways and try to make it look like you also come from the vicinity of Stepford, within commuting distance at least. The ironing is her only chore and they have in the past couple of years employed a cleaner. Her guy does virtually all the other household duties, including arranging flowers and following her around with a J-cloth, while also managing sparkling, witty conversation during authentic Italian suppers he rustles up for unexpected unStepford friends of his wife.

Stepford Guilt sets in for her when what they call the "corridor of filth" at her side of the bed gets so filled with tea cups and make-up wipes, he is tempted to disobey the cleaning moratorium that exists around the area. She usually gives in and makes a pretence at clearance that keeps him off her back for another couple of weeks.

I know it might sound like these men are getting a raw deal, but there must be some reason they stick around. I quizzed Stepford Boyfriend about this the other day as he wiped down the cupboards. He paused for what I considered to be an offensively long time before saying that he supposed my carefree approach to cleaning was at times a positive antidote to his more disciplined methods. At that point, I gleefully told him about the sticky end the Stepford Wives come to in the movie. I could have sworn I saw a puff of steam coming out of his ears.

Losing My Religion

Swim for the Soul

If Brian hadn't come back from Bombay for Peter and Aoife's wedding, I would never have known what it was like to swim with a dolphin. Brian, known variously as Yoga Boy or Siddhartha to his friends, is the kind of brother who comes rushing over to your apartment and says: "Oh my God, man, guess what? There is a dolphin swimming in the exact place on the west coast where you nearly drowned. We are totally going to swim with that dolphin. Biba says it has healing powers, man. It's meant to be. We have got to check it out."

For reasons entirely to do with Brian's arrival in the Western world, my resistance was already low and I knew that trying to change his mind on this one would be pointless. The same week he had more or less frogmarched me to the East Wall Community Centre where I was introduced to his newly invented form of yoga. I'll be the first to admit those three days of Soma Yoga were an edifying experience, both for body and mind, but after a few too many Downward Dogs (don't ask) this yoga novice felt dog rough. And I just didn't have the energy to argue.

So I meekly accepted the fact that on the first Sunday in October, we were going to be driven by another yoga teacher, Biba, to Fanore in Co. Clare, where Dusty the Dolphin has been delighting observers since she legged it from her previous hang-out at Doolin.

"That Fungi in Dingle is a bit of a tart," said Brian, who overnight had metamorphosed from a yoga teaching osteopath into an expert on the personalities of seafaring mammals. "Dusty is the alternative dolphin."

Apparently that Kerrymaid ad ("a dolphin is a man's best friend, ha, ha, ha, ha") hasn't done poor Fungi's reputation much good. Some non-believers say Fungi probably expects royalty cheques and appearance fees, while newcomer Dusty is like one of the freshly plucked contestants on *Popstars: The Rivals* and hasn't become jaded by all the attention.

The night before the day trip, some family skeletons had been dragged out of the cupboard by Brian and there were lots of tears before bedtime. I had been acting as a sort of mediator during Brian's trip home. We were emotionally hung over as we left Dublin. Dusty, named after Dusty Springfield who had her ashes scattered in the Atlantic, represented 'the cure'. As Brian had pointed out, I nearly drowned at Fanore in the early 1980s in the days when being bashed about by 20-foot waves was my idea of fun. I was ten years old and I remember thinking "this is it, this is the end". It was dark and we really shouldn't have been swimming at all.

He was a family friend, a father figure really, whom I loved. When I finally reached the shore, I looked back into the sea and he was gone. I hadn't been back since. He was buried in Fanore, just a few minutes away from where Dusty lives now.

We found his grave and I realised for the first time that he was only 34 when he drowned. I walked out to the spot where it happened. There is a sign there now: 'Bathing Is Unsafe In This Area.' Better late than never, I suppose.

We saw the caravan where we waited all night to see if he might come back and make us a cup of tea and laugh so hard his curly black hair would shake. I closed my eyes and imagined him waving from his blue Renault 4. I was glad I had come.

After that, and a break for what we prayed were dolphin-friendly tuna sandwiches, we were ready to meet Dusty. Brian and Biba wore matching wetsuits. I wore my swimming togs and, inexplicably, a black Prince Naseem T-shirt.

The cove was crowded with boys in canoes and people in boats and children paddling among the rocks. Every few minutes, we would hold our breath as the dolphin flipped out of the water, sometimes far away and sometimes so close you could reach out and touch her.

There was something magical about all these people who had just come to spend time with or to observe such a magnificent wild creature. Even swimming in the Atlantic Ocean, for the first time since the time I nearly drowned, was an incredible experience. I don't know if it was Dusty or the fact that I was returning to a special place I had tried to forget about for too long.

Anyway, as corny as it sounds I felt at peace bobbing around in the seaweed, the sun shining down as Dusty seduced us all. And I thanked her as I got out of the water. For drawing me back here, for reminding me of the good times. Tired, depressed, emotionally hung over? You could do worse than head west for some dolphin therapy. Like my brother says, "It's healing, man."

Any Dogma Will Do

Are you a Roman Catholic? Culturally the answer may be a resounding yes. The catechismic truth for many of us, however, is rather less clear cut. Can we be in full communion with the Church while rejecting several of its most fundamental teachings? Is the Pope a Buddhist? Clearly, no.

We all have at least one friend or relative, probably more, who got married in a church for reasons that had nothing to do with their belief in Catholicism. Maybe her dream from early childhood was that the echo in the cathedral and the smell of incense burning would be the icing on the cake. Maybe his respect and love for his deeply religious parents overrides his ambivalence towards the Church.

From discussions with some of my married and unmarried friends, I have learnt that being a Catholic often means picking and choosing the bits that suit you. Like mixing so many items of Burberry or Gucci – you love the check print on the scarf but draw the line at the matching shoes. "I don't believe in any of it," said one acquaintance who was preparing to walk down the aisle, "but in this country it is just handier."

I have given up having these discussions with people because I always end up looking like a Catholic-beating ogre when actually I have a healthy respect for anyone with the self-discipline and faith to live up to the dogma of organised religion.

Some of the Catholics I have argued with in the past tell me they agree with divorce. And sex before marriage.

And contraception. They also insist on a woman's right to choose. They don't accept the notion that a wafer and a goblet of wine is transformed into the physical presence of Jesus Christ at mass. And yet they insist they are Catholics.

This has confused me since the days when I stopped going to mass with the blessing of my mother, and my friends had to grab a mass leaflet before hitting the shopping centre so they could pretend to their parents they had been to church.

The subject seemed more pressing after listening to several harrowing days of *Liveline*, hearing stories of clerical abuse and the clerical protection of abusers. One woman who had suffered for years at the hands of a priest said she still had faith. "But my God has nothing to do with those people," she said.

I have to admit I am a little jealous of those with faith. I would love to be one of those who wakes up every morning and resolves to try to live according to their Church's teachings. Sometimes they stumble but they ask forgiveness and try to do better the next day. I just wonder about the ones who imagine themselves part of this club while living their lives happily rejecting its core beliefs.

I went to a higher authority to learn the Church's position on the increasingly puzzling phenomenon of plastic Catholicism. One expert explained to me that the Catholic Church was not a conventional human organisation like, say, the Bray Golf Club, and therefore things were not as black and white as I seemed to think.

But after a few minutes of theological discussion he conceded that it was "wildly hypocritical" of people who rejected vital elements of the Church's doctrine to get married there. "I would certainly advise them to get married elsewhere," he said. But how many newlyweds do you know would 'fess up to the parish priest that their ideals and the way they live their lives is at complete odds with the Church?

The same people who exchanged rings while pretending to sign up to the Rule of Rome will proceed to baptise their children into a belief system they don't adhere to. Again, a lot of people I know say it is just less hassle.

Baptism means a better choice of schools and, for them, that is the beginning and end of the argument. Being a believer doesn't come into it. And who can blame them? While the government is beginning to invest in non-denominational schools, it is still 'handier' to have the kids baptised just in case there isn't an alternative in the area.

It seems more and more that the Church is being used merely to invest ceremonial significance into rites of passage such as birth, marriage and death. If somebody told us they were members of a group called Communists for Privatisation or the Vegetarian Steak Lovers' Society, we would laugh in their faces. But somehow, it has become acceptable to be a Catholic Who Only Believes In Some Bits Of The Religion.

I will continue to respect those who live their life in communion, or even in partial communion, with their chosen faith. For the rest of us, I recommend a spot of spiritual anarchy which doesn't have to mean abandoning the notion of a god.

It's time to stick our heads above the Church parapet and find a set of personal beliefs that we can live up to. Like that esteemed philosopher Roy Keane once said, Only dead fish go with the flow.

Go Forth and Multiply (Safely)

If, as some believe, libel letters are the Oscars of journalism, getting a tongue lashing from the clergy is surely equivalent to a Golden Globe. And it's wonderful to discover, as I did recently, that today's priests aren't all namby-pamby forward-thinking types.

Funny, but if I was ever going to incur the wrath of God/Allah/Buddha/Roy (delete according to your conscience) because of my contributions to this newspaper, I thought it would have been for my sins against the fine art of punning. Writing about the Irish Family Planning Association's sensible request that soccer fans pack contraceptives when travelling to Japan for the World Cup, I mentioned that those hoping to "score off the pitch" should stock up on condoms. I know, I know. It's worth ten Hail Marys at least.

The *Sunday Message*, the excellently produced parish newsletter of St Andrew's Church, Westland Row in Dublin, was posted to me anonymously, so a big thanks to that particular cowardly custard. It was within those hallowed pages that I, and anyone else who thinks safe sex is good sex, was accused of "moral bankruptcy" by the church's administrator, Father Arthur O'Neill. The good Father also recalled that, in the past, "the old lady of D'Olier Street" (as *The Irish Times* is known by some) used to "feign a lofty distance between herself and the gutter press". "Unfortunately," he continued, "if Ms Ingle's comments are indicative of her present-day standards, it would seem that the old lady is being tempted to take to the streets herself so to speak . . . shame on all those associated with such crass comment – sex is not a recreational past-time and any attempt to even hint that it could be is a shameful (mis)use of journalistic influence." Told you he was peeved.

I briefly considered legal action on the grounds that Father O'Neill had sullied my good name by associating me with street-walking ladies of the night. Then I thought about the many witnesses the defence could call, all with a similar story to tell: "Your honour, in one night alone I spent 20 old pounds and 40 old pence procuring pints of cider and cheese and onion crisps for the plaintiff, a transaction which eventually enabled me to gain access to her grotty bedsit for the purpose of recreational sex." The whole thing began to sound like a bad episode of *Ally McBeal.*

I really don't know why he is picking on me. I hardly think readers of *The Irish Times* were going to rush off to Japan for a mass orgy just because I'd made a bad joke. He might have been better served ticking off past seminarians at Maynooth. According to one member of the clergy writing in *The Irish Catholic* (always an enjoyable read, by the way), some priests who studied there openly admitted they had got ordained in the belief that the celibacy ban would be lifted in a few years. Father Joseph Briody remembered cases of trainee priests dating girls and having condoms on their person in preparation for a bit of extracurricular how's-your-Father. Not to mention the seminarians who were having 'inappropriate' relationships with other men. And while the Roman Catholic Church decrees that baby-making is the only moral justification for copulation, is the hierarchy or Father O'Neill seriously suggesting, for instance, that sterile couples should never, ever make love because their passion will never result in conception? Doesn't sound very Christian to me.

I passed St Andrew's Church the other day. It's an

appropriately forbidding-looking building beside Pearse Street DART station in Dublin. (By the way, if you want to get married, an old German tradition says you should sleep naked on the night before St Andrew's Day and you will dream of your husband. Best check out the Church's position on sleeping naked first, though). Anyway, if the gates of the church hadn't been locked, I would have gone in and said a prayer for Father O'Neill. "Dear Whoever, please help Father O'Neill to understand that if you do exist, it's likely you are a loving, non-censorious type of spiritual being who, despite centuries of man-made dogma, is really just asking people to love one another and never leave the lid off the toothpaste."

And I know it's not based on any theological philosophy, but I don't think such a being would mind us engaging in safe and consensual bedroom activity, especially as it's been raining so much this summer. No offence, Arthur, but I would be more inclined to seek guidance on matters of morality and sexuality from my mother. She is a little more experienced, having done the deed at least eight times in her life, resulting in my four brothers, three sisters and me.

Having once had a husband who was a total looker, and a few boyfriends since he died, I wouldn't be at all surprised to find she had done it at least a dozen more times for purely recreational purposes. The heathen. Father O'Neill might benefit from studying the lyrics of George Michael. He once sang "sex is natural, sex is good, not everybody does it, but everybody should". Hallelujah! Now go in peace, and in case you didn't hear me the first time, my children, always use a condom.

Vinnie Claus

Battling through a busy toyshop with two Stretch Armstrongs and a talking Tweenie, I found time to ogle the Action Man display. When I was a kid, there were two variations – the one who had fuzzy hair and swivelling eyes and the one who didn't. Now there is the One Who Swims With Dolphins, the One Who Has His Own Spaceship and, I imagine, the One Who Paints and Decorates The Front Room.

I couldn't wait to escape toy central on a busy Sunday afternoon recently.

If darling Joanna wasn't belting out the little known dance version of Beethoven's fifth on a giant keyboard in aisle eight then the parents of Damien were throwing evil looks at their offspring who was making inappropriate gestures with a pogo stick in aisle ten.

The will to live was seeping away and the shop had become a terrifying blur of Barbies, Barney and "Bloody Hell, Marcus, if I have to tell you one more time!" I got weary and ended up buying the same toy for two lucky nephews.

These Stretch Armstrongs are heavier than they look. The ones I remember were half the size and after a few stretches could be known to leak blue gunk all over the carpet, which my brother thought a most excellent bonus.

Now he looks like a steroid munching surfer dude (the toy not my brother) and if you are thinking of buying one as a Christmas present, study his squidgy arms carefully before you take him home. I think the word I am searching for here is phallic.

I am aware that it's a little early for a Christmas column but I've been looking forward to the holiday ever since I changed my mobile phone ring tone to 'We Wish You a Merry Christmas' back in November. Sure, this may have moved some colleagues to throw stationery at my head but it gave me a little warm glow every time the phone rang.

Excuse me while I go all *Angela's Ashes* for a few paragraphs but when we were young our Santa presents came from charities such as the Society of St Vincent de Paul (SVP) or Vinnie de P as my sister calls it. And, even though the toyshops in Dublin are packed with an astonishing variety of singing, dancing and exploding toys, I actually think we got a better deal. There was history to the contents of our bulging pillowcases, left at the end of the bed by my mother who had spent the night sorting through bags of one-armed teddy bears and games with missing pieces.

It never occurred to us that there was something wrong with a talking doll that instead of saying "I love you Mommy" mumbled "luvuommyughwaadugh" when you pulled a string on her back.

The St Vincent de Paul food hamper was another Christmas highlight, if you ignored the obligatory packets of Angel Delight (yuck) and cans of marrowfat peas (ditto). Again, I don't think we saw this annual gift as an indication of our family not having as much as other families. It was more a Christmas tradition that no one else we knew enjoyed.

Like the Christmas Eve chips marathon. There are good things and bad things about growing up three doors down from a chip shop, even if Borza's in Sandymount is one of the best examples of this gastronomic delight on the southside of Dublin. There is a risk of developing an early addiction to batter burgers for example, one I am still fighting to this day. But it was worth it when the night before Christmas each year, Bruno and his family brought around all the freshly cooked fish, chips, onion rings and spice burgers that hadn't sold, and sat with us while bread was buttered and one of the best yuletide traditions ever invented ensued. Happy, if not particularly healthy, days.

Vinnie de P has just launched its annual Christmas campaign. I am reliably informed that one-eyed dolls are a thing of the past due to the fact that most donors buy new toys as gifts for the thousands of SVP clients. And instead of six packs of Tayto and Angel Delight, they give out gift vouchers so families can buy their own food, cutting out the annual Marietta biscuit conundrum: to bin or not to bin, that was the question.

What the organisation needs most is cold, hard cash and so in churches on SVP Sunday, volunteers will be hoping to collect enough funds to increase the level of Christmas cheer in homes all over the country.

These days, the miracle of Christmas is more about the ungodly amount of money we manage to spend. My prezzies are all bought and I just got paid so I'm going to enter into the spirit of SVP Sunday and give something back. Even if that means darkening the door of my local church tomorrow morning and sitting through mass read by the same priest who not so long ago questioned my morals in the parish newsletter. Now that's what I call a miracle.

Desperate Measures

Stand outside your local off licence this Thursday and watch how religiously we Irish observe this most sombre of seasons. Holy Thursday, a day not generally associated in Christian circles with revelry and merry-making, is one of the busiest days of the year for those in the off-licence trade. Father forgive us, we know exactly what we are doing.

The owner of one of the most popular establishments in Dublin tells me that only Christmas Eve beats Holy Thursday in the alcohol stockpiling stakes.

In Cork, a man at the head office of a chain of off licences says that, in his experience, most people stock up out of panic, others because they want to have enough booze to hold a house party on the night Jesus Christ was nailed to the cross.

In Galway, a busy off-licence manager rates the day among his top five busiest and says it is traditional for bar and restaurant staff to have parties in their homes, taking advantage of the fact that their profession allows them access to cheaper kegs of beer. Crucifixion parties, he says, are all the rage among people who want to turn Good Friday into a Very Good Friday Indeed Thank You Very Much. It is worth pointing out that the Church itself does not request the closing of pubs and there is nothing in its teachings about abstaining from alcohol on that day. And while Good Friday continues to be one of the busiest occasions for churches around the country, I don't know one person who will abstain from alcohol this Friday in the name of religious observance, or even tradition. In fact, there are some for whom the State's locking of the pubs presents the challenge to drink as much as possible, in the manner of a bold child told not to go near the biscuit tin for 24 hours.

But most people simply want to do what they do most Friday nights of the year, which is have a sensible amount of drink in a venue of their choosing. It is for these people, and the tourists who are often bewildered to find they can't get a pint of Guinness on the first day of their weekend break, that I present this guide on How To Get A Legal Drink On Good Friday. The first option may be expensive, but if you book into a hotel on Good Friday and order a portion of chips or some nachos, say, from room service, you can also request the tipple of your choice. This is thanks to exception number one on a list sent to me by the Department of Justice, which states that "persons lodging in a licensed premises may be sold and supplied with intoxicating liquor to be consumed with a meal in such premises".

Those in search of alcohol should also make Good Friday as cultural an event as possible, because "intoxicating liquor may be sold to patrons attending the theatre or other cultural institution". The problem is a good number of theatres close down on that day, "because it's Good Friday", a woman at a popular Dublin theatre told me, as though no further explanation were needed for closing its curtains on an unofficial holiday.

To find a cultural event with a bar, you may have to travel to Ennis, Co. Clare, to view the Bollywood classic, *Lagaan: Once Upon a Time in India* at the Glor film club. This martial-arts romance is almost three-and-a-half hours long, and as result there is a 30-minute interval during which drinks and snacks will be served. The club has a full bar and intends to serve alcohol as, unlike pubs, it is legally entitled to do so.

Another option is to go racing because alcohol can also be sold at race meetings, or greyhound sales or trials, on Good Friday. Unfortunately, it is unlikely that there will be either horse or greyhound activity on that day.

For some reason, it is also perfectly legal for alcohol to be sold in a military canteen on Good Friday, although an army spokesman said that, without exception, army messes are closed for the day, whatever the law says. So a more feasible plan is to take a trip by rail, air or sea in order to buy your friends a round on Good Friday. Drink is available to ticket holders at airport bars, pubs at train stations and on the ferry.

The manager of a pub in a top secret island location tells me he always keeps the place open on Good Friday, the local gardaí being some distance away. In addition to the legal places where you can have a few pints, it is generally accepted that a good number of establishments, in more out-of-the-way areas, keep the back door open for customers. Into thy hands they commend their spirits. Sláinte.

Friend of the Bride

I had been dropping hints for months about the wedding. Are you sure there isn't something I can do, I'd asked more than once, a pick-me-please smile plastered on my face. Amanda is extremely vague about the arrangements for today's big event so she probably isn't the one I should have been talking to. Naturally, she is very interested in getting married to Brian, but not at all fussed about table arrangements and buttonholes and canapés. A bit of a circus all that, she tells me, without realising how very much I would like to be her personal clown.

It's unfair really, because I have all manner of expertise to offer. Perhaps she was unaware of my impeccable wedding singer credentials. My repertoire ranges from gospel numbers, aimed at appeasing religious relations, to secular sixties numbers that will have the congregation swinging in the aisles.

My brother Peter signed the register last September to the strains of Diva Olivia and me harmonising on 'When I'm 64'. Particularly poignant was our jazzy rendition of 'Memories Are Made of This', a version of which Dean Martin himself would have approved. But for some reason, and your guess is as good as mine, Amanda felt her two stunning and classically trained sisters could somehow do a better job at the vocals. I had never felt so unloved in my whole career – which incidentally spans three weddings and a christening. (I still have some slots available in July.)

It happened just when I had given up all hope. The

groom-to-be had kindly sent me the latest IKEA catalogue and a dinky little tape measure by way of congratulating us on our new house. I have gotten over the terror of living in a dust bowl for months and am at that drooling-over-bookshelves-and-wine-racks stage. I'm thinking big abstract oils in the hallway. Pink and white tiles in the bathroom. No lightbulbs – how last century – only brushed silver spotlights everywhere, thank you very much. And no Bakelite, obviously. Can't stand the stuff. Even though it must be acknowledged I didn't actually know what Bakelite was until the electrician came round the other day. I'm pretty good at interior design, I have discovered – something else Amanda might have kept in mind when doling out jobs.

Anyway, along with the catalogue and the tape measure there was a little note from Brian. He wasn't sure if Amanda had mentioned it but they would absolutely love me to do a reading in the church. Not only that, but I was to be in charge of the other readers. Telling them where to sit, how to genuflect at the altar and offering elocution tips as and when required.

Then I got scared. When I was asked to become godmother to Hannah, I had the same dilemma. How could I take such a significant role in a religious ceremony when I was not a member of that religion and actively disagreed with it on many significant levels? The answer for any of you in the same position is to quietly say "No" instead of "Yes" to all those questions they ask at baptisms like do you think the "devil" is really bad and will you promise to bring the baby to mass if its parents are away skiing in Gstaad. Technically, you could say I'm not her godmother at all but at least my conscience is clear and I don't think Hannah cares as long as I keep the *Jungle Book* videos coming.

So no matter how much I wanted to have a role in the wedding, I didn't think I could stand up on the altar and read out something I didn't believe in. I thought about writing my own contribution, having gone through this marriage business myself once – but not having made a very good job of it, I reconsidered.

Another option was doing a serious editing job on the text and hoping the priest wouldn't notice. But I've just looked at the reading for the first time and I don't think editing will be necessary. It's a letter from Saint Paul to the Romans:

"Hate what is evil," he wrote, "cling to what is good. Be devoted to one another in brotherly love. Honour one another above yourselves Be joyful in hope, patient in affliction, faithful in prayer. Share with God's people who are in need. Practice hospitality. Bless those who persecute you. Rejoice with those who rejoice; mourn with those who mourn. Live in harmony with one another. Do not be proud, but be willing to associate with people of low position. Do not be conceited. Do not repay anyone evil for evil. If it is possible, as far as it depends on you, live at peace with everyone."

I couldn't have put it better myself.

Gotta Get a Guru

It's a small little India world, remarked the boyfriend as we crossed the Lakshman Jhula Bridge in Rishikesh for the first time. Although only a couple of wet weeks in the country, he is already surprised to find himself exchanging greetings with spiritual tourists he has met along the way. As monkeys scampered up suspension wires to catch packets of peanuts thrown by women in saris, he spotted at least two Westerners we had previously encountered on trains or in meditation halls. Rishikesh may be Pilgrimage Central, but it's also the place to recharge the batteries when the noise, pollution and bizarre animal life found in the bigger cities gets too much for a pair of weak-bowelled Irish people desperate to begin the holiday part of their holiday.

We left the brother back in Lucknow teaching the sister-in-law yoga, but you never feel lonely in Rishikesh. A charming middle-aged German lady we got to know back on the Buddhist trail, who had a penchant for canary yellow leggings, turned up in our favourite coffee shop. At an ashram we met the young, yoga-mad girl from Sweden who was a student on a retreat we did. She is in seventh heaven in this place, where every corner offers ashtanga or iyengar, hatha or Bikram. Meanwhile, our dusty mats remain stubbornly strapped to our rucksacks as we exercise our elbows sipping grape juice on the balcony of our hotel watching the bottle-green Ganges flow by.

We went white-water rafting the other day. The boat picked us up on the silver-speckled sands of the river and we surged through baby rapids as though they were Niagara Falls. When the waters grew calm again, we rowed in silence past holy men carrying tridents and washing themselves on rocks, and stunning ashrams, where the gurus are in residence, with terraces so numerous they appeared as extravagant wedding cakes perched on the river's edge.

After two months in India, the eyes tend to glaze over when a Westerner opens his or her mouth and the words "my guru" come out. My guru says this. My guru does that. In the south, at the beginning of my trip, I met an Israeli who plays a mean mandolin. His song, 'My Guru is Better than Yours', is a perfect parody of the spiritual scene – a scene which, despite his irreverent ditty, he takes very seriously indeed. Swopping guru stories is the dinner-party equivalent of discussing property prices at home.

In Rishikesh, it took around five minutes before the man in the hotel room next to us, an American with white swirly hair, uttered the magic words. "My guru," says he, "gives Satsang (a spiritual get together) every day at 3.30 p.m. if you are interested."

He offered detailed directions to the ashram, which we found ourselves following later that day. We sat on mats and looked around, taking in the shaven-headed disciples in the white robes, the man with a Mohican haircut, the women who wouldn't have looked out of place on that old US sitcom *The Golden Girls*. Then she appeared. Tottering along in a peach shawl and white robes, her wet blonde hair scraped into a pony tail. A surprisingly normal-looking American woman, wearing small hooped gold earrings, she was followed by various devotees bowing and scraping and kissing her feet along the way.

I have been back every day. Not bowing or kissing her feet, but becoming expert at everything from Native American to Sanskrit chants and marvelling at how after each Satsang my eyes are shining and my mood is elevated. There is no less corny way of telling you why I think this happens, except to say that the woman lives every moment of every day in her heart and that I've found it's kind of infectious.

But as everyone knows, there are teachers on every corner in India, some more reputable than others. Take the man in the beauty parlour, who thought a head massage involved other parts of the body you might not necessarily want massaged. The lesson here is buyer beware. Or the 70-year-old man on the night train to Rishikesh, who laughed like a drain when he heard I had spent 250 rupees (around €5) on a comic book depicting the life of the Buddha. "You Westerners, how you love to waste your money," he chortled, before expanding on his lesson in discernment.

One teacher, a man wearing white robes, with a matching, flowing, wide, candyfloss beard, appeared as we sat rowing in a raft on the Ganges. He would walk, with difficulty, for ten metres in one direction on the riverbank before turning back and walking the same distance the other way. It was mesmerising. Frail step following frail step. A man going nowhere, with elegance. He is probably treading the same riverside path at this moment, the living embodiment of a philosophy you hear time and again here. What is the path to true liberation? That's the question on the lips of both the mildly curious and the perfectly cross-legged. There is nothing to do, the gurus almost without exception enigmatically reply. Nothing to do. And no better place to do it in than India.

From Incense to Incensed

I was devouring chunks of a duty-free chocolate bar for breakfast and digesting the astonishing news that Jordan is dating Peter Andre when it struck me that sticking to my post-holiday resolutions was going to be even harder work than I realised. The plan was to prioritise sitting cross-legged in a room covered in meditation cushions, but I arrived home with a craving for celebrity gossip and, of all things, Yorkie bars. I need to wake up and smell the incense. And fast.

Convinced that a few packets of frankincense-scented sticks and my chanting CDs would help me remember what I've learned during two months away in India, I was almost looking forward to coming home. I had discovered a previously unexplored part of me, a place so powerful I would have no choice but to remember and honour it 24 hours a day.

But when I unpacked my spiritual reminders – a ten-rupee statue of the Buddha, some pictures of the gurus I encountered in India, a dinky elephant figurine – and put them on the mantelpiece, the mother threw a Jaysus-so-you've-joined-a-cult-now style wobbler. It's not easy, this transformation from insatiable consumer to ultra-equanimous being.

Obstacles are everywhere on the path. At the airport in London I felt an intense pull to the magazine stand and, before I knew it, I was shelling out the price of a three-course meal back in India on *Heat* magazine. I haven't thought of the thing for two months and somehow survived, but here I was, almost salivating at the thought of reading about Kerry McFadden being voted Queen of the Jungle. At home, it turned out that *You're a Star* was in its final hours and two cousins of Daniel O'Donnell were the last men standing.

I watched, of course, somehow I couldn't resist, but oh, the shame afterwards when I thought about what I had done with that portion of this precious lifetime.

We have decamped to the mother's apartment – I think she hopes she can de-programme us or something – because the heating in our house has gone on the blink. I rang the nice man in the gas company to set up an appointment to get the boiler fixed, but found this wouldn't be possible for at least five days. He gave me the number for some independent plumbers who might help, but they told me the boiler in question was a dodgy make that none of their workers were willing to touch.

Naturally, I was as Zen as the Dalai Lama while trying to negotiate with the nice man from the gas company when I phoned him back. That's a lie, actually. My jet-lagged voice rose to a whine as I patronised and then verbally abused him in a frenzy of uncontrolled rage.

When I put down the phone, I seamlessly continued the Dharma lecture I had been giving my mother, a lecture about how all mankind's problems and all suffering stems from our reactions to the behaviour of other people. "Other people are not the problem," I explained, "it's the knee-jerk negative reactions that take us over all the time that we need to work on." "Really," said she, making for the door, claiming she was late for some extremely urgent appointment.

Five minutes later, I was back on the phone to the gas company apologising for my rudeness. It was progress of sorts I suppose but I couldn't help feeling that the New Me was on a slippery slope edging closer and closer to the Old Me all the time.

This post-India adjustment period is enough to make you want to voluntarily quarantine yourself. To slip inside a comfy cocoon where the world can't disturb your inner calm. A place with padded walls, where there is nothing to react to and, as a result, no suffering. I walk past pubs and nightclubs struck with an abject fear that were I to walk inside I might be sucked into a gin and tonic vortex, never again to know the peace that can be gained simply from keeping still and clearing the mind.

There has been some serenity along with the scares. My older sister was amazed when I stayed calm in the face of remarks made by my younger sister, remarks that would normally have had me up in arms.

I am getting out of bed earlier than usual to meditate, and so far it doesn't feel like a chore. Subtle changes are taking place as I begin to understand that the Old Me is an intricately constructed thirty-something institution that cannot be flattened overnight.

I came home to hear that my friend, who has been finding it hard to breathe lately, has been taking a five-week course in Buddhist meditation. We met and spent the night talking about all the things that have moved me and moved her over the past two months. It's good to talk, and at the same time I know that all this spiritual stuff is something that many people view with suspicion. But, honestly Mum, I haven't joined a cult. I'm just relearning how to live.

Best of Intentions

It's on my bedroom wall. A piece of cream linen, hanging like a scroll between two short pieces of wood. Just 92 black words, printed in a deceptively ordinary font, a simple design for life. The brother brought it back from India with him, along with enough bags of spices to open quite a decent takeaway. He was going to use them to cook all these exotic meals for his new housemates. Things didn't work out. Things went from close to cool between us. He's staying somewhere different now.

'A Precious Human Life.' That's what it says on the top of the scroll. And like all my brothers and sisters, he is precious to me. He doesn't think that now, though. I began to distance myself from him in an effort to avoid the confrontation I knew would come. But it happened anyway, the emotional distance making the meeting more cruel than it might have been. I said too much. Didn't hold back. Put it all out there on the table, just the way he says he likes it. But he didn't like it this time. "She hates me," he told my mother. "She really hates me." How to find a way back?

'Every day think as you wake up: Today I am fortunate to have woken up,' the scroll says. Sometimes I feel it. A box-fresh morning. The sun shining in where we haven't put up curtains yet, a snippet of good news on the radio and my dream job waiting at the end of a short cycle ride. It's not hard to feel fortunate when the off-side rule is being explained patiently to you over a lazy Sunday salad. When you are moving little feta cheese defenders around a

cucumber goal. On these days, anything is possible. Other days are harder. Brooding over an argument. Disturbed about things said and unsaid. Feeling, as though it were my own, his heart breaking slightly from the hurt. But even then, I know I am fortunate to have woken up. It's just on these days it's harder to remember.

'I am alive, I have a precious human life. I am not going to waste it.' What's wasteful, though? What's more wrong? The hours spent watching live streams from the *Big Brother* house, glued to that precious human zoo, or the guilt that sets in afterwards? The guilt is more wasteful, I've decided, because at least what's going on in that house is real. Muscleman Jason's boredom and isolation. Michelle's all-consuming crush. Stuart's cowboy obsession. I'm not going to waste my life feeling guilty about my own big brother, either. Not if there is something more positive I can do. Maybe this is it.

'I am going to use all my energies to develop myself, to expand my heart out to others, to achieve enlightenment for the benefit of all beings.' This is different for everybody. I know what this means for me. I need to develop my creative side. Nurture it. Give it space. I need to stop splashing around in the shallow end where there are no risks to be taken and, where, if I stumble, nobody will laugh at me for not being able to swim. I know diving into the deep end will help me expand my heart out to others. I don't know much about enlightenment, I don't think we can know until we achieve it. But we can nurture that which opens our hearts. I need to let my imagination run wild.

'I am going to have kind thoughts towards others, I am not going to get angry, or think badly about others.' Yeah, right. These words have a deeply aspirational feel. But even reading them once or twice a day, forcing myself to spend a few seconds taking them in, tends to melt something in me. I have not been kind. I have been angry. I have thought badly

about him. I may well do it again tomorrow. But reading the words aloud, saying with conviction – I am going to be kind, I am not going to be nasty – reminds me of my intention. It seems unbelievable, unthinkable that I would forget that this is how I want to behave. Somehow I do, though. Every day. I read it to myself morning and night and at least for those brief moments in time, I remember.

'I am going to benefit others as much as I can." This line concludes the advice from His Holiness The XIV Dalai Lama hanging on my bedroom wall. I met him in Belfast four years ago. I'd appreciate meeting the man in saffron robes more now, I think.

'I am going to benefit others as much as I can.' All I can say is that I will try. I don't think this means asking my brother back to stay with me. I don't even think it means taking back what I said. But I don't hate him. That knowledge may be of some small benefit. I hope with all my heart it is.

Living for Now

I hadn't listened to the radio or looked at a television the day my brother rang. The morning after Christmas was all about me.

My bad cold which had sent me to bed when I should have been out at the races. My bad luck at getting a set of coat hooks from my beloved for Christmas when what I really wanted was, well, anything but coat hooks really. A news text alert appeared on my mobile. Something about a tidal wave. My bad mood. I didn't even look to find out where.

"I'm all right," said Brian when he rang half-an-hour later. "I'm alive." In my ignorance my first thought was, what do you want, a medal? I knew Brian was in Auroville for Christmas as part of his latest adventures in India. We had gone there together almost exactly a year before. We swam together in the sea, spent a few nights in a beach hut on stilts, sat together in the Matrimandir, a giant sphere with a magnificent white meditation room at its core. "I'm OK," he said, shock rendering his voice unfamiliar. And then he told me how that morning he had gone out to bodysurf and survived the biggest wave of his life.

In keeping with the theme of the magazine this week, this column was supposed to be about where I think I will be in 20 years, but I can't think beyond 20 minutes at the best of times. While trying to sort out our finances recently, I was asked to plan the year ahead, which I did under protest and then found that I couldn't venture into the future beyond September. It just felt wrong. I love that cliché, "sure you could be run over by a bus tomorrow" because it reminds me that even when we try and exercise it, we really have no control over this life. You could be run over by a Luas tomorrow. You could.

I used to dread going to a former boss for a chat because he always asked the same question: "Where do you see yourself in five years' time?" The truth – that I didn't see myself anywhere because I didn't view life that way – wasn't going to improve my employment prospects, so I would make up a reasonable lie.

I try not to look back either. At a party over Christmas, a girl with an all-singing-all-dancing mobile was making short videos of people and then showing the results to them straight afterwards. "Why live in the moment," the girl beside me remarked drily, "when you can relive what happened a few moments ago."

For some, there is no looking back. The sight of an Irish banklink card on the front page of this newspaper, a scrap of plastic among other everyday effects of the missing, was as painful to look at as the most gruesome television pictures of recent weeks. An instantly recognisable logo bringing the human tragedy, already unspeakable in its awfulness, even closer to home.

I wonder how far 27-year-old Eilis Finnegan from Ballyfermot had planned her life beyond her post-Christmas holiday in Thailand. Had she pictured herself smiling that beautiful smile as a proud mother one day, and did she think she would still be living in Dublin? Perhaps she looked into the future with certainty, or maybe her thoughts only reached as far as New Year celebrations with her boyfriend. Did she have solid ambitions kept to herself, in case sharing them, like a birthday wish revealed, meant they would never come true? In the end it didn't matter. All she ever had was the moment. It's all any of us has. A series of heartbeats from the day we are born until the day the wave comes.

It's how well we live those moments, not how well we plan for the future, that counts. It could be putting our hands in our pockets to help our brothers and our sisters in southeast Asia or the many other troubled places in the world. It could be meditating for three minutes in silence on the vulnerability of human life.

Spending our precious moments nursing past grievances and slights is an awful waste, but we do it. Highlighting the negativity of a situation when there is always good to be found, is an awful waste, but we do that too. In each moment there are choices to be made. The biggest choice is whether we want to suffer or not to suffer. Even in the bleakest of circumstances, that choice is always there.

It could be as simple as seeing beyond your superficial desire for a big romantic gesture and appreciating something as simple as being able to hang up your coat on a proper hook. Understanding, or at least trying to understand, that being here now is all we can do. We waste so much time. There is no time to waste.

It's a Holy Show

When the Pope came to Ireland in September 1979, I was just a little girl. His visit made about as much impression on me as his recent death. That is, it made virtually no impression.

When he was busy telling the young people of Ireland he loved them, I was playing in the house of some Protestant friends. His visit didn't distract us from making tents from bed sheets or eating instant noodles from a plastic bowl. The frenzy of yellow and white bunting, of prayers and of piety, completely passed us by.

I remember the day well, and I remember that feeling of being out of step. I didn't wave a flag. I didn't say a prayer. I didn't even care about the dinky Popemobile. I have fallen out of step again in the past couple of weeks as, on radio, in newspapers and on television, commentators relayed the latest details about the funeral, our official mourning protocol or the interpretation of John Paul II's legacy. This holy show has been impossible to escape.

I'm not a little girl any more. I understand that the vast majority of the billion Catholics around the world view this man as someone who took the papacy to new spiritual heights, and I understand that their love for him is real. It is not my intention to disrespect those feelings. But a few years ago, when millions around the world, myself included, felt genuine sadness at the death of Diana, Princess of Wales, I didn't begrudge those critics who felt the need to examine the validity of that outpouring of grief.

He was the first superstar Pope. The first globetrotting

Pope. The first media Pope. He was probably the first Pope to grant an audience to an Irish rock star and an Irish football team. As a historical figure who battled against communism and fought for justice, he was truly great. But he was also a Pope who clung fast to the vital tenets of his Church even as many of his followers were calling for rules about women priests, homosexuality and contraception to be relaxed.

Let's be clear. He preached that homosexuality was unacceptable. He rejected all appeals to introduce women priests. He excommunicated one of his flock for writing a document that made Jesus more accessible to other faiths. Catholics who used artificial birth control, he said, were denying the sovereignty of God. With their coils and their condoms, these people were essentially atheists. That's the way the late Pope saw it.

I think a healthy proportion of the billion Catholics around the world would happily admit to pretty much ignoring the moral stipulations that formed part of the late Pope's Christian mission. Even as their Holy Father cautioned against these things, his flock continued to use contraception, to discuss the possibility of women priests, to have sex outside marriage, to tolerate homosexuality.

I can't help wondering whether this unapologetically strict and dogmatic Pope would have wanted the tears of people who live their lives in complete contradiction to the faith they profess to hold.

But this is the part I really don't understand. The Pope travelled the world with a message that poverty should be eradicated while condemning the global imbalance of wealth. Then he would return to the Vatican, the centre of one of the world's richest organisations, to sit on a throne amid the Church's vast and priceless art collection. The tradition of poverty and humility present at the founding of the Church has long since been abandoned by those at the top of Catholic Church Inc.

John Paul II, if he was serious about poverty, could have done something about this. The late Pope worked hard to change the attitudes of everyone from the well-off to the poorest among us, but what of the attitude of the senior figures in the Church? He could have led by example: sold off the statues, the jewels, the art, the silver and the gold. Yet with one hand he condemned the material world, with the other he gave his blessing to the existence of the Church's own incalculable wealth.

Jesus enjoyed none of the trappings of the modern Church and had no time for opulence. He didn't need robes or pointy hats or even stained-glass windows. Wherever a few people were gathered in his name, that was enough. It's not enough any more. It hasn't been for centuries. Not in the Vatican. And not around the world, where the church owns vast swathes of land and precious treasures that to me are unjustifiable.

In the US, young Christians wear a bracelet with the initials 'WWJD'? It stands for 'What Would Jesus Do'? It's a reminder of the figure true Christians try their best to emulate in their everyday lives.

It's nothing personal against John Paul II, but watching his funeral, seeing the cardinals in their flowing robes and marvelling at the strange uniforms of the Swiss Guards, I felt as if I was watching a very elaborate circus.

Bishops live in palaces. Popes sit on thrones. What would Jesus do?

Game for a Laugh

Running to Stand Still

I am sitting here in a team Brazil T-shirt, trying very hard to think like Sonia O'Sullivan. The shorts I bought don't fit, baggy and tight in the wrong places which I suppose is understandable because – as I discovered when I got home – they are men's. I found them in Belfast shop where the assistant smirked as she told me about their special offer: three pairs of horrible white sports socks for the price of two. Oooh, yes, I inexplicably said, and give me two of those towelling wrist bands, please.

I thought this get up would make me feel a bit sporty, ready for the mini-marathon in Dublin on Monday, but I just feel like an egg. Round and white and Brazilian yellow in the middle. I take comfort in the realisation that I am a hard-boiled egg because I don't feel a bit runny. And, marathon or no, I don't plan to do any running. The information sheet says you don't have to. I could crawl the six-mile course for all they care. Women "of all shapes and sizes" have been squashing themselves into lycra for years, raising squillions for good causes all for the pleasure of seeing Sonia and Co. flash past them in a blur of more appropriate sportswear. Now I am among their number. And I am not happy. I am not happy at all.

First off I feel I have been kind of hoodwinked into this. As I recall, I was drinking a pint of Guinness, minding my own business at a pub quiz (which, I should point out, my team would have won except for a mix-up with complex Roman numerals) when my friend popped the question. Not for the first time I am wondering what possessed me to answer in the affirmative. All I can say is that I was of good cheer and it seemed very far away at the time. What is bothering me more than anything else is other people's reactions. This has not been pleasant. Mostly people just think I am joking and launch into a conversation about *Big Brother* and whether they can train themselves not to watch it this time. Or, when the election was looming, the more politically minded got out bits of paper and counted up how many seats Fine Gael might lose (even the most conservative of estimates was way out).

More hurtful, though, are those who have stopped in their conversational tracks and guffawed in my face at the thought of me and a marathon. They didn't actually say "the closest you have come to a mini-marathon is eating a fun-size Snickers bar", but they may as well have. Still, it's a walk, right? A walk on a bank holiday Monday with my friend down to the Merrion Shopping Centre and back into town. There is nothing to stop me reading *Heat* magazine if it gets boring, or practising my song for a friend's wedding (another imminent event that has me regularly questioning my sanity, but I promise to do my very best, Catherine and Liam) and stopping for a refreshing Cornetto on the way.

I have seen some vaguely normal-looking runners in a shop and when I find some more elegant shorts I will surely feel like a mini-marathon type person. But my mother, who says I didn't actually walk as a child – I slouched – keeps banging on about training. I can't have a single conversation with her without the "T" word being mentioned. So I checked out Sonia O'Sullivan's website for some tips. Former mini-marathon winner Sonia has the right approach, I feel. She says it's amazing how many non-running folk don't understand that you actually do less training in the run up to a race. Exactly my point.

I haven't actually done any training as such yet. I think about it a lot though. Sometimes, I travel mentally from town to the Martello Tower on Strand Road in Sandymount, without once letting my mind drift down to the village for fresh cod and chips from Borza's. Anyway, I know someone who did the mini-marathon last year and she says, and I quote, "Jesus, you'll be grand. I did nothing before it and I smoked en route."

I am not advocating that approach by the way of course it is more sensible to have weekly exercise plans and the like but the notion of training to go for a walk brings me out in a cold sweat. My friend and I – we are raising money for Focus Ireland – have tried to get together for what we on the circuit call 'meet and train' sessions. The problem is that I had to go to Belfast and she had to go on a glamorous press trip and so unfortunately it looks like there won't be much 'training' and the only time we will be 'meeting' is at the starting line. I just hope we are still together at the finish.

Harry Potter and the Mystery of the Disappearing Balls

Another Christmas miracle. I finally found a place to play pool, have a drink and watch David Beckham on a giant screen. Some secrets are too good to share but when I wrote bemoaning the lack of billiard facilities in Dublin a while ago, a few readers corresponded in agreement. So, seeing as it's the season of goodwill I will say this only once: lo, follow yonder star to Fireworks, on Pearse Street. There is plenty of room at that inn.

The other day I met my regular pool partner there for a club sandwich and a cocktail. He has a Stephen Hendry-esque playing posture thanks to a misspent youth in Co. Armagh snooker halls. But with his boyish looks and spectacles, unkind people say he looks more like Harry Potter, especially since Daniel Radcliffe who plays the young wizard grew eight inches and his voice broke.

But all slagging stops when this Potter clears the table like a pro.

I love watching him beat other people. The way he pushes his glasses up onto the bridge of his nose, the utter concentration on his face as he makes an impossible shot look easy. Sometimes, he even bends the white ball like Beckham to escape a nasty snooker. Then he'll chalk his cue wearing an expression that suggests defying the laws of geometry is the most natural thing in the world.

Naturally, I don't manage to beat him often. But I have improved lately and that night I fancied my chances. I was like Paul Newman in *The Hustler*, zipping around the table, erratic yet skilful, pausing only to sip my Blue Lagoon or go to the bathroom at crucial stages in the match, a little psychological trick I find quite effective. I beat him three games to nil.

Normally placid Potter was not impressed.

My three in a row was a genuine achievement. We don't have the kind of relationship where he lets me win occasionally because I am a girl. Whether it is Swingball or Scrabble, I take games seriously, and for me the only thing worse than losing is being let win. My youth was filled with happy hours of Buckaroo, Operation, Frustration and Sorry! They were happy for me anyway, but the people searching for the pieces I had chucked all over the room in disgust might not agree. These days I am determined to learn Bridge but still enjoy playing board games such as Balderdash, Articulate, Cluedo, Cranium and, the king of them all, Monopoly.

Three years ago I entered the World Monopoly Championship. I didn't tell the organisers I was a journalist because I hadn't planned to write a story.

I just wanted to try to become the Monopoly Champion of the World. Is that so wrong? Apparently, yes. A colleague in a Sunday paper had also seen the tiny ad encouraging participants to bid to be the Irish champion and then continue on to be the world champion in Canada. Finding the idea hilarious, he decided to do an article on the kind of people who would enter such a competition.

The organisers gave him my name. "Duh," I told him when he called. "I am only entering because I am writing a story. Do you really think I am that sad?" Ahem.

The big day approached and we assembled in the Bank of Ireland on College Green to play Monopoly. I spent the night before in training. Worryingly, I lost every single game.

Halfway through the championship, I was bankrupt and scared.

The winner, Nigerian-born Ekamundo Badmus, was like no other Monopoly player I had encountered before. "Come on guys, just give me your houses," he snarled from behind dark shades as the rest of us neared financial ruin. "You have gone bust, man, just turn it all in." My usual tactic of throwing the board up in the air in the face of certain defeat would not work here, I surmised.

I grew fonder of the Monopoly master when I heard he later changed his name from Badmus to O'Badmus to represent Ireland in the finals in Toronto. He came a respectable fifteenth.

Meanwhile, I am a permanent contestant in a pool tournament that never ends. The only other competitor is a bloke who looks like Harry Potter and says "hard lines" with a smirk when I miss an easy shot. I may have won three games in a row but, by the end of that night, the score stood at 20 games to three and if his pool cue was a broomstick he would have been doing loop-the-loops on it around the bar. "Wizard!" I thought I heard him say as he potted the black to win his twenty-first game of the evening.

That's when I lost it. The unfailingly courteous staff at Fireworks still haven't located some of the balls.

Ask a Silly Question

Cheating is in, a fellow competitor in a table quiz informed me brazenly the other night. I'd been monitoring her team's performance with the zeal of an eagle-eyed member of the production team on *Who Wants to Be A Millionaire?*. Let's just say Tecwen Whittock couldn't have wedged a hanky between her team and the one she spent the night whispering answers to, they were that close.

Not having realised that since Major Ingram's Oscar-winning performance, cheating was the new black/brown/neon pink leg-warmer, I had relied purely on brain power. Well, other people's brain power at any rate, and assembled a crack team for the night. We had all the bases covered. Sport (Jonny), politics (Liam), cinema (Ben), ever so slightly irrelevant facts gleaned from *Heat* and *Hello!* magazines (me). Despite this breadth of expertises, we only achieved a sorry 10th place, narrowly missing out on what I considered the prize of the night, a box of Taytos each.

I managed to successfully name the president of South Korea while successfully forgetting absolutely every other piece of trivia that clogs up my brain. Not remembering that Jonathan Franzen wrote *The Corrections* is one thing, but forgetting the names of the brilliant McIlhinney twins from *You're A Star* – unforgivable.

Table quizzes bring out the worst in me. Due to my desire to win but not actually to do any pre-quiz swotting, I have unrealistically high expectations of my team-mates. But it never even occurred to me to cheat, which is strange because

I have been known to make up two-letter words in Scrabble and nick £500 notes from the Monopoly bank. When watching *University Challenge*, I'll admit I have consulted reference books and I consider it a viewer's privilege to get the dictionary out during the *Countdown* conundrum.

But there are some programmes that cheat us, so we don't have do it ourselves. Yes, I am talking about *The Lyrics Board.* I watched it the other night and I'm still not the better for it.

As you know, the premise of this televisual swizz is that the 'contestants' – usually members of defunct girl bands or refugees from *Fair City* – must work out which song is on the big screen as words from the lyrics are revealed one by one. When a 'contestant' works out the song, someone is nominated to perform it. But despite the fact that it is plain to everyone that the whole farce has been worked out in advance, the 'contestants' enthusiastically participate in the charade that they are winging it. I say clear to everyone but apparently there are some viewers of RTÉ 2 who are convinced Shirley Temple Bar, the drag queen on *Telly Bingo*, is actually a 14-year-old schoolgirl, so *The Lyrics Board* scam is probably about as clear as mud to them.

The night I tuned in, Barry from *Eastenders*, surely one of the most annoying characters in soap history, was on one of the teams. Watching him pretending to try to remember a song – "Oh, oh, is it? It might be. Yeah, yeah, sorted, apples and pears, luvaduck, etc, etc,"– had me covering my face with a cushion in embarrassment for him. I mean, he is supposed to be an actor, for goodness sake. "Will you sing it for us?" asked host Linda Martin, who is worth watching just for her extraordinary clothes and make-up alone.

So off went Bazza up onto a stage where he belted out whatever Elvis standard he had carefully rehearsed for days beforehand. Do the people who make this programme think viewers are completely out to lunch? Personally I think it would be much more successful (and honest) if participants were made to sing random songs they hadn't rehearsed in advance. And if at least one of the 'contestants' had even a tiny bit of street cred – surely Sinead O'Connor would come out of retirement for it – all the better.

In fairness, *The Lyrics Board* is not quite as terrifyingly bad as it was in the old days when 'contestants' relied on just a piano for accompaniment and Aonghus McAnally was the host, but it still makes Brendan O'Carroll's ill-fated *Hot Milk and Pepper* quiz look like intelligent TV. This is where defenders of *The Lyrics Board* start mumbling about how the groundbreaking programme is syndicated all over the developed world and rights are pending on the Moon and Uranus. And maybe that's the case, but it's still rubbish.

Naturally, I watched *The Lyrics Board* from start to finish. The whole excruciating hour. There is something horribly addictive about it and I may end up having a look tomorrow night. But, really, the whole point of watching Z-list 'celebrities' on game shows is so that they can make total and utter eejits of themselves, *à la* celebrity *Stars in Their Eyes*. If they had those McIlhinney twins on, I would definitely watch. Shauna, I think she's called, and umm, whassernameagain? No coughing at the back.

Celebrity Street Cred

In the past few weeks I have had the pleasure of the company of two wealthy and deliciously handsome movie stars. Nobody is more amazed than me at this development. Yes I know the way Colin Farrell gets around everyone in Dublin and their granny is bound to bump into him at some point, but I didn't think it would be so soon. If I had, I might have made a little more effort with the lip gloss and not been so drunk I had to lean on him for support.

Why is it that things involving fabulous people always happen when you are feeling less than fabulous yourself? I seem to be having a run of those days when all you want to do is crawl home to the sofa for several doses of *Dr Phil* and *Murder She Wrote.* On one such rain-sodden afternoon, I was sent to interview Pierce Brosnan and gently forced by the organisers of the interview to wear a bib. I repeat. A bib. The fact that it had MEDIA written on the back did not, I would like to point out, make the bright blue scrap of windcheater material appear any more glamorous.

In the excitement, my bib slipped over one shoulder slightly so I suspect – a suspicion later confirmed when a photo of me interviewing Brosnan appeared in another newspaper – I looked like an inmate from *One Flew Over the Cuckoo's Nest.*

For the benefit of anyone who hasn't met the former James Bond, I'd like to outline what Pierce Brosnan looks like in real life. I should warn all women and gay men, that if you ever do meet him, the overall affect of an encounter viewers are completely out to lunch? Personally I think it would be much more successful (and honest) if participants were made to sing random songs they hadn't rehearsed in advance. And if at least one of the 'contestants' had even a tiny bit of street cred – surely Sinead O'Connor would come out of retirement for it – all the better.

In fairness, *The Lyrics Board* is not quite as terrifyingly bad as it was in the old days when 'contestants' relied on just a piano for accompaniment and Aonghus McAnally was the host, but it still makes Brendan O'Carroll's ill-fated *Hot Milk and Pepper* quiz look like intelligent TV. This is where defenders of *The Lyrics Board* start mumbling about how the groundbreaking programme is syndicated all over the developed world and rights are pending on the Moon and Uranus. And maybe that's the case, but it's still rubbish.

Naturally, I watched *The Lyrics Board* from start to finish. The whole excruciating hour. There is something horribly addictive about it and I may end up having a look tomorrow night. But, really, the whole point of watching Z-list 'celebrities' on game shows is so that they can make total and utter eejits of themselves, *à la* celebrity *Stars in Their Eyes*. If they had those McIlhinney twins on, I would definitely watch. Shauna, I think she's called, and umm, whassernameagain? No coughing at the back.

to swear in interviews or he'll never work in this blah blah blah. Also he says things like "I was just Mickey Mousin' around" and he wants his not-yet-born baby brought up here and not in some spoilt-rich-kid enclave in LA. To put it simply, as far as us Type Bs are concerned, Colin Farrell could dangle a baby from a hotel window and we would still cheer.

I'd like to think I managed the encounter quite well when I found my champagne-fuelled self standing next to him at the bar of a nightclub. I'd like to think that, but it's all a bit of a blur. I do remember watching five lissom young ladies vying for the space on his armchair while an oblivious Farrell chatted away to the equally adorable Keith Duffy. I confess I was feeling a little envious and depressed knowing that I – with my kaftan and chipped nail varnish – would never be welcome on such an very important armchair when one of the young ladies fell off and landed in a heap of Versace on the floor. If you can't join 'em, chuckle at 'em from a discreet distance, that's what I say.

with Brosnan will be the cause of serious stomach acrobatics and much face reddening.

But that's the effect of the whole package. Unfortunately, when you break it down, the thing falls apart. You see, he has lovely dark hair with grey flecks at the temples but he likes his hair a little too much. We know this because when he isn't signing autographs he is running his hands through it with alarming regularity. This affectation cannot fail but to make you feel ill.

His legs. Ah yes, his legs. They are very long and when clad in denim appear to go on forever. Then you look down and see the carefully frayed bits on the ankle of his jeans which appear to have been hand ripped by Shabby Chic of Beverly Hills. Speaking of cheek, his bottom area is so well formed it makes you drop your pen. However, you soon get over this when it becomes obvious that Pierce loves his bottom even more than you do and starts wiggling as he walks and generally thrusting the thing into the camera lenses as he bends down. His mouth is like an overripe raspberry but when he smiles he purses his lips in a bizarre fashion. He is, however, only gorgeous and very generous with his time – when I met him he was presenting medals to Special Olympics athletes – and yet . . . he's no Colin Farrell.

There are two types of people in Ireland today. Type A think Colin Farrell is a tulip who needs to be reminded several times a day that he is from quite a respectable home in Castleknock and not, as his accent suggests, the outer reaches of Talifornia. Type B think Colin Farrell is the best thing to come out of Castleknock since . . . well it doesn't matter. He is simply the first and therefore best bona-fide, love-'em-and-leave-'em, drink-from-the-bottle, spittin'-and-cursin' goddamn movie star this country has ever produced.

Plus, he is easy on the eye. Plus again, he quite clearly does not care about the Hollywood agents who tell him not to swear in interviews or he'll never work in this blah blah blah. Also he says things like "I was just Mickey Mousin' around" and he wants his not-yet-born baby brought up here and not in some spoilt-rich-kid enclave in LA. To put it simply, as far as us Type Bs are concerned, Colin Farrell could dangle a baby from a hotel window and we would still cheer.

I'd like to think I managed the encounter quite well when I found my champagne-fuelled self standing next to him at the bar of a nightclub. I'd like to think that, but it's all a bit of a blur. I do remember watching five lissom young ladies vying for the space on his armchair while an oblivious Farrell chatted away to the equally adorable Keith Duffy. I confess I was feeling a little envious and depressed knowing that I – with my kaftan and chipped nail varnish – would never be welcome on such an very important armchair when one of the young ladies fell off and landed in a heap of Versace on the floor. If you can't join 'em, chuckle at 'em from a discreet distance, that's what I say.

Roysh and Wrong

Growing up in Sandymount, in the heart of Dublin 4, I got used to assumptions being made about my world. That I must be wealthy. That my family must own two cars. That my dad was something big in the Four Courts. And of course that I spoke with what has become recognised in common parlance as – "OK, roysh, we'll get the Dort and I'll meet you outside BTs" – a fluent D4 accent.

As soon I was old enough to understand that this was a stereotype, I began to find the humour in these observations. The stereotype didn't fit my life but it still had enough of a basis in truth for it to be spread liberally around and put to whatever use the commentator, the comic or the activist desired. An inner-city politician might remark that something was "typical, arrogant D4 nonsense". And, wherever you came from you would know exactly what he meant. Just because the stereotype didn't fit my experience of that world didn't mean I was offended.

I happen to think that without such stereotypes, much of the best comedy – *The Office*, *The Royle Family*, *The Lyrics Board* – would be confined to some politically correct telly-prison by people who just don't understand the concept of "it's funny because it's true". I've been thinking about this ever since I wrote a column about Colin Farrell and received correspondence from a lot of angry people who don't like stereotypes at all. Especially if they are about Tallaght in Dublin. I upset these people by using the following line to illustrate why some misguided folk can't stand the sight of an actor I personally consider a national treasure: "Type A think Colin Farrell is a tulip who needs to be reminded several times a day that he is from quite a respectable home in Castleknock and not, as his accent suggests, the outer reaches of Talifornia."

Oh dear. They really were very cross those people who mailed me from London and Scotland and Tallaght to call me a racist and assume that I thought a strong Dublin accent was something to be ashamed of. All of these people, including the lady who was so angry she had to call me directly on the phone, made me feel terribly guilty for a couple of days. So guilty that I was all ready to write a grovelling column apologising for the insensitive nature of my comments and confess that I had made a heinous error and would they please, please forgive me when . . . well then I woke up and realised that they were the ones with the problem and all I could really do – and I have a sneaking suspicion this won't be enough – was try to explain.

These furious people, some of whom have now decided I must be a D4 princess with a Daddy rich enough to land me a job in *The Irish Times*, seem to have missed my point, so I'll try one more time. My point was that Talifornians, most born and bred Talifornians, like my cousins, for example, possess strong Dublin accents. My point was that middle-class people like Colin Farrell have been known to adopt that accent – in rather the same way posh English director Guy Ritchie has cultivated a cockney geezer guise – in an effort to inject their public personas with commercially valuable street cred.

I was not, by referring to Farrell's "quite respectable" home, making any kind of judgement on Tallaght people and the kind of homes they come from. Unfortunately, my disgruntled friends chose to take that meaning from what I wrote.

Limerick is sometimes called Stab City, yet I don't think

everyone I meet from there is hiding a butcher's knife behind their back. Cavan people are, the stereotype goes, stingy but it doesn't surprise me when a person from that region acts generously. D4 people are loaded, privileged and have everything they need but hang on a second, my family – and others in the D4 area – were recipients of charity from the St Vincent de Paul. So what?

Incidentally the ingenious Talifornia tag is widely thought to have been made up by locals and was first seen as graffiti on a wall in the area, as witty a bit of self-deprecating humour as you'll find anywhere in Dublin. Soccer player Robbie Keane boasts proudly of coming from Talifornia, as well he should.

Some of the angrier correspondents complained that all their lives they had been discriminated against because of their Dublin accents. That they had been told "you don't sound like you come from Tallaght" or worse "you don't look like you come from Tallaght".

I suppose having to deal with that kind of idiocy is bound to leave a few chips on your shoulder but let it be recorded that this column is a fan of all kinds of Dublin accents weak, strong or Talifornian.

And now that's sorted, I'd like to thank the Tallaght woman who wrote to inform me that Colin Farrell was way out of my league. Because, you know, for a second I really thought I was in there. Well you would, roysh?

Night Moves

The evening of my first night class dawned, as they are destined to do, dark and damp and miserable. I was busy dreaming up excuses for not turning up to Guitar: Intermediate. He was busy inexpertly pummelling my shoulders in preparation for his class in Aromatherapy and Massage: Beginners. For the most part they were valid excuses. As in:

a) I might miss the first gay kiss on *Coronation Street*;
b) I am not actually sure if my basic strumming of *Gypsy Rover* qualifies as Intermediate; and
c) the price (a measly €150 for ten weeks) didn't exactly inspire confidence in the course.

Perhaps there was a misprint. Perhaps it was Air Guitar: Intermediate. I gave a half-hearted after-dinner rendition of Shania Twain's 'Still The One' while he drowned himself in Issey Miyake. When I suggested he might have overdone it on the smelly stuff, he threw me a withering look that said, "It's aromatherapy, stupid."

Maeve Binchy had the right idea when she recently began her Writers' Club night class in the National College of Ireland with an open lecture on what exactly the course would be all about. Having signed up for classes in the past and dropped out after the first or second night, she knows well how the idea of a night class is often much more attractive than the reality. A course in, say, stock-market trading may sound like the type of place where you will meet exciting Nick Leeson-types and learn how to make your first million by the age of 35, but invariably it is not. That's the mistake a friend made. She now knows that a course in stock-market trading actually means sitting in a draughty prefab next to a scary man with hair growing wildly out of his nose, while nodding wisely at an incomprehensible lecture on bull markets.

So, you see, the idea of a guitar night class appealed. For too long I have bored myself and countless people at parties with my three-song repertoire. At a recent house party, the kind where there are caterers and rock stars in attendance, I even forced the lead singer with Bell X1 to sit and listen to a song my friend and I had composed. In fairness to the man – who had earlier performed the best Justin Timberlake cover I've ever heard – he made encouraging noises as I told him it was a song about Jamie Oliver and his quest to take homeless people off the streets with his Fifteen restaurant. Sample lyric: "Monosodium satellite makes him the dish of the day."

"It's about the love" is what the hostess says I actually said to him, although I am hoping she is making this part up. "Of course it is. The love," he allegedly replied. Fighting a thundering hangover the next day I circled Guitar: Intermediate in my well-thumbed night-class book and vowed to learn bar chords if it killed me.

There are two types of evening class people. Fair-Weather and All-Weather. The All-Weather ones are the kind who declare, "I want to learn at least one new skill a year" and actually mean it. One year they do welding. The next, wine-tasting. They master Italian. And sign language. You probably know some of these people. They may even be related to you. What they don't know about marine engine maintenance just isn't worth knowing, and they would find a way to get to Calligraphy: Advanced if a force-nine gale was raging outside.

Fair-Weathers are another breed entirely. You will find

them at the back of the class, stifling yawns, eyes glued to the clock on the wall. That's if you find them at all. Come the end of September, Fair-Weathers, who have normally signed up to at least two classes a week, develop a variety of ailments ranging from laryngitis, if the course is Public Speaking: Wrestle Your Demons, to an abject fear of heights, if it's Rock Climbing: Indoors.

I don't yet know which camp I fall into. The first class flew. I didn't look at the clock once. I learned all about something called tablature, although not, as yet, how to avoid embarrassing oneself in front of established musicians at parties. Meanwhile, over in Aromatherapy and Massage: Beginners, he's discovered a new calling. You will know what I mean when I say I cannot recommend highly enough getting your boyfriend to do this course.

But I should also include a cautionary tale that will make you think long and hard before you encourage anyone to enter night-class land. A few years ago, an acquaintance suggested that her childminder – the best one she ever had before or since – should go on an assertiveness course. She was a sweet, if slightly shy girl, and duly signed up. By week seven, she was talking about setting up her own health-food store; by week ten, she had handed in her notice. Don't say you weren't warned.

Guess I'm a Luas Girl

How do I love him? Let me count the ways. The ding-ding-ding-ding that announces his arrival and, less happily, his departure. The view from behind as he slinks around corners like a caterpillar in an old-fashioned video game. The high-pitched whine he emits when accelerating through Peter's Place and then up over the canal. The voice of the posh, bilingual lady announcer who manages to make Windy Arbour – who even knew there was a place called Windy Arbour? – sound vaguely sexy. There's just no getting away from it. He's the tram of my dreams.

I love the Luas or, as we've taken to calling it in our house, the Danny Day. A friend insists on calling it the Rebecca but I think that kind of lowers the tone. I have to confess I skipped the queue on the first afternoon which would have been fine had I not been caught rapid by my eight-year-old niece who just happened to be passing. "You cheated," said Bláithín accusingly down the phone when I rang. I tried to explain. That I was running late. That I wanted to make sure I got on it before the last tram left. That being on the Luas on the first day was really, really important to me. "You cheated," she repeated. Pesky kids.

Two days later I returned to St Stephen's Green and took my place behind the beaming masses all waiting patiently for a free ride. Most of my fellow queue inhabitants were busy announcing their surprise to each other that they didn't really have anywhere to go. "We are literally just getting on it to go to Sandyford and then come back here," said one woman amazed at herself. "Literally." "Same here," replied a smiling man, while behind him a little girl lost her grip on a yellow helium balloon. We all looked skyward until it disappeared behind a puffy cloud and then we gave each other these silly Luas grins.

I don't quite know what it is about Luas that brings out the ten-year-old in us. I was only a bit older than that when the first DART came through Sandymount and we packed like pilchards into the green train, marvelling at the stunning views when we got to Killiney.

The Luas doesn't have the same open vistas except for that sweeping glimpse of water and greenery before you go over the nine arches bridge at Dundrum, but it's got a gritty urban feel which I like just as much. You can see people hanging washing out on the line. Watch people working in stuffy offices. Here's a top tip for voyeurs: if you sit on the left side of the tram at Charlemont you can gaze right into the offices of a bank and watch as glum-looking suits shuffle bits of paper around. There is a man working there with a desk almost as messy as mine. Almost.

If you haven't had a ride on the Luas yet I'd recommend standing during your maiden journey – the views are better and you can move from side to side. Just be careful to keep hold of the yellow safety bars when it's slowing down or speeding up, and keep an eye out for low-flying elbows at peak times.

And don't be afraid to strike up conversations with strangers on the tram. I'm positive we can get away with those "Jaysus, isn't this great altogether" kind of chats for a good few months.

One of the highlights of my first trips on the Luas has been answering the mobile phone while zipping through places I've never been to like Cowper and Balally. "I'm on the Luas," I say louder than I need to, loving the newness of the phrase.

Personally, I enjoy the tram so much I'll be taking the Luas not to get anywhere necessarily but just to, literally, take the Luas. It's going to be pleasure trips on the Green Line forever – or at least until the novelty wears off. You see, apart from my sister's house in Ranelagh, I don't really have any reason to alight at the Luas stations. At the end of the line at Sandyford Industrial Estate it's all finance and software companies as far as the eye can see. Not even a coffee shop to distract you from jumping back on the next town-bound Luas, although hopefully this will change.

So far there seems to be pretty much unanimous affection for our newest, old form of public transport. But this being Dublin, it stands to reason some people are not going to afford Danny Day the respect he deserves. Like the young man at the St Stephen's Green stop last week who, announcing he was about to become the first person in Ireland to use the station as a toilet, proceeded to relieve himself all over the shiny new ticket machine. It's the Luas not the Loos, people. Let's all try and remember that.

Freeloading Blues

Forget Summer Lovin', Summer Liggin' is where it's really at. I was invited to the opening night of *Grease* at the Point Depot recently and, as a bonus, our free tickets enabled us to mingle with virtually the entire cast of *Fair City*. I spotted the *Celebrity Farm* one, the Russian one, the one who had a relationship with her brother and the one who used to go out with a teacher twice her age.

There were Marty Whelan, Larry Gogan and Chris Doran. All the greats. Best of all, the seats were so good we were in spitting distance of Simon Casey, who stole the show singing Beauty School Drop Out, while dancing suggestively in a pair of silver lamé pants.

I wouldn't class myself as a professional in the ligging Olympics, but I am a definitely a hard-working amateur.

These events are better if you bring an LP, a non-media 'Ligging Partner' who can turn even the blandest launch into an enjoyable social event. At *Grease*, when the star of the show Jonathan Wilkes (a.k.a. Robbie Williams's Best Mate) came near us in the green room, myself and a similarly excitable ligger screamed so much we scared him off. You just wouldn't have the guts to do that on your own.

Lately I've been trying to curb my enthusiasm for ligs, or at least to be more selective about which ones I go to. It's not always easy to say no.

I broke one of my golden ligging rules (never go solo) the other night, when I turned up on my own to the launch party for a dinky new range of phones. It was on my way home and anyway I was hoping that the company might take pity on me and offer to replace the falling-apart phone which I borrowed from the mother when my own phone fell into a foot bath. Don't ask.

After depositing my name and phone number in a raffle to win one of the phones, I spent ten minutes talking, some might say stalking, the marketing manager who was over from the UK. Accidentally on purpose, I let him glimpse my poor excuse for a 21st-century communications tool. Unfortunately, he didn't bite but after he escaped I did, into some particularly gorgeous fish and chips served in paper cornets, so it wasn't a total waste of time.

Though I don't frequent these events quite as much as I used to, from what I've seen lately they are increasingly elaborate. Once, the most you could hope for was warm wine in a plastic cup and, should you manage to mug a passing waitress as she hovered around the room, you might manage to snaffle a chewy sausage roll. These days you can get dinner, entertainment and as many free cocktails as you can swallow in two-and-a-half hours.

Ligs can be educational too. Once, the makers of a cranberry juice flew a New York barman over to show us how to make the finest cocktails. They can also be great autograph-hunting opportunities. At the unveiling of Louis Le Brocquy's portrait of Bono, my favourite LP got Mr Hewson to draw a self-portrait on her copy of Peter and the Wolf.

The mobile phone press reception had everything a free-loading journalist could hope for and a whole lot more. It was like Fosset's Circus in there – a man on stilts, a live snake, a tarot-card reader, a magician, two portrait artists and a jazz band.

Perhaps it started with the Celtic Tiger but *Sex and the City* definitely consolidated the trend. We had got so used to seeing Carrie and Co at stunning New York launch parties eating canapés that looked like mini works of art that I think it forced PR people here to raise the bar. Literally. We want cute mini-cheeseburgers now, not smoked salmon and cream cheese. We want Cosmos, not cheap red wine. And while, we are, of course deeply interested in the specifications of your all-singing-all-dancing product, we have more pressing questions such as, "Excuse me, young lady, but where's my goody bag?"

These days the wine may be sparkling but there will always be something a bit soulless about these events: corporate types talking about their product while you try to work out whether the free portion of the bar is still in operation.

If you have forgotten to bring an LP, you stand with other journalists in what you hope is an industrious-looking huddle. Some of us are genuinely working, some of us are genuinely in search of a free lunch. But we all adopt the purposeful demeanour that we hope elevates us from the ranks of your common-or-garden ligerati.

I still get a kick from free champagne but it turns out those summer nights were even better fun back when your name wasn't on the door.

Having a Pre-Ball Ball

Sartorially speaking, this summer was supposed to be different. I wasn't supposed to be still looking for an outfit that would see me through a ball and two weddings, just 48 hours before the first event. In fact, in order to avoid this very scenario, a few weeks ago I cunningly employed my younger sister – who happens to work in a boutique recently frequented by Ms Spears – as my personal stylist. The only problem with having your sister as your stylist is that she is not bothered about being diplomatic when it comes to telling you things you don't want to hear. What Not To Wear? Get That Thing Off You Immediately You Big Eejit, was more like it.

I'd be fondling a particularly covetable chiffon wrap-around dress, for example, and she'd snatch it out of my hands with a dismissive "that won't go anywhere near you". In more sympathetic moments, she'd offer a soothing "sure, maybe you'll grow into it one day".

"Your only hope is Wallis" meant she was in a really bad mood and I nearly staged a walkout when I emerged from a changing room one afternoon and she shouted at the top of her voice, "Would you ever go to Arnott's and get yourself measured for a piece of underwear that actually fits you?" I tell you, she'd scare the hipsters off Trinny and Susannah.

As the businesslike woman with the measuring tape did her embarrassing thing a few days later, I tried to work out whether the stress caused by the build-up to these formal functions was worth the few hours of fun that would be had at the occasion itself. Caroline and Barry's nuptials in Derry. Fionnuala and Mick's wedding reception on a canal barge. I wasn't doubting that they'd be special events, I was just wondering why I always had to get myself into such a state of anxiety in the run-up to these big days and nights out.

I don't think I'm alone. It seems that frenzied preparation has become more and more the point of these functions lately. What with the dress search, the fake tan, the hair removal, and the accessories hunt, I'm estimating some people spend at least a week in pre-production for gigs that are over in the blink of a fake eyelash. Never mind what they say about staying in, by my reckoning getting ready is really the new going out.

I decided that instead of stressing about it, I would embrace this trend. With the help of the sister stylist and a supportive friend, I found an acceptable skirt and top combination which didn't make me feel like a frump. The skirt even had ribbons, which is always good. Then I asked a make-up artist friend, who lives around the corner from me, to work her magic for myself and a couple of other ladies who were also off to the ball. She kindly agreed to come to my gaff and bring her pots, lotions and brushes with her. By Saturday afternoon there were six women lined up on the make-up conveyor belt.

One friend, who was wearing a gorgeous little black dress, was having an underwear issue and wanted an honest opinion on these "smooth support cups" that were supposed to mould invisibly in a gravity defying manner to her bust area. This was a difficult one because the instructions were in German and it was almost impossible to figure out what we were supposed to do with the curved pieces of sticking plaster.

One of the token boys present at the Getting Ready Party

came into the room at the precise moment when we were assembling the cups, and if we had been sticking pins in a voodoo effigy of him he couldn't have looked more offended. "Have some respect, there are some things a man should never have to see," he said, scooting sharpish back to the kitchen.

I left the ladies at one stage to pop across the road to the local hairdresser, Dora Jeans, where I sat beside pensioners getting perms and had my hair put up for one-third of the price that I normally pay. When I got back to the house with my lovely bridesmaid hairdo I passed around some olives, popped a bottle of champagne and let all my pre-ball cares melt away.

So, if getting ready is the bit that gives you the biggest headache, make it painless by doing it in company and in style. Get the canapés out. Hire someone to make you look as lovely as possible. Take pictures of each other to record the moment. After you've done all this, you might even decide that's quite enough for one day, take off all your glad rags and watch DVDs all night instead. Me? What can I say? I had a ball.

Do You Come Here Often?

I see the days in a line. From Monday right through to Sunday. In my head they stretch out as if perched on a ruler, the space between each one and the next always the same.

This line never ends, although when Saturday is over the indentation in the ruler is a little deeper. The months are arranged in an oval. January is at the bottom, with the Christmas festivities sparkling drunkenly behind it and the spring and summer months curving around to meet September, then back along the gently sloping path to December.

A friend sees the days spread out in an expansive circle while the months are stiff and upright, like soldiers standing for inspection. We see the same things, but we see them differently. That's just the way it is. For example, not too long ago my friend and I were out for one of our far-too-occasional meetings. Two men approached our table. The one with slightly more hair asked my friend whether they could "pop ourselves down" with us on the two spare chairs that were beside our table.

The mood I was in at the time – hassled, frazzled, slightly depressed – meant I wouldn't even look at them, and it was left to my friend to tell them that of course they could sit down. We didn't own the chairs, she said later when I began to harangue her for giving away the seats that were acting as a buffer between us and the rest of the bar.

Almost immediately the man with slightly less hair started talking to us, with some inane comment designed to draw us into their company. I murmured something noncommittal and continued to chat to my friend while she wavered between responding fully to their attempts at conversation and chatting to me.

At each lame gambit – "So, what are you girls doing here?" and "It's not very lively here, is it?" – I, in my bad mood, became increasingly agitated. She was the picture of politeness. After what seemed a very long time both men stood up and walked to another part of the bar, leaving their coats on the seat. "We'll be back," their anoraks weakly implied.

My friend found it offensive that I was so annoyed by their innocent attempts to befriend us. The way I saw it, they shouldn't have assumed that we would want them to interrupt our conversation – a particularly meaty one about relationships, as I recall – just because we were two women out in a bar. "Neither of us has any interest in being with them, so why should we waste any energy, or give them the wrong impression, by talking to them?"

It sounded cold when I said it, but then I reversed the situation in my head. Imagine, I said to her, two women popping themselves down and presuming that permission to pop meant permission to interrupt the night of two men who were obviously deep in conversation. Some level of arrogance would be required to assume they were fair game just because the men were out drinking at night.

I didn't think it would happen. And, if it did, the men, in my view, would have been quite justified in ignoring them.

But my friend insisted there were ways of dissuading unwelcome attention without being rude. She would have had no problem waving her 'wedding' ring in their faces and telling anecdotes about her 'husband' until they retreated, having got the message she was sending out. Her tactic would have allowed them to keep at least some of their dignity.

She went on to accuse me of being unnecessarily cruel.

She said it wouldn't be enough for me that they left with their tails between their legs. "You want to see them whimpering all the way home," she tutted. It wasn't exactly true, but it made me feel guilty. Not quite guilty enough to call them over and ask them whether they came here often, but guilty all the same.

She said that, taken to an extreme, my rudeness – I preferred to call it honesty – could have made the men angry enough to wait outside, to accost me. I suggested that her politeness could have made them get the wrong idea enough to accost her in a display of overly amorous zeal.

We sipped our drinks and thought about this as we watched the men take their coats off the chairs beside us and attempt the same trick rather more successfully at the other side of the pub. I see the days in a line, she sees them in a circle. We decided that, on balance, a courteous but firm blend of our reactions would be more appropriate the next time someone attempted to seduce us.

If, as she quite reasonably pointed out, there ever was a next time

Jogging the Memory

The first column I ever wrote for this magazine back in 2002 was given the deeply appropriate headline 'Running to Standstill'. In my debut outing as a columnist, I shared with readers the details of my training – I use the word extremely loosely – schedule for the women's mini-marathon.

Back then the schedule consisted of going for approximately three walks before the big day and diverting to Borza's chipper in Sandymount for post-training sustenance. Athletes need their carbs, I reasoned, and I made sure I got more than my fair share.

Some background on my athletic record; I walked the mini-marathon that year. It felt like I had run a marathon. I have done nothing like it since.

Now, almost three years later, I have made a decision to attempt jogging the 10k race. Even typing that last sentence made me laugh. I haven't so much as run for a Luas in the past ten years. Up until very recently I didn't know if I still could.

I decided to find out on Sandymount Strand, around the corner from where I grew up. I thought I'd feel at home there, looking out at the ESB towers and the rock pools where I used to play. My personal trainer – who also happens to be my annoyingly fit boyfriend – suggested we start with a brisk walk along the seaside path but, by the time we reached Sandymount Tower, my lower back was aching so much I had to pause for a pit stop.

I was about to give up on the project altogether, on

health grounds you understand, when on our way back to the car I thought I would see if I could jog the distance between the lamp posts. Success! Of sorts. I walked between two lamp posts and then jogged between two lampposts and when I got home I needed a long lie down.

On rising the next day, I realised that if I was to do this properly I would need the right equipment. An army never marched on one pair of pink backless runners bought on impulse at the airport because they were half-price and looked cute on the shelf, as the saying goes.

The runners I purchased the other day in a proper sports shop feature some class of hydraulic lift in the heel which I assumed practically did the running for you, making them well worth the nearly €150 they cost. But they don't, in fact, do the running for you. Apparently, I have to do that.

The next important issue to which I turned my attention was the matter of appropriate running attire. The last time out I wore a voluminous yellow Brazil football jersey which I can't seem to lay my hands on anymore. Having surveyed the skin tight selection of Lycra on offer at the sports shop and having ruled out going down the short shorts route, I was left with my own sorry collection of tracksuit bottoms and a bright pink Go Dublin! T-shirt. (The latter is available in selected sports shops in the run-up to the race.)

Having donned the tracksuit, I made the huge mistake of asking my personal trainer/boyfriend whether the bottoms were as unflattering to my bottom as I imagined them to be. Note to all personal trainer/boyfriends: Do not answer this question with a phrase such as "well, at least you are doing something about it now". Obviously, I fired him.

After hiding under the duvet for an hour in recovery position, I ventured alone down to Fairview Park in my bouncy runners and my unflattering bottoms and did a warm-up walk. Then, using the stopwatch on my mobile phone, I measured just how long I was capable of sustaining a slow jog. That would be 30 seconds then. A disappointment, sure, but not really a surprise. The surprise came later when I improved that time by another 30 seconds. I wasn't quite in the grips of what they call the running high but I was definitely out of the duvet slump which had preceded the walk in the park.

After he grovelled sufficiently, I re-hired my trainer and the next day we went down to the Grand Canal Basin, where we got a glimpse of what the Docklands will be like when they are finished. On our warm-up walk by the water, the urban waterside scene reminded me of one of my favourite parts of Manhattan, along the Hudson where joggers, walkers and rollerbladers make the place come alive.

The roads and paths around the Basin are now beautifully paved, in readiness for all the apartment dwellers, restaurant owners and members of U2 who will shortly be hanging out there. One of the paths doubles as an excellent running track. And that's where I discovered I'm now a two-minute jogger. By the time you read this I am hoping to be able to go five minutes. Whether I walk or run the mini-marathon is immaterial. I actually think I will be having fun.

And I'm looking forward to watching this part of my city evolve as I return for what I hope will be daily jogs. The air tastes different in a place that is waiting patiently to happen. In physical fitness terms, I'm waiting to happen myself. Paula Radcliffe, be very afraid.

It's a Beautiful Game

For about five minutes, at the beginning of our relationship, I feigned an interest in football. I found out that he supported Liverpool FC. I found out that he supported Portadown FC. And then I found out that not even love could make me sit through 90 minutes of a sport in which I have zero interest, aside from every four years, when the World Cup spices the game up with a spot of rampant nationalism.

I am aware that, as a revelation, "woman not a fan of football" is up there with "claustrophobics don't like lifts" and "animal-rights activists are not really into McDonald's". I only bring it up because in the past couple of weeks there has been a slight shift in my views on the beautiful game.

Part of being a non-football-friendly girlfriend is an acceptance that, no matter how important you are to him, sometimes a game on a television will be more important. At certain times during the year – from experience, every weekend except in the summer, when there is a break of around two months – there are matches on. Mostly he doesn't tell me until I have arranged something else for us to do. "Sorry, there's a match on," he says, as though no other explanation is necessary. Which, of course, I've learned is pretty much the case.

In addition, I have learnt to accept that, during these periods, he will not be accessible to me in any way, shape or form. I also now accept that when I go to his family home, in Portadown, and there is a match on, I will be banned from talking. In the early days his football-crazy brothers and sisters did not actually say that; they just glowered in my direction when I tried to be polite, commenting on a player's haircut or what I considered to be a skilful pass. Now they say: "Róisín, if you don't have anything intelligent to say, just keep quiet." So I do. It's humbling, actually.

In the past couple of weeks the soccer thing has acquired even more significance. Apparently there is a competition in which all the European football teams take part, and Liverpool have managed to get into the final, which will take place later this month in Istanbul.

This is very important, and not just to him. I've spent five years trying to make my boyfriend change his footballing allegiance, because Liverpool don't seem to be very good at winning things, and I don't like being associated, even at a remove, with such sporting underachievers. He claims that switching teams – to, say, Manchester United – is not possible at this late stage, citing family heritage and team loyalty. So I'm genuinely glad Liverpool seem to be achieving some kind of success. Long may it continue.

As if this weren't enough footballing good fortune, his other team got into the final of the Irish Cup. This is also very important. Portadown were playing Larne in the final last Saturday, and while it would have been a big shock had they not won, the 5–1 victory was still the cause of much joy around the town. To celebrate this great soccer triumph, we went to a disco at the local rugby club. The choice of venue made no sense to me, but what would I know?

At the disco, it felt as if I'd just hitchhiked back to the 1980s. I haven't heard some of those songs since I went to discos as a teenager at Marian College. They even played 'Time Warp', which was exactly what it felt like for much of the night.

Anyway, there I was, marvelling at the colourful language

of the DJs and their penchant for running offstage to rub their faces in some young woman's breasts, when the footballers arrived.

"There's Vinny Arkins," somebody said, adding that this pleasant-looking tall man was from Dublin. It would have been rude not to go over for a chat with my fellow Dubliner, and when Arkins heard where I was from, he wanted to know what the hell I was doing in this Protestant heartland.

"Well, my boyfriend is from here, and, you know," I said warming to my theme, "I support your team as well. Congratulations, you were great out there today, scoring all your goals and all the rest."

Thankfully, I found out later that Arkins had in fact scored goals, two of them if you're interested. He's something of a local hero around these parts apparently. And the fact that he was also the first Dubliner I'd ever met socially in Portadown made it a deeply auspicious occasion. As the night wore on and I chatted to Arkins again, I realised that I was in danger of developing an interest in Portadown FC. And if I could just meet that Steven Gerrard fellow, the same might happen with Liverpool.

The next day my boyfriend's nephew Stefan taught me some chants. "Vinny super Vin, Vinny super Vin, Vinny super Vin, super Vinny Arkins" is lyrically limited I'll grant you, but I am assured that, when sung en masse, it is a powerful composition. Portadown fans are so enamoured of the Donabate striker that they also chant a warning to the opposition when he comes on. "Vinny's gonna get ya, Vinny's gonna get ya," they roar. He certainly got me.

I Am What I Eat

You Ain't Seen Muffin Yet

This McCafé establishment, the new addition to McDonald's on Grafton Street, is going to take a bit of getting used to. It's all leather sofas and stone tiles, fancy pastries and china cups. Sometimes you walk past and there are people just peering through the windows scratching their heads trying to figure it out. In corporate-speak, McDonald's are trying to, um, like, gain credibility with the cappuccino market. In other words, some bright sparks at the Hamburger University woke up and smelt the coffee. And it smelt like dollar bills.

Profits are rising like never before at McDonald's. A lot of people think this is a very bad thing. Entire websites are dedicated to dissecting the golden arches, a symbol they say represents all that is wrong with multinationals. Other anti-McDonald's arguments include the fact that fast food feeds the obesity epidemic and we shouldn't be eating meat at all. Some of the things you read about Ronald would make you choke on your Chicken McNuggets. I would like to feel strongly enough about it to risk a McLibel case by handing out leaflets condemning them. But for reasons that only have a little to do with freshly made Big Macs, I couldn't. Too many good memories and milkshakes I'm afraid.

All the same, I think this McCafé is a terrible idea. Like a fish and chip place putting caviar on the menu. It makes sense for the McBosses because, while they have cornered the young children and teenage market, they lose customers between their late teens and thirties who don't come back until they have children of their own. The McCafé is supposed to tempt these lost souls back with the promise of a grown-up coffee with junk food on the side. I was in the McCafé recently and some kids who had spread out their fries and burgers on the wooden tables were told they had to buy something from the McCafé to eat in that part of the restaurant. I cheered inside when one guy said, okay he would take a sachet of sugar. But his mates caved in and went to buy a chocolate muffin between them so that they could continue their lunch in peace.

It reminds me of when McDonald's tried to have a Valentine's evening in the upstairs section. They advertised it for weeks before: little home-made posters in the restaurant that people laughed at, wondering who on earth would spend Valentine's night in a burger joint.

You had to make a reservation, which a friend and I did enthusiastically confident that we would secure dates before the big day. Unfortunately, we were stood up, but we went along anyway. The ten or so couples who had also booked looked suitably embarrassed to be there but were even more annoyed at having to share their special night with a couple of giggly girls who some presumed were lesbians.

We really got on their nerves by coming first in the game where you had to hop around the candle-lit banquettes with a balloon between your legs. The prize was enough free vouchers to keep us in chicken sandwiches for weeks.

I remember my first burger in McDonald's. I'd been taken out shopping with a friend and her parents. She kept telling us we were going to a place called McDonald's later and I decided it was a shoe shop. Maybe they put an addictive substance in the hamburger patties, but from then on I was hooked. McDonald's was where you went after getting drunk in town for the first time, where you met up with boys and spent hours chatting over two Diet Cokes and a small fries.

I had a ritual with another friend when we got together for lunch. I would go with her to the vegetarian restaurant Cornucopia where I'd watch her eat soup and a brown scone. Then she'd follow me over to Mickey D's and wait for me to finish a burger. It became a habit that in any foreign county I visited I would go to at least one of their burger emporiums just to see if things tasted the same. That's how I got a burger with brown lettuce in a Manhattan McDonald's. You would think it might have put me off.

In darker days, I'd buy loads of magazines and sit in a corner of the Grafton Street branch on my own, with only a strawberry shake, large fries, six chicken nuggets, a quarter-pounder and an apple pie for company.

The trick was to make sure you didn't bump into anyone you knew. That was a social disaster. Luckily it didn't happen often. Maybe everyone else was hiding too. Last week I had a broccoli and mushroom bake in Cornucopia followed by an espresso from a pristine china cup in the McCafé. I read the newspaper and people-watched until I just couldn't take it any more. What will they think of next? Will we get our beer in McPubs, work out in McGyms and pay for it all with dosh from the McBank? They have already opened McHotels. (A double room with fries please.) Maybe they really are trying to take over the world. Oh, if only their cheeseburgers didn't taste so fine. The McDiet starts here.

Water on the Brain

Advertising is deep and mysterious and just a little evil. There I was innocently examining the fridge compartment in the supermarket, when I spied a product I hadn't seen before. Chicken sausages. Chickages. Chausages. Call them what you will. At the time, I didn't know what stopped me purchasing regular sausages – made of pigs as opposed to chickens. But something told me to ignore that voice in my head shrieking "chicken sausages – are you out of your mind?" I glanced up to make sure nobody was looking and grabbed the chicken variety instead.

They sat in my freezer at home, making friends with the turkey rashers that had also found their way into my Bag for Life. Then I heard the ad and realised that once again I had fallen foul of subliminal advertising; "Dear Brain," the voiceover said, "your unwillingness to try something new is truly disappointing, I'm delighted that I chose to ignore you and try those new chicken sausages. Your body will thank your mouth for ignoring your brain."

It got me thinking of other things your brain tells you are really bad ideas but you go ahead and do anyway. Like saying "make it a double" to the barman at closing time. Or planning fun outdoor activities on a rainy day.

Recently we had a weekend visitor from out of town. A pub crawl on the Saturday night was a bit of a failure, mostly due to the fact that I was no longer familiar with which pubs were good for meeting eligible young gentlemen. Our single female visitor was decent about it, but the following (very rainy) day, I felt a desperate need to make amends.

And so, ignoring my brain, which was muttering something like "I wouldn't if I were you", I declared in my best hostess voice, "Let's do the Viking Splash thing!" The Viking Splash is that weird-but-wonderful amphibious vehicle, full of tourists wearing Viking hats and doing the Viking roar, that Dubliners see roaming their city centre.

Our driver was not in a good mood. Who could blame him? His Viking costume had got saturated so he was in his civvies, but on his head he sported a rather soggy looking Viking hat 'n' wig combination. He should have been at home with his feet up, instead he was driving around the city talking history to a load of high-spirited Italians and a few locals.

The tarpaulin roof started to leak as soon as we moved down Patrick Street and the grumpy Viking proceeded to treat us to Bernard Manning's entire back catalogue of rejected mother-in-law jokes. "See that house? That's where Bram Stoker lived, the fella who wrote a book about my mother-in-law." Boom, Boom.

We hoped things might improve when we splashed into the Grand Canal Basin but he was only getting started. "See that derelict warehouse over there? An estate agent tried to sell it to a dyslexic pimp. Har, Har." On the driver's behalf, I would like to express my sincere apologies to dyslexics, estate agents, pimps and good comedians everywhere.

In hindsight, it would have been wiser not to complain, but freezing rivulets of water were running down my nose and I was embarrassed at bringing my guest on another less-than-successful outing. As the tour neared its conclusion, I asked the Viking why he had felt the need to tell so many lame and discriminatory 'jokes' during his guided tour of Dublin. The plaits on his Viking Hat started to shake. He told me not "to take it so personal love", that he "didn't make up the stories" he only "passed them on". He said "don't shoot the messenger" and claimed he had "never had any complaints before".

I want to say a big thank you to the woman who braved the Viking's wrath and told him that she agreed with me. "Never had any complaints before," he parroted. "Don't shoot the messenger." By the way, I know a lot of people who have been on the Viking Splash and thoroughly enjoyed the experience, but it's an experience to be avoided in a downpour, I respectfully suggest.

On a Thursday a few weeks later, it was lashing so heavily the man on the radio said that in just one day, a whole month's worth of rain had fallen. We had the afternoon off so I said, "Let's do the ice skating thing" while my brain shook its cells sadly and said: "I give up."

My first mistake was to expect that the ice-rink at the IFSC actually featured ice. It didn't. Now I am no Torville and my companion is no Dean; still we reckoned if we held hands we could emerge with our dignity intact. But when we tottered onto the watery surface we discovered it was like trying to skate on freshly mopped lino. I blame no one but myself for the fact that I fell over three times and twisted my left ankle. Later, I found a novel use for frozen chicken sausages and even my brain had to agree that they brought the swelling down.

Diet of Denial

He occasionally eats tomatoes on toast for dinner. Because I am on a diet he thinks I will understand. He can't remember a time when he had a normal relationship with food. It has always been a game. Eat enough to stay alive but not enough to allow extra flesh to develop anywhere it shouldn't. That, he says, is how you win.

He makes a killer Irish breakfast. Does the bacon nice and crispy, fries the eggs sunny side up in the pan. But when the gang is gathered around, he doesn't eat any of it because he knows how much fat it all took to make. He will have a slice of toast. The trick, he says, is that you don't spread the butter to the edges, that way there are less calories, less fat, less chance that your belly will stick out. There is nothing worse, he thinks, than developing a sticky-out tummy. He remembers his father teasing him gently about his own belly when he was 12 or 13. Maybe sticky-out ears would be a worse affliction. But on balance he doesn't think so. Not really.

He is almost 30, my friend, and he eats tomatoes on toast for dinner. When he ate his first burger, it seemed like gluttony. A burger all to himself. It didn't make sense. Now that he has grown up, he likes his fillet steak but will chew it carefully in his mouth so he is still eating when everyone else has finished. If he comes across a bit of steak that seems somehow stringy or fatty he will spit it out just, he says, "to be on the safe side". At the end of the meal, a pale brown pile of regurgitated meat is left at the side of his plate.

Nobody has ever mentioned it to him. He uses a napkin and is very discreet.

He was packed off to school with a pound for pocket money. The pound was spent on a school dinner that he always felt was too much. At home, eating meals in front of the TV, he took smaller portions than everyone else and eventually there came a time when nobody laughed at his sticky-out tummy any more.

To this day, if he buys chips from a takeaway he will only eat three or four. If the fish looks remotely greasy he will throw it in the bin. He buys a box of choc ices and won't open it because he knows there is a danger he might eat them all in one go.

When he eats Italian food, he notices how the Parmesan cheese sticks to the plate and he thinks how happy he is that he didn't eat it. Stuff that sticks to the plate is bound to be unhealthy and difficult to digest. He doesn't eat anything that will be a challenge to his digestive system.

Every now and then this man I know adds something else to his made-up list of nutritional guidelines. Sausages should not be taken at face value; inside, some of them are leaner than others. Better to investigate than just devour indiscriminately. He eats no carbs after 6 p.m. because he heard that is how Catherine Zeta Jones regained her figure after giving birth.

Because I am a woman and I am on a diet, he thinks I will understand. He sees no difference between my regime, which is more a programme of healthy, balanced eating than a diet, and his own food issues. He reads about people with eating disorders and doesn't recognise himself. That's a girls' problem, he says, it's a thing that happens to the Rose of Tralee or Calista Flockhart. Men don't deny themselves.

He plays hockey and spends too much time in the gym. He thinks he will bulge out all over, like the Incredible Hulk, if he doesn't keep it all in control.

He is tired most of the time. His face is drawn and he has no energy. Sometimes he wakes in the morning and he doesn't want to get up. The day ahead looks like an obstacle course, too difficult to negotiate. On Sunday, friends are planning a brunch after football and he can't be bothered making excuses to avoid this inevitable pig-out. So he doesn't answer their calls.

He looks at the TV guide and circles the Oscars. He is going to stay up all tomorrow night to watch it. He will admire the dresses and laugh at the speeches. In Hollywood, the evening sun will be shining and Jack Nicholson will be smiling. Afterwards when the awards have been given out there will be private parties with quails' eggs and caviar on the menu. He thinks he would like to go there. Where nothing is real and nobody clears their plates.

Mon Sherie

It was the hangover from Hades. My head felt like a DART had run through it. My mouth was drier than a Pioneer's reunion. Peanuts and half empty whiskey glasses littered the table, shrapnel from a night that left casualties all around. I had slept for exactly four hours when the telephone rang. "Breakfast at Sherie's?" he asked. "I'll be there in ten."

As far as I am concerned breakfast at Sherie's beats breakfast at Tiffany's – and anywhere else in the world you care to mention. The Luas-works outside on Lower Abbey Street might mean that there is some all-day drilling to contend with as you plough into your all-day breakfast, but that is a small price to pay. It doesn't look much from the outside. To the untrained eye, it doesn't look much from the inside to be honest. It's a liver-and-onions, Sunday-dinner kind of place. But since 1948, Sherie's has been a magnet for everyone from weary shoppers to paint-splattered builders, to those of us who discovered it by accident and still can't believe something so wonderful actually exists.

I always take a seat at the long formica counter that stretches the length of the restaurant down to the kitchen hatch at the back. It reminds me of that cheesy Hollywood Boulevard print where Marilyn Monroe and James Dean are having a drink at the counter. Or a little piece of Manhattan in the inner city. Most of all it feels as though the place hasn't been touched since the late 1940s when Mr Isherwood, the grandfather of Adam, who runs it today, bought the place.

Go often enough and you'll get to the know the faces of the customers. Two air hostess friends, who were regulars at Sherie's in the 1960s, returned the other month and waited until the table at the back was free. It was the one they always sat on when they wore their uniforms and wheeled their trolleys down Aer Lingus aisles. And it was where they wanted to sit for their trip down memory lane.

A girl to my right is putting her purse back into her Gucci handbag. The middle-aged woman to my left is ordering a tomato and mayonnaise sandwich. She used to come here with her mother as a girl after a hard day's shopping. A smartly dressed man comes a few times a week and always sits in the same spot. Adam has invented a special hamburger for him with toppings that include sun-dried tomatoes and pineapple. Pineapple? "Oh we put it with a lot of things here," says Adam. "You'd be surprised."

There's a jazz diva Makin' Whoopie in the background when my friend joins me. We order the big breakfast, an Atkins-lover's delight. And we talk because Sherie's is the perfect place for an old-fashioned heart-to-heart. He likes the service, affable but never intrusive. He likes the way when you come in on your own, the staff know when you want to chat about the weather and when you want to read your paper. It's like going to your granny's, he says, the staff at Sherie's would hate it if you didn't leave satisfied.

My friend orders tea, and Adam asks, "Would you like hot milk in that, it's all the rage on the continent." I order coffee, and he says, "Would you like cappuccino?" It's like another world here with the dark wood and the red fittings and the canopy that stretches the length of the counter overhead. On Saturday nights they stay open until nine. You can eat downstairs served by Breda or Angela who have both been working there for 20 years. There is a chef in the kitchen who has been cooking there for almost 25. Creamed chicken and ham pasta. Corned beef and parsley sauce.

Another friend calls Sherie's "the poor man's Trocadero", because the place is a magnet for loads of resting thesps, as well as those rehearsing in the Methodist Mission a few doors down. The WeightWatchers and the AA members who meet at the Mission use Sherie's too. Nuns, laden with bags from the Veritas shop next door, come in and order roast chicken. When it opened, Sherie's had the first rotisserie in the city and the smell of the chicken on the spit hit you when you walked in the door, so Adam says.

Nothing beats a toastie in Sherie's on a Saturday afternoon. Except, perhaps, an omelette with everything in it. Hold the pineapple, please.

"It's all theatre really", says Adam, whipping up a creamy coffee, adding a drizzle of exotic flavouring that he is aghast to hear costs an extra 45 cent in other more upmarket cafes. "Where," he wonders aloud, "is the fun in that?" And that's why we keep coming back.

Weighty Matters

I'm sick, looking at Carol Vorderman's body. I can't even watch *Countdown* without feeling queasy. This is because I accidentally caught sight of her on the cover of a magazine wearing that most horrendous item of clothing, the stretch-satin, plunge neck leotard. I can't get the vision of pale-blue awfulness out of my head.

Yes, I admit that perhaps it was a mistake to actually buy the magazine, but I simply couldn't resist. "Get my body in two weeks," gushed good old Carol on the cover. I needed to know how.

Turns out it's pretty simple. Eat fresh food, says Carol. Drink water, says Carol. Eat when you are hungry and enjoy it, says Carol. The Detox Queen has a very good reason for squeezing into dodgy gym gear and spouting such hoary nutritional chestnuts. She has released another version of her massively successful diet book where you basically live on oatcakes, vegetables and brown rice for a couple of weeks.

The woman has an IQ of approximately seven million and here she is insulting our intelligence by peddling the idea that after 14 days of sweet potatoes, soya yoghurt and millet we can all look like her. It's a blatant lie, of course, but even if it was possible, the question I kept asking myself was, did I really want Carol Vorderman's stretch-satin-friendly body?

There was a time when I'd have jumped at the chance, but I'm not so sure any more. I've had a lifetime of feeling uncomfortable in my skin. Walking into and slumping out of changing rooms. A lifetime of hoping my personality would make up for the bulges and the shirts that never quite fit. Shopping in Evans. Refusing to shop in Evans. Losing a stone. Gaining two. Searching for the hidden codes in other people's words.

"You look well," they might say, but what they really mean is, Thank God you've lost a bit of weight. Or they smile hello and say nothing, covertly looking you up and down. This, you soon learn, means, God, look at the state of her, she's let herself go. Again.

I've counted points. I've ditched carbs. I've supped on cabbage soup. I've given up every single regime, every single time. I can't even laugh and blame my fat on the fact that I love my food, which, it should go without saying, I do. The real problem is that I've always used and abused food, treating it as an emotional life raft that I could cling to when the water got too choppy. I do it much less now than I did when I was younger, but I still do it all the same.

The other week, for example, I was facing into a whole load of work and stressing about stuff I was powerless to change. I went, naturally, to the supermarket. Half an hour later, I had guzzled down a chicken tikka wrap, two caramel slices, two crisp sandwiches and a slice of apple pie. An hour later, I went to a friend's house for dinner and consumed a beautiful beef stir-fry with brown rice followed by ice-cream and slices of fresh mango smothered in Baileys. It's an old trick, this using food as ballast to get through a stormy day. But it just doesn't work. I see that more clearly now, which is why these food attacks occur less frequently. But they still happen now and again.

I don't know whether Michelle McManus, the large young woman who won *Pop Idol*, has food attacks. She was pictured recently on a holiday in Barbados wearing a modest black swimming costume. The captions to these pictures which made the front page of one tabloid were depressingly predictable and utterly offensive. Michelle's response? "I'm big, happy and sexy." She even had the audacity to sound like she meant it.

Then someone made the point that if an anorexic woman was photographed splashing listlessly about in the sea and later heard declaring herself to be "skinny, happy and sexy" there would be an outcry and she would be packed off to the nearest hospital. They had a point – political correctness has gone too far when morbid obesity is seen as an acceptable rather than unhealthy condition – but it brought home to me how difficult it is for some people to accept that happy and fat are not mutually exclusive states.

It took me a while to make up my mind about whether I should be offended by the woman who wrote to me recently asking if I wanted to join her "shed a stone from home" programme. I decided not to take offence. It's hardly wrong for her to have thought that, being overweight, I would want to do something about it in the comfort of my own home. And I do, in a way. But not because people like Carol Vorderman have the arrogance to think I want a body like theirs. What I want is a body like mine. But could I have it in a slightly smaller size, please?

Fête Accompli

Recently, I spent a sunny Saturday afternoon at a church fête up on the gently sloping fields of Drumcree, Portadown. I was taken there by Iris, my Protestant mother-in-law-in-waiting, who some readers will remember from a previous column as the woman from the North who has an unnatural fondness for cheap bleach.

There was an auction in a garage and a cake stall in a white tent where beautiful blooms and ancient books shared space on trestle tables heaving with bargains. Outside, women sat on benches enjoying the live country music. I couldn't resist phoning a friend to tell him where I was. "Is it a fête worse than death," he not unreasonably wanted to know.

For the record – and there was plenty of gospel vinyl for sale on the bric-a-brac stall – it was actually a grand day out that reminded me of the sales of work that used to be held in the Presbyterian church hall next to my childhood home. Even though the lovely Mrs Smith, a stalwart member of the local ladies' club, who lived next door on the other side, produced magnificent apple tarts, there was an unspoken assumption that Protestants baked the best cakes. Take the classic Butterfly Cake, for example, where the top of a fairy cake is sliced off, cut in two and then stuck back onto the cream covered confection like a pair of crumbly wings; a little piece of heaven in a fairy cake case.

Only they don't call them cakes up in Drumcree. They call them buns. Or pastries. Or, in some cases, traybakes. Reverend Pickering – a charming man who in the South we only hear about during the marching season, when he is being interviewed about the protests on the hill outside his church – was on stage reminding those in attendance that there were teas all day in the tent. So that's where we went. It would have been rude not to.

Queuing up in the tea tent, I counted at least 231 varieties of pastries/buns/traybakes laid out like buttery jewels on the table. There was everything from your common-or-garden iced bun to your 15 bun, so called because this dentist's nightmare contains exactly 15 ingredients including biscuit, coconut, mini-marshmallows and glace cherries. Yum.

Top Hats, I learned, were chocolate-covered marshmallows with a smartie hat on top. The unfortunately-named Sticky Jimmys, it was explained to me, are a sweeter version of your average Rice Crispie cake, made with toffee instead of chocolate. There were mini-lemon meringue pies, crisp chunks of shortbread and baby éclairs. They all cost 20p each. And, yes, we had more than one.

Later, strolling around the life-sized *Dr Who* exhibition, complete with tardis and daleks – don't ask, I didn't – Iris explained to me that it wasn't only local Protestants who came to the annual fete. To illustrate that this really was a mixed event, she steered me towards Willie Nugent ("Willie's a Catholic," she said proudly) who was standing beside a sign which read 'The Motionless Farmer'. Some years ago, Willie got into the *Guinness Book of Records* for standing motionless for 13 hours in a shop window in London. These days, he travels around the country, sitting totally still on a tractor festooned with cuddly toys, for hours at a time. County Armagh's own David Blaine is a regular at the Drumcree fête, where, one year, he lay in a bath of ice. Reverend Pickering was actually quite worried about him that year, but Willie survived and went on to push a pea along the road with his nose for two miles.

A few days later, I rang Reverend Pickering to thank him for an enjoyable afternoon. He confirmed Iris's claim that over the past 15 years of the fête, Catholics have supported the event, which raises money for Drumcree Church. I happened to phone him the day after Mary Holland's funeral in Dublin, which had been a deeply moving celebration of her life and work. Something Nell McCafferty said during the service had stuck with me. She told the story of how as far back as the 1960s, Mary was writing about both sides, holding up a mirror to the troubled communities, somehow being able to tell them more than even they knew about who they were. She was a great teacher, Nell said.

Reverend Pickering remembered meeting Mary during one particularly bad July. She sat quietly in a pew at the back of his church. People were milling around but she was relaxed, he said, and didn't look at all uncomfortable to be there. They had a pleasant conversation and she went on to write a perfectly pitched piece for *The Observer* which laid out the case for both communities.

Reverend Pickering said he was hoping for a calm July. A prayerful July. But whatever happens, it would be great if, like Mary Holland always did, we could try harder to see both sides. That would be even sweeter than a Sticky Jimmy and so much better for our health.

My Bubbly Personality

There are a few rules that should be adhered to when indulging an occasional champagne habit. Rule Number 1: It's best not to order champagne if you can't afford to, even when said champagne is the least expensive stuff on the list.

I broke Rule Number 1 in a most embarrassing fashion recently. We were celebrating a monumental musical event at the time. OK, so we had just been to a Rick Astley gig. But if you loved him like my companion for the evening did back in the 1980s, you would totally understand the need for a celebration. Once, she actually wrote to his grandmother asking her to put in a word for her. She wants to remain nameless. Obviously.

Even more gorgeous than in his Stock/Aitken/Waterman days, Astley performed a storming set of covers that included a bit of Deano and a lot of Sinatra. He even did a cheeky little version of his biggest hit 'Never Gonna Give You Up'. Oh how we screamed.

At the end of the gig, we rushed down to the front of the stage with all the other shameless 30-somethings as he shook our sweaty paws and looked right into our eyes. I hadn't been that moved since I first saw the video for 'Last Christmas', particularly the bit where George Michael drops a crucial bit of tinsel, thus locking eyes with his erstwhile lover, whom subsequent events have taught us he wouldn't have fancied in real life.

We were on a high as we left Rick, and it wasn't our fault that we passed a bar on the way home where we knew we could toast our encounter with the cream of 1980s pop with a trip down the Champagne super-nova. The last time we had been to the Dublin club Renard's we could have sworn a glass of the cheapest champagne on the list had cost €10 a glass. And we had exactly €20. Ah, the serendipity of it all.

Well, yes. Until we order the champagne and it's being poured and we have kind of drunk half of it by the time the barman gets around to handing us the bill and actually it turns out the cheapest glass of the fizzy stuff is now checking in at €15. That'll be €30 girls. Oh dear.

The manager was very understanding. He even helped us count out the 5 and 10 cent coins found in hitherto unexplored crevices of our handbags as the bemused bar staff looked on. An urgent call was made to the brother at this point. He refused to bail us out, suggesting the experience might teach us a lesson and unhelpfully reminded us about the last time we had called into the same club for a glass of champagne "for the road".

We had just enough money for our two glasses of champagne that time. Not only that, but actor Patrick Bergin just happened to be nursing a drink right beside us. She who will not be named was also in attendance that night and worryingly revealed she harboured a bit of a crush on Bergin back when he played the wife beater in *Sleeping with the Enemy*.

No matter how much I told her it was him, she wouldn't believe me, which is how I wound up asking him if he wouldn't mind telling my friend he really was Patrick Bergin. "Yeah, right," she sniffed when Mr Bergin introduced himself. He had to practically do a mime of the bit in the film where he fishes Julia Robert's engagement ring out of the toilet before she would believe him.

Eventually, she was persuaded, and, thanking Mr Bergin for his patience, I clinked my full-to-the-brim glass of champagne in his direction and said cheers. At which point a delighted Mr Bergin took the glass from my hand and said "that's very kind of you". Rule Number 2: Don't wave full glasses of champagne at celebrities, because they might think you are rewarding them with your hard-earned bubbly as a token of your admiration, and not just saying cheers.

On the occasion of breaking Rule Number 1, we did eventually manage to get the money together using some long-lost card my bubbly buddy had found at the bottom of her bag. Sensibly, we vowed never to return to the celebrity haunt, at least until we had enough spare cash to buy two more glasses of champers and thus prove to the manager we weren't total chancers.

Strolling nonchalantly past the bouncers the other night, we retained our cool until spotted by one of the managers, who shouted over, "Have the right money this time, do you?" Not the most elegant of entrances.

Once inside, we downed our solitary glass as quickly as possible and then a generous man with gorgeous kids – he showed us their pictures in his wallet – decided on a whim to buy us a whole bottle of the stuff. It seemed rude not to accept. Rule Number 3: It never champagnes but it pours.

Food for Thought

According to my guidebook, staff at Ethiopian Airlines still get asked whether food is served as part of their in-flight service. It's 20 years since Bob Geldof's global fundraiser, since Band Aid, since Feed the World and those harrowing images of skeletal pot-bellied children, flies buzzing around them as they dropped like flies. The slightly misleading slogan of the country's department of tourism is 'Ethiopia – 13 months of sunshine'. But to most people the country means famine and, if we travel there, we want the airline to offer vacuum-packed chicken, chocolate mousse and bottomless supplies of bite-sized cardboard masquerading as snacks.

There are things you feel uncomfortable saying even in the capital, Addis Ababa, where food shortages are never as extreme. "I'm starving," you moan, only minutes after visiting a feeding centre where people with dead eyes and protruding bones queue up for the local pancake injera and a bowl of soup. Drought has hit some rural areas hard and these people who have travelled miles to get here might not eat again for days. "I could eat a baby's arse through a tennis racket," someone else in the group remarks later.

You stop yourself thinking about any of it too deeply until you come back and find yourself pushing 1,000 calories around your plate. "Think of all the starving children in Africa," we were always told. Funny, but you could never imagine them fully until now.

In Ethiopia, you are suddenly more conscious than ever

about your weight. "I'm going to Ethiopia," I told my friends. And we laughed. I imagined myself, this bona-fide EU Butter Mountain, being the target of bitterness in a land where in some parts a square meal is untold luxury. But the Ethiopians I met, even if they did occasionally do discreet double takes at my largesse, were gracious, kind and proud. The men, from the Junior Minister for Foreign Affairs to the staff at our hotel, were polite and charming. Well, most of the time.

We were walking through the Merkato, the biggest market in Africa, when it happened. I had just haggled successfully for a couple of ebony statues and traditional children's dresses. I was strolling through this wonderfully chaotic market with a middle-aged local man who asked me a million questions – Ethiopians are endearingly inquisitive – only some of which I could understand. He asked me was I married. I said no. "But you are so fat," he pronounced admiringly. "So, so fat." Luckily, there was no one in our group to witness my mortification. It took me 15 minutes to explain to this nice gentlemen that this kind of talk was not the way to a *faranji* (foreign) woman's heart. He looked utterly confused.

"So what should I say to Western women when I want to talk nice to them?" he asked. I could only advise that he stay away from the F word, and he still looked puzzled when we said our goodbyes.

The Miss Addis Ababa competition was being held that night in the Sheraton Hotel – a marble-covered monument to obscene wealth stuck smack in the middle of the poverty and disease-stricken community – and after my chat with Mr You're So Fat, I did briefly consider entering. Then I saw some of the competition, most of whom could out-pout Naomi Campbell, and I thought better of it.

At home, we crash-diet our way through life while

Ethiopians forage through bins for their next meal. At home, we pray the rain stays away while in Ethiopia the lack of rain has brought the country to the brink of another food emergency.

According to projections from Ireland Aid, the recent drought means at least seven million people will be in urgent need of food assistance in the coming months. But this best case scenario is extremely unlikely. A more realistic assessment is that nine million people in rural regions in the north and south of the country will face famine. At worst, if more international assistance is not given, 12 to 13 million people will starve.

Food supplies have almost run out – the government says it has only enough stocks until the middle of October – and while the crops all over the country look green and lush, they have not matured enough to be harvested. In the Afar region, where the Irish charity Goal is active, 40 per cent of the cattle have died. Rains have failed in Tigray, where the worst scenes of the famine in the mid-1980s were played out, and around 2.5 million people there are in urgent need of food assistance.

At the moment, it's a crisis. But if there isn't an adequate international response, there could be a catastrophe. Can we stomach those scenes again? It might not be too long before we find out.

Some of My Best Friends Are Aliens

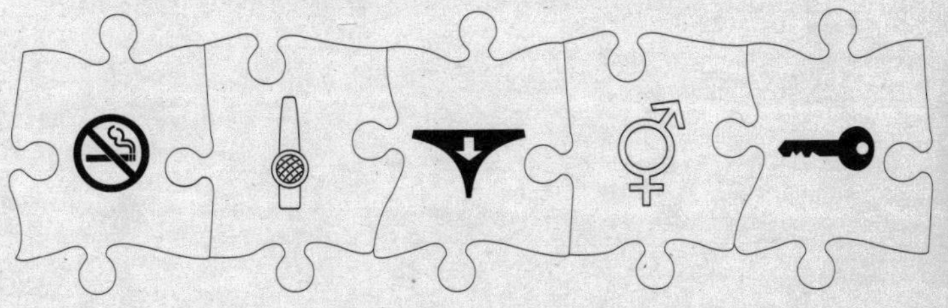

Living in Oblivion

There's this friend I have known for longer than I haven't. I call him Jagger in honour of his all-time hero. He is 53, thinks he looks 26 and says he feels about 90. I hadn't seen him in years but I knew I'd find him. He is an agoraphobic and couldn't go far even if he wanted to.

His hair was still wild but streaked with grey. His face was worn, but he hadn't lost his corny sense of humour. "Did ye hear Elton John wrote a song for Mother Theresa," he asked me. "No," I replied. "Well he did, it's called 'Sandals in the Bin'."

We used to play cards, me and Jagger. For money that neither of us really had. There were games of poker late into the night and more frequent games of Don, a brilliant game that I had forgotten the rules of until he reminded me. His flat was where I went when I bunked off college. His girlfriend would cook me fried eggs and chips. She left though. He's been on his own since.

So here was Jagger telling me that he had a place in Pembroke Road in Dublin, after being evicted from the flat. His previous landlord didn't want to take Jagger's Eastern Health Board cheques anymore. He was doing the place up and wanted Jagger and his dog and his bicycle and his racing pages out of the way. He was doing fine now, he said. Grand. Not a bother. The other day my mother told me she had heard some news about Jagger. He was living in a container in the heart of Dublin 4. A container? But he's got a flat in Pembroke Street. No, she said, he's living in a container and waiting to get housed.

That evening, I took a walk as the sun set over the docks. I knew where he was but wanted to warn him before I turned up. I called the place where he is a part-time cleaner and he answered the phone. He sounded annoyed and put me off with the excuse that he had to visit his grandchildren. I wandered along anyway. Saw the metal container, standing gloomy in the twilight, 12 feet by 10.

That night I rang his mobile phone. "You're living in a container?" Silence. "Well, yeah. Yeah, I am." He told me his story.

After getting evicted he bought a tent and pitched it on some wasteland in this Dublin 4 suburb. After five weeks, Dublin City Council told him to pack it up but he had nowhere else to go. Some local benefactors gave him access to this container. He has a key. And an airbed. There's no electricity but he has a gas camper stove, a candle and a radio. The rats running around outside are the size of horses, he told me. He doesn't think they can get in. He hopes not anyway.

Jagger wants to walk up and down outside the home of a local TD with a placard reading: "I'm Irish, please house me." He is the type that, once he starts talking about something he feels strongly about, can't stop. "I'm Irish and I'm homeless and it's a disgrace. I'm not the only one. They are everywhere, these forgotten people, the ones on the streets, and nobody seems to care. People come to this country in containers from foreign places and get housed in places I couldn't afford to live. I live in a container and can't get housed. If I painted my face black I'd have a better chance of getting a proper place. If I sailed over from Holyhead in this container, I'd be sitting in an apartment right now. You won't see a refugee sleeping on the street. Is this what our ancestors fought for? Is it?"

And on and on. And I didn't know what to say. The liberal,

hate-racism-with-a-vengeance, politically correct part of me was appalled. I told him, but look, we Irish were forced to leave and go to other countries and what would have happened if people over there had the same attitude as you? But he is living in a container. And all he can see is the colour of the skin of people he believes have decent roofs over their heads. And here am I. Safe and warm in a place where rats don't scurry outside, or if they do it doesn't matter because I can't hear them. He's lying on an airbed, trying to read his newspaper, by the flickering light of a candle. The local authority put him on the priority housing list. "I might get housed by the time I'm 65," he says. "And Róisín?" "Yes Jagger?" "Who invented camping?" "Don't know, my friend." "Henry the Tent(h)". If you didn't laugh you'd die.

Down with this Sort of Thong

There's a protest going on in Milltown, Co. Kildare, that sounds uncannily like a scene from my favourite episode of *Father Ted.* Remember that scene where Ted and Dougal picketed the local cinema because there was a blasphemous movie being shown? The home-made placards they carried read: 'Careful Now!' and 'Down with this Sort of Thing!'. Their display did more to promote the film than prevent people watching and *The Passion of Saint Tibulus* became Craggy Island's most popular movie of all time.

In the tiny village of Milltown, locals are protesting against the opening of a lap-dancing club in the local hostelry. The Chicken Ranch operates out of the Milltown Inn from 8 p.m. Reporter Nicola Tallant was informed by one villager that theirs was "a good-living community and we do not want this sort of club, it certainly isn't for locals". While it made me laugh, I found myself sympathising with the villagers even if they did sound like unemployed extras from Craggy Island. Maybe it's because I have finally realised that there is more chance of me shinnying up a pole backwards while gyrating in time to 'Falling' by Alicia Keyes than of me formulating a consistent view on the lap-dancing phenomenon. To be appalled or not to be appalled, that is the question. And I don't have an answer. Even after two nights of probing research and several strawberry daiquiris.

Despite the outrage of the Milltown-placard wavers, it seems the practice is gradually gaining more credibility here.

Drinking men under the table used to be the ultimate display of girl power, but these days, all a woman has to do is sit quietly while a peachy bottom is thrust in her face, and look like she is enjoying it, to really be one of the lads.

I thought a visit to one of these clubs might concentrate my mind a little, but all I got were plaudits I didn't really deserve. I was voted best girlfriend in the world, and not by my boyfriend. He and three male friends of mine went to a lap-dancing club in Dublin where, with an indulgent smile, I gave permission for him to be danced upon by a girl in a barely-there catsuit. Giddy with the delicious anti-feminism of it all, I laughed louder than anyone else when he left the private dancing area and returned to his seat. And then I allowed the same girl to dance on me. "Best girlfriend in the world," cheered the three lads when I returned.

Aw, shucks. It's easy when you know how. Within half an hour these lithe creatures had enticed around €200 out of our little group. Exploitation? It certainly felt like it. These women may look soft and seductive but underneath, they are just cool, hard businesswomen with sparkly dresses instead of pinstriped suits.

There is Tanya. And Danielle. Or Suzanna. Or Chantelle. Take your pick from dozens of mostly foreign young women in any of the ten such clubs around the city. They might have been the ones taking their tops off but – and like I say, I still haven't fully worked out why – it was me who felt exposed. The venue was Lapello on Dame Street. A place which, in former incarnations, was always cramped and stifling, but now it was cramped and stifling and stuffed full of girls with fake tans and fake smiles. The Merrion Inn with implants, if you like. The lads had a great time. All I felt was uncomfortable ambivalence. And that was almost worse than being disgusted.

When I mentioned to a colleague that I was going to

write on this subject, he insisted I should hold off until I had visited Dublin's most exclusive lap-dancing dub, Barclay's in South William Street. The manager, Conor Merry – his real name by happy coincidence – confirmed that *Irish Times* journalists are among the clientele, so I figured it must be the real deal. The women are beautiful, the dancing rooms posher than most exclusive nightclubs in Dublin and the staff polite and handsome. They feed you oysters and strawberries, and even Carrie would be impressed with the cocktails.

My girlfriend and I brought two guys; both had dances and both came back beaming ear to ear. "Fantastic" was all one of them could say until several minutes had passed. My girlfriend needed some Dutch courage but eventually disappeared upstairs for the first lap dance of her life. Twenty minutes later, she hadn't come back. It turned out she had got chatting to the girl in question and then found she couldn't go through with it. Too weird. In any case, a man who was being danced on in another corner of the room started singing 'The Wild Rover'. She said afterwards that any lipstick lesbian tendencies that might have been hidden deep inside her died at that precise moment. I, meanwhile, had the second and last lap dance of my life and, as I drained my fourth daiquiri, could only be heard muttering, "Down with this sort of thong!" like the confused ladette I am rapidly turning into.

Save Our Schemes

My first major interview was with the Hothouse Flowers some time after 'Don't Go' but before 'Sweet Marie'. I got the scoop beside the ATM machine in Sandymount. I had my notebook and pen ready, even though I had only popped out for a sliced pan and a few rashers. Our brief encounter went something like this.

Me: "Hi, would you do an interview for *NewsFour*"? Them: "What's *NewsFour*?" Me: "It's the local free newspaper serving Ringsend, Irishtown and Sandymount that comes out a few times a year. I'm a reporter there. And the advertising manager." Them: "OK, then." Me: "So, um, like, er what are you guys up to at the moment?" Them: "We are getting money from the cash machine."

Back then my advertising manager skills were almost as bad as my interview technique. One day I ran delighted into the editor telling him Big Bad Polluters and Co. wanted to place a full-page ad. He gently pointed out the fact that since *NewsFour* was running a campaign against the incinerator Big Bad etc were planning to erect, it might not be the best idea.

NewsFour was set up as a community employment scheme in 1986. Some of the most entertaining and frankly strangest people I have ever met passed through its doors. It was, and still is, a place for those who have been termed the 'hardcore unemployed', the folk for whom the boats will never rise, the ones who just don't fit.

There was the man who suffered from Schizophrenia and

found it impossible, because of his illness, to hold down a regular job. But he mastered the battered computer and became meticulous in the layout of the paper. I remember a kind guy who looked after the office and made coffee; his physical disability closed doors to other employment opportunities. But he was needed at *NewsFour*. For a few years, they had a chance to prove to themselves and to FÁS and to whomever cared to know that they were worth something. It was a reason to get up in the morning for some and the beginnings of future employment for others.

In relative terms, we all had our problems. I had returned from waitressing in London without a degree and with a "it'll never happen" notion of being a journalist. Others were trying to get back into the workforce after a gap of several years. *NewsFour*, paying slightly more than the dole and requiring our presence for a mere 20 hours a week, gave us all a start.

So I am watching with interest to see what Mary Harney is going to do with these schemes: the community-based crèches, environmental projects and help-the-aged ventures. They were originally set up to combat high unemployment figures, and she said last week they were being reduced to reflect the "significant reduction in the numbers of long-term unemployed".

But even the projects that at first glance don't appear to be particularly empowering or productive are acting as a lifeline for thousands – for people who may be eminently unemployable but want the chance to lead a useful life. And deserve one. It's incredible how many journalists, photographers and broadcasters got their start on *NewsFour*. A rock critic of a national daily. A deputy editor of a Sunday newspaper. A 2FM newsreader. An *Evening Herald* sports reporter. A successful freelance photographer who now travels the world.

Other community schemes have their own success stories, happening quietly across the country. And while that kind of success is important, the real value of the schemes is the effect they have on the participants. I know people who started work on the scheme without being able to hold a simple conversation and with a few months of interaction had been transformed.

I should declare another personal interest here. My mother, Ann Ingle, is the current supervisor at *NewsFour*. She says it is the most fulfilling job she has ever had. "The community rallied to the cause when the government asked for these projects to be set up," she says. "And now it looks as though the resources people have worked so hard to create together are going to be wiped out."

The Taoiseach's view of Community Employment Schemes, 40 per cent of which it is thought will be shut down, was that "some give value and some don't". I'd like to know how their value is measured. If it's in terms of how many go on to actual employment or further education, then the officials who are deciding which of these schemes to axe are looking in the wrong place. I am just one of tens of thousands of people who owe more than can be measured to projects such as *NewsFour*.

Faith Restored

When I last wielded a Trocaire box, I had a haircut like Purdy from *The Avengers* and a nylon jumpsuit in electric blue. Incredibly, these cardboard institutions have been around for 30 years. In our family, we stopped bringing them home when we left primary school, and when we gave up giving up things for Lent, the boxes came to represent one of the flimsier relics of our past.

When Trocaire sent me one this year as part of research for an article, I knew I would have felt like a selfish spoilt child if I didn't make full use of the box. I spent a few minutes assembling the ingenious piece of charitable origami and positioned it on a shelf on my desk.

Everything comes around. My old jumpsuit, for example, would be the height of fashion in some circles today although not, sadly, the circles in which I move. As diligently as I did all those years ago, I have been putting my spare change in the slot provided. I've been collecting all those coins that congregate in crevices and under mugs and in pencil holders and at the bottom of bags. I have wiggled my hand down the back of the sofa and discovered, among the biscuit crumbs, an occasional €2 coin.

And each time I deposit my booty, Maria (ten) from Guatemala smiles down at me from the box. An information panel assures me that if I raise even €15, it will provide food for one week for 50 displaced children in Colombia. The box was half full when I lifted it last week. Or half empty, depending on your world view. Two days later and the same box was suspiciously light. On inspection, I discovered that a solitary old Irish pound coin, donated by a colleague, was all that remained.

I am used to items being stolen from my desk. Small radios, batteries, concert tickets, books. I put it down to my carelessness and my head-in-the-sand approach to the inconclusive evidence that industrious thieves are at work in the building. When I assembled the Trocaire box, I wondered for a split second whether it was wise to leave smiling Maria guarding the money. But like an old woman lamenting a time when you could leave the key in the door, I said to myself that things had come to a sorry pass if you had to keep a Trocaire box under lock and key. I have now taped up the bottom of the box in a bid to deter the thieves. Things have indeed come to a sorry pass.

When developments like this occur, you can get cynical about trying to be good. What's the point if there are people around whose conscience allows them to tip out money from a cardboard box destined for children in Guatemala, who don't have school books, or crops, or medicine or access to legal aid, and put it in their pockets? When things like this happen, you are momentarily disgusted with the world, filled with shock, never mind horror.

I was due to go to an awards ceremony that night, but not the kind where people wear fancy dresses, sip champagne and air kiss each other to death. The Sean Moore Community Awards do was at the Clanna Gael GAA club in Dublin's Ringsend. Sean Moore, a former Fianna Fáil lord mayor, was a local politician dedicated to his community. This awards scheme, a kind of Oscars for good people, has been going since 1988. It was a night to marvel at good deeds in small doses, a night to restore your faith in trying to be good.

There were ten winners. People like Joe Donnelly, who runs the Anchorage playgroup with his wife. "I really felt

Joe showed his caring and kindness during the time of the floods in the area last year," wrote the woman who nominated him. "He knocked on doors, including mine, offering his services, whether it was knocking down walls, tearing out kitchens or sterilising floors." Kitty Crowe, of Bath Avenue, was nominated for her "exceptional community services" over the years. "Not so much as a sweet paper can be found on her road and she also maintains the grotto of Our Lady at Margaret Place." Gerry Browne was nominated for his work at St Andrew's Resource Centre on Pearse Street, where he teaches older people about the internet. "When he tells them to type www, most of his group respond in the knowledge that he is taking them on a journey that many never envisaged was possible just a few years ago," his nomination read.

Good deeds in small doses. As the Lord Mayor of Dublin, Dermot Lacey, said that night, "If Volunteer Ireland went on strike, this country would collapse." Thankfully there are thousands of Joes, thousands of Kittys, thousands of Gerrys making life easier for others all over this island while asking nothing in return. And when somebody fills their pockets with the proceeds of a Trocaire box, it helps to keep remembering that.

Up My Nose

There was a match on. For this reason, the fare from Cork to Dublin was cheaper, and the train fuller, than it would normally be on a Sunday. One of the teams who were playing wore blue and yellow colours. I'm not sure if the blue and yellow team beat the other team, but the fans seemed in good spirits anyway. A boy who couldn't have been more than 15 had managed to buy himself a few bottles of cider. He sat drinking them at the next table with a pained expression on his face while his friend snored gently beside him. I wondered what President McAleese would say if she could see him. But I didn't mind. There was, after all, a match on.

And I didn't mind when the blue and yellow-clad men at the bottom of the carriage started what I believe they would describe as singing. Tuneless voices shouting about men behind wires and lonely prison walls and some other things I couldn't make out. I didn't mind when they banged their fists on the table in an attempt to emulate a bodhrán. Well, not much anyway. I had a pile of Sunday papers and a nice comfortable seat. And a radio with earphones if it came to that.

But I was bothered when the first wisps of cigarette smoke wafted in my direction. This development, quite literally, got up my nose. I looked around and spotted at least four people at different seats smoking. On each window there was a sticker that said smoking could lead to a €500 fine and or imprisonment. It was bright red. You really couldn't miss it.

I gritted my teeth and thought about saying something, wondering what words I could use so that I wouldn't end up sounding like a killjoy or a busybody or both.

I practised it in my head. *Excuse me, would you mind putting out your cigarettes?* No, too soft. *Excuse me, this is a no-smoking carriage.* Too snooty. *Stop smoking you morons and what about taking a break from the table-banging antics while you are at it?* Hmmmm. That one certainly had potential.

While I was thinking about all this, an Iarnród Éireann employee from the dining car came into the carriage and asked the men for some change. She chatted with them for a few minutes, as they puffed happily away, before thanking them and leaving.

At the next table, a man and his wife took out their cigarettes and lit up. I caught the man's eye and pointed wordlessly at the sign on the window. His wife glared at me while he sucked at the fag and blew the smoke out with relish.

I decided to take the coward's way out. The next time the guard came past, I mentioned to him that people had been smoking. But, of course, suddenly nobody was. He said he had been up and down the carriages asking people to put out cigarettes. He was sick doing it. "They won't go to the smoking carriage," he explained. When the legislation banning smoking completely on trains comes out next year, he certainly wasn't going to be enforcing it. That would be impossible.

A few minutes later, one of the jolly GAA supporters came and sat at the next table to make a call on his mobile. As he talked, he lit up a cigarette. I called the guard. He came over and asked the man to put it out or go into the corridor to smoke it. The smoker went into the corridor where, strictly speaking the guard told us, it is illegal too. But what can you do? Er, fine them €500 I suggested. He laughed. And then so did I.

As the train approached Heuston Station the smoker's friend came over to the table with a view to setting me straight about a few things. "You have to understand something," he said. "The guy didn't see the signs. He didn't realise it was a no-smoking carriage, had he realised there is no way he would have been smoking. Actually, his father is a former EU commissioner so, you see, he really is an upstanding member of the community." And on he rambled. I nodded in all the right places. His friend wasn't being rude, he repeated, he just didn't see the signs. Did I understand? Perfectly.

My new acquaintance was about to leave when he remembered something else. If that is all you have to complain about when there is a match on, you are very lucky. "You are lucky," he said, "that you didn't get drink spilled on you or get caught in a fight because that's what sometimes happens on the train when there is a match on. A little bit of smoke? Sure you got off lightly," he said. "When there's a match on, you have to expect it." Maybe that's why they lower the fare.

Bringing Out the Best

I armed myself with Louis Walsh-style cynicism to cover the Special Olympics World Summer Games 2003. It was the only way to get through it, I figured. When Bono was holding hands with Nelson Mandela in Croke Park I was in London visiting old haunts, relaxing in a back garden, nibbling vegetarian kebabs and discovering an intense hatred of Tofu. When I rang home I heard choked voices talking about how the opening ceremony of the games made them feel proud to be Irish. It was exactly the kind of sickly-sweet sentiment I'd legged it to London to avoid.

My lost weekend of roof-top parties, bargain hunting in Brick Lane and dozing on the grass in Highgate Cemetery was over far too quickly. I returned to a country consumed by the event. Returning home from the airport in a taxi, I lost count of the number of gardens festooned with Irish flags and patriotic paraphernalia originally purchased for the World Cup, now being put to another use. They're getting good value for their green, white and gold, I observed from the back seat. The driver threw me a dirty look. Like Walsh, I had misjudged the mood. But there is nothing like the vast majority of people feeling one way to make the rebel in me speed off in the opposite direction. Professionally, I was enthusiastic and anxious to do my best. Personally, I wasn't sure I could stay afloat on this tsunami of goodwill.

At the beginning of the week I remember finding out that there could be as many as ten gold medal winners in, say, the

50-metre back stroke because the athletes were put in different divisions according to their ability. I raised a cynical eyebrow at this news.

One colleague, a broadcaster, said his bosses were getting annoyed because he was supposed to be covering the news angles but all he could feed them were tear-provoking stories of triumph over adversity. No news, only good news, which in their eyes was no news at all.

You probably know where this is going. Well, you know if you had anything at all to do with the games. Days pass and the emotion you thought you might have to simulate creeps in on you with each story you hear, each medal-winning athlete you meet. You have to turn away to compose yourself when a brother tells you how proud he is of his sister. He lists her qualities with genuine awe – "She sings, she dances better than any of us, she is so brave, so bubbly," he says.

By the third day, I was walking around with a permanent lump in my throat, devouring all the newspaper coverage, embarrassed by this emotional U-turn. Little things. Outside the National Aquatic Centre, a bus for the athletes emblazoned with a sign that reads 'Transporting Heroes'. A garda hugging an athlete, his cap tipping to one side.

I've been waiting an hour for a taxi and I don't really mind because I know the taxi company in question has dedicated drivers transporting the athletes around Dublin. Normally I would be fuming. Now, I'm just a little concerned about an appointment I will no longer be able to keep. A bus passes. I make a pleading, any-chance-of-a-lift, face at the driver. With a smile, he rolls down the window and tells me to hop in. He's been doing this all week, driving from venue to venue transporting family members, volunteers and athletes. "Great craic," he says, "the stories you hear."

After dropping the passengers in the Phoenix Park, the bus driver goes completely out of his way to drop me a two-minute walk from where I urgently need to be. He is almost apologetic about his generosity. Confesses he is not used to being this nice. But the Special Olympics, well, it's turned him into a 24-hour Good Samaritan. He can't help himself. His mouth keeps forming the "Yes" word where he confides he might normally have said "No".

And it's not just him. "Have I ever seen so many people with smiles on their faces?" he wants to know. Well, no, now that you mention it. Exactly. Everyone has a more useful, honourable purpose. That makes them happy. Simple, really. But what he also wants to know is whether we will all return to normal when the last aeroplane full of athletes has departed. Will it be 'business as usual' when the glow of the games wears off? Or have we been infected with some class of benign disease, deadly contagious, the kind that won't kill us but, if we could just be sure not to forget how it feels, will make us so much stronger? He beeps the horn, I raise a hand in reply. Hoping the answer is "Yes."

Hector the Great

Hector Grey didn't like the word cheap. The vast selection of light hardware, ornaments and souvenirs imported from the Far East and sold in his shop in Liffey Street, Dublin, were not cheap, which he thought implied a certain tackiness. They were, more accurately, inexpensive. Even today, if you suggest to his son Alex that Hector Grey's was the original pound shop, he will tell you it was never a pound shop. "We were the original bargain store, he corrects," as Hector looks down proudly from a large photograph on the wall of his office above the shop.

Of course his real name wasn't Hector, but that's what half of Dublin called him anyway. His real name was Alex Scott. He got the name of the shop from Hector Grey, a jockey in Australia. Alex, or Hector, wasn't from Dublin either. He travelled from Scotland to this country to investigate why the Irish were all emigrating. He married an Irish girl, but she didn't take to Glasgow life so they moved back to Dublin and he started selling things from a tray on Henry Street.

Then he started importing toys from Japan. Hector was one of the first to travel to Japan after the war. He had a tiny shop on Middle Abbey Street, across from the old Adelphi Cinema, selling toys and souvenirs. Souvenirs were the only item that had to have the country of origin stamped on them. But some English people didn't like the tag 'Made in Japan' and wanted the souvenirs to be made in Ireland. Canny Hector got around this by printing 'An tSeapáin tír a dheanta' on the back of the ashtrays and the porcelain figurines, so the fussy English customers were none the wiser.

But it was toys and stocking fillers that made Hector Grey famous. My family used to get all our Christmas presents there. For £5 you would be able to buy for your brothers and sisters, and still have enough left over for marbles. It was like a treasure trove. It still is.

On a busy Thursday evening last week, I made one of my regular visits to the shop. There are clothes organisers for €4.50 or 24 colouring pencils for €2.50. Giant chalk sticks are competitively priced at €1.35 while a packet of eight kazoos is only €2.50. (We always got a kazoo in our stocking. It was the only other constant apart from a tangerine and chocolate coins).

You can buy a pocket-sized travel brush with built-in shoehorn and a multi-purpose, spring-loaded holder for tea towels and still have change from a fiver. Mousetraps sit beside Sisal play mice for cats. And, of course, there are miles of tinsel and hundreds of tree ornaments all over the shop.

Hector Grey also stocks a range of religious paraphernalia. There are 3D Christmas cards featuring Jesus and Mary which have to be seen to believed. And they are flying out of the shop, apparently. Alex says people his age, in their late sixties and seventies, are buying them. The cards are even more popular than the Jesus address books, which are inspired examples of the Christian collectables that sit easily alongside oil paints on the shelves at Hector Grey's.

This year our family are doing Kris Kindle for the first time, so we only have to buy one of our siblings a present, instead of all eight. This decision was driven by economic factors, but I'm thinking now that I could get something useful for all of them in Hector Grey's without breaking the bank. I mean, everyone needs cotton buds and at Hector

Grey's a packet of 1,000 sells for €2.25, which, incidentally, would also buy you 100 incense sticks.

The shop is as much a part of Dublin folklore as the Ha'penny Bridge. Hector used to call it the metal bridge, and even at 81 he could be seen selling stuff out of boxes there before going up to The Oval for a few glasses of whiskey. That's what he did on the day he died in the 1980s, before he went home and fell asleep in his longjohns. "It was a nice way to go," says Alex.

Alex has been working in Hector Grey's for exactly 50 years. He keeps telling his wife Sally that he will stop, but she doesn't believe him. She says, "If you are giving it up, then why do you keep walking out the door every morning?" As a young man he won a scholarship to Trinity College to study history, but his father told him that history wouldn't put meat on the table and that was that.

Alex doesn't know how long more he will be working, but he reckons his younger brother Robert will keep the business going for as long as he is able. After that the future of Hector Grey's is unsure. Alex's children are doctors and lawyers and dentists and computer programmers. None of Hector Grey's grandchildren has any interest in taking on the shop. We should treasure this gem while it's still around to sell cheap (sorry Hector) Jesus address books and Sacred Heart candles. Alex says they drew the line at religious ashtrays. Well, you would.

Believing in Aliens

I married a man who wasn't Irish. We got hitched in London where we met, and when we moved to Dublin a few months later I accompanied him on his compulsory visits to the immigration centre. There was a sign in the office that read 'Aliens, This Way'. Suddenly I was starring in a bad B-movie: *Mom, I Married an Alien!*

It was the mid-1990s and we were both on the dole. We would sit in a cafe near the social-welfare office on Marlborough Street and drink watery coffee while we waited to see how much money they'd give us. We got jobs collecting glasses in a quayside nightclub where we started to notice people were drinking more water than beer. As you passed by with your leaning tower of glasses they would try to massage you. This was Generation E, we discovered. They wore white gloves that shone under UV lights and they smiled too much and too wide.

After a couple of years of my Alien being a good boy, we had to undergo the interview process so that he could be naturalised and become an Irish citizen. We were so nervous about it, I rented the movie *Green Card*, hoping for some tips. I was Andie McDowell and he was Gerard Depardieu. I mean, what if they asked him my favourite perfume? What's his shoe size again? In the end, the process was pretty painless. He got his passport and we set off to live in that place called happily-ever-after. But a few years later, to the genuine sadness of both of us, I starred in a sequel called *Mom, I Divorced an Ex-Alien*. It wasn't half as good as the original.

I think this experience of seeing things from an alien point of view must be part of the reason I get so emotional about the upcoming referendum on immigration. I've been devouring the press coverage, informing myself on the issue like I've never done for other referenda. I didn't want to just have a knee-jerk reaction to such an important change to our Constitution. The fact that, for the first time in my life, I find myself in agreement with both Sinn Féin and William Binchy is just a cross I have to bear.

This is what I feel. Anger at people who think the referendum is all about keeping foreigners out, and more anger at politicians who, as long as it's passed, don't really mind if that's the reason people vote Yes. Disappointment at a government which can't be bothered to hold a proper debate on the subject, and more disappointment that they hold us in such contempt they feel they don't have to provide proper facts and figures to back up their claims. Confusion. More confusion. Is such a major change to our Constitution of so little importance that homes in Dublin received the Referendum Commission's booklet a measly ten days before the vote? Apparently so.

But it's not just my personal experience that makes me so emotional. The main reason is that I smell a rat. Why, when the health services are in crisis and homelessness is still a huge problem, is this issue considered such a priority? Exactly how many babies are being born here to parents who just came to get citizenship for their child? Why does Minister McDowell keep dismissing rather than addressing the arguments against his proposal? There are too many questions and too few answers for me to even consider voting for this amendment.

I was on the hustings last week and when the politician I was tailing moved on from a couple of young girls having a pint outside a city-centre pub, I asked them did they know anything about the referendum. "What referendum?" they said. They will be voting for the first time in their lives next Friday. They are interested in the issue, they agreed, after I had explained the basics, but if I hadn't mentioned the referendum to them they didn't think they would have heard about it.

So it's no wonder that a recent opinion poll indicated the amendment will pass. But it might not pass if people who don't normally vote take some time to examine the issue. They might see that there hasn't been enough time to properly assess the arguments. They might feel they don't trust this government and the arrogant way they are trying to rush this through. They might decide our liberal citizenship laws – the kind that make us unique in Europe – honour our rich heritage of immigration and emigration by bestowing Irishness on all babies born here.

They might look at how they have embraced the multicultural Ireland of today and how they want that Ireland to thrive. They might decide that babies should not be born aliens while other newborns in the same ward arrive in this world with a superior set of rights, modern Ireland's version of a silver spoon. *Mama, The Baby's an Alien!* Coming soon to a Constitution near you.

A Worthy Winner

Several years ago, not long after I began working as a freelance reporter for this newspaper, I was asked to write an article about an Irish dentist called Dr Lydia Foy. The 49-year-old woman was in the news because of her struggle to have her birth cert put in her name, the name she chose after she underwent successful gender realignment surgery 12 years ago. She wanted the birth certificate to reflect the fact that she was a woman called Lydia, not a man called Donal, the name given to her at birth. Lydia was granted leave to challenge a refusal by the registrar to change the entry on her birth certificate. Two years ago, she lost the fight when the High Court rejected her claim.

"It is like a witch-burning," she told the *Carlow Nationalist* at the time. "It is being used as an instrument to punish us, to ridicule us and to deny us basic rights if someone throws a stone at me, which they have done on many occasions, and says to me 'you are not really a woman anyway because you don't have a birth certificate, you are an old transsexual', what can I say? I don't have a birth certificate. I am a lesser citizen in Ireland until I get it."

I found my article about Lydia's struggle extremely difficult to write back then. We journalists get used to turning into temporary experts on subjects we are not overly familiar with, but the transsexual experience was so utterly alien that I agonised over every word. The result was a perfectly acceptable, factually enlightening 900 words explaining the complexities of gender dysphoria. Reading it back now, I see I was trying so hard to understand the issue that there wasn't any room for heart or soul in the oh-so-worthy article that I wrote.

I've been thinking a lot about Dr Lydia Foy over the past two months. About the two children she fathered when she was Donal, the children that as Lydia she was not allowed to see. About the taunts and jeers she has lived with ever since she underwent the long-drawn-out and painful surgery. I've been marvelling at the bravery of her ongoing battle to be seen as a woman in her own right and not to be dismissed by society and by the State as some kind of freak.

A determined, tenacious woman, Lydia is currently appealing the High Court decision. Meanwhile in Strasbourg, the European Court of Human Rights has since granted several women, including a British transsexual, the kind of legal recognition they deserve.

I've been thinking about Lydia because of *Big Brother*. I really hope she has been enjoying the programme over the past couple of months, particularly the antics of Nadia, the 27-year-old Portuguese woman who laughs like a hyena and always fights for her rights. At the time of writing, I have no way of knowing what the outcome of the contest is, but I know that if there is any justice in the world, this stiletto-wearing, cleavage-obsessed, lip-gloss lady is currently contemplating her future as the winner of BB5.

It's incredible what Nadia's presence on *Big Brother* has achieved in developing our understanding of a much-misunderstood condition. From the minute she teetered into the house laughing that laugh, giving voice to her every emotion, there was never a question but that she was a woman. At an all-female champagne soiree I attended recently, where everything from shaving body hair to shotgun weddings was discussed, some of us were forced to admit that she was more of a girly-girl than we would ever be.

Unfortunately, Nadia's last days in the house were tainted by concern that she was being ridiculed or condemned by the outside world and by her nervousness about the reaction of her remaining housemates when they finally hear her secret. Some fool shouted, "Nadia, you are a man" over the wall of the house and while the others pretended they hadn't heard the intruder, she went into temporary depression in the privacy of the Diary Room.

What Nadia didn't know is that, against all the odds, she had emerged as one of the most popular housemates in the history of *Big Brother.* When this vibrant, brave, glamorous, hilarious woman was thrown an inevitable and heartfelt love bomb from the public, she probably got the sweetest shock of her life.

It has to be said that on her own, Portuguese national Nadia Almada has done more for the cause of transsexuals than a million earnest articles on gender dysphoria. We shouldn't imagine that all transsexuals will be as loud and as in-your-face as Nadia. Sometimes they will be as quiet as Dr Lydia Foy. But at least now when a male-to-female transsexual stands up in work or in court and says she is all-woman, a whole new generation will respond with fresh understanding. And they say reality television rots your brain.

There Goes the Neighbourhood

Who are the people in your neighbourhood? The man across the road who is trusted to mind the spare keys of almost everyone on the avenue. The woman who comes off like a busybody but is really just keeping an eye on things when most of the residents are out at work. The teenager who knocks on the door at 9 a.m. because you have left your wallet, containing €80, in the basket of your bike all night. They're the people you meet when you're walking down the street each day.

These are the people in your neighbourhood. Three boys and a girl, they can't be more than 19, who have nothing better to do at night than mess with people's cars. It's ten p.m. A man in his thirties is relaxing at home. He hears some noise outside and lifts a slat on the blind to peek out. He sees the teenagers at his car – one on the driver's side and one on the passenger side – then puts on his jacket and goes out to confront them.

One of them, he notices, has written their name in the dust on the bonnet. He is not afraid of these kinds of neighbours. Never has been. He tells the gang to get away from his car. He demands that one of them wipe the name off before leaving. He turns to walk away. He feels a blow to the back of the neck and falls to the ground. All he can remember are the lights from the port tunnel shining between the trees, first from this angle and then another, as his head moves from side to side in rhythm with the kicks.

These are the people in your neighbourhood. As two

teenagers stand kicking a man who lies in the foetal position, trying to shield his head, two cars approach the scene. Both drivers make an instant decision. A decision to slow down. A decision to steer the cars around the huddle of bodies on the road. A decision to drive away without alerting anyone.

A third car, containing a woman and a man, drives up. They stop, and the man presses down hard on the car horn. When that doesn't stop them the man emerges from the car. Only then do the youths run away. Blood is everywhere. An ambulance arrives. As he is taken into the ambulance the man's shoulder pops out of its socket. The man has a dislocated and fractured shoulder and broken ribs.

A policeman sits at the end of the bed and says, "Yes, we know who they are, because we passed them earlier in the night." They will call to his house to take a statement, they say.

These are the policemen in your neighbourhood. They do not take a statement from the woman who caught the people in the act. The woman who described what she saw as a frenzy of kicking. Despite his constant requests, they do not arrange a line-up so the man can identify his assailants. They tell the victim that a prosecution is unlikely. They have 80 or 90 cases like this on their books and don't have the resources. They call to read the statement that he typed with one hand, but they do not take it away with them. They know who they are.

The neighbours send cards and nod when he tells them the police don't think anything will come of it. He won't let it lie. He asks the policemen whether they would have investigated more thoroughly had he died. He thinks it's a sad indictment of society that you have to die before a decent attempt is made to catch people like those who attacked him.

He has had enough of civil libertarians who cite poverty and lack of education as factors when the majority in the same situation don't resort to violence. He knows the truth. That we have all developed a creeping complacency towards violent crime.

Two months later, the man can't sleep at night with the physical discomfort. He is facing into ten months of physiotherapy. It may seem strange, but he wants to meet these people in his neighbourhood.

He used to sleep with one arm crooked above his shoulder. It was the way he was born, a perfectly formed caul covering the arm like a blanket. After half a lifetime sleeping this way, he can't get used to the new position. He thinks about his neighbours, about the name he saw on the bonnet of his car. He phones the police to ask who they are.

He will get their names and addresses whether the police give them to him or not. He knows what he will do when he finds them. He will watch them. See how they live. He might call to their door and ask: "Do you remember me?" He might ask them why they did it. They know where he lives. He thinks it's only right and proper that they should know that he knows where they live too.

Bully for Me

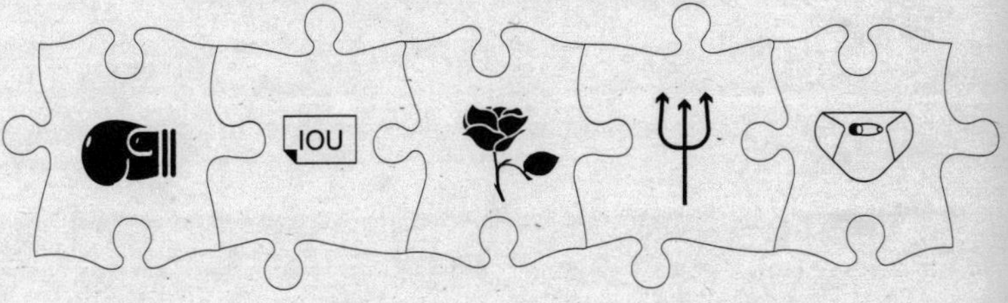

The Game of the Name

I received a few snotty e-mails recently after writing what I thought was a pretty innocuous article about *Star Wars: Attack of the Clones.* It wasn't written for the benefit of anoraks, which in hindsight is why I probably ended up annoying some of them.

This guy, who signed himself "A Man" and began his missive "Dear Woman", instructed me to make sure the next *Star Wars* piece that appeared in the paper was written by a male because "I'm sick of your prattle". Even more thought-provoking was the one who told me that the time had evidently come for me to "settle down and have babies".

I replied to them both and tried to make up for my weakness in the sci-fi department by asking after their collection of Light Savers and Luke Moonwalker figures but my mail came back as undeliverable. Attack of the anonymous anoraks. George Lucas take note.

When I stopped laughing, I felt glad my new e-mail friends had narrowly missed the opportunity to really annoy me. They could have done that by suggesting I "settle down and have babies with names such as Chloe, Shaun and Dylan". Those were some of the most popular baby names in the country last year, but if I ever do have babies I will be steering well clear of helpful books such as *What Everyone Else in the Country Calls Their Children* by E.Z. Money.

No offence to the parents who favour names shared by the rest of the English-speaking world, but I am with Posh and Becks on this one. I always think it's unfair when people such as the Beckhams, Bob Geldof and Jonathan Ross get ridiculed for christening their kids with names such as Fifi Trixibelle, Peaches Blossom and Brooklyn. Is it so bad to want your children's names to resonate a little bit in a world overrun with Johns, Marks and Emmas? And what's so wrong about wanting to celebrate the uniqueness of a child by giving it a name which, just like them, is one of a kind. There were three Róisíns in my primary school class, so I have good reason to complain. And I can sympathise with the confusion that lies ahead for the three Marys sitting around the new cabinet table. On the plus side, they can always get away with ignoring Bertie by pretending they think he is addressing the other two.

It's still rare to meet anyone with an unusual name, apart from the Irish ones which have the added bonus that outside Ireland you are constantly mispronounced and misspelt. I answer to Raisin or Resin depending on the time zone.

Last summer, during the Cathedral Quarter Arts Festival in Belfast, I interviewed the English author Will Self, and later the subject of baby names came up. I was very nervous talking to him, as I often am when faced with overtly intellectual types, but this time I managed to keep up. I even relaxed enough to discuss a literary question that had been bugging me. Namely, how to write a book without knowing very much about anything.

When he asked me to join him and a couple of his friends for a drink after reading from his new novel, I have to admit I was paranoid about saying something stupid. I'd had a few gin and tonics, but I was doing fine until the talk turned to Self and his partner, an English journalist, who were pondering names for the latest addition to their family. "We've been thinking about Lucifer," he said. I sipped my drink and waited for the punchline. But there wasn't one.

The other two people there seemed oddly enthusiastic

about calling a child the equivalent of Damien, the Omen. Will said he had been running the name past his mates, and they quite liked it too. Now, as I have explained, nobody is a more vocal supporter of off-the-wall names than I am. Perhaps christening your offspring Satan had some kind of divine irony that I just didn't get. And, as Kylie has rightly pointed out in the past, it's better the devil you know. But then again, naming a child "Lucifer" was surely tantamount to abuse, and even if it did turn out to be a clever post-modern thing to do, I simply couldn't condone it.

My silence and the fact that I was choking on the ice in my tonic didn't go unnoticed, and Will eventually asked me if I had a problem with the name. So I told him. "You just can't name your child after the devil and expect me to think its OK, I mean Lucifer for God's sake," I said. There was a pause while this literary luminary looked deep into my eyes. "You think," he said. "I was going to call my son after the devil?" Turns out I'd misheard. Turns out he said Luther not Lucifer. Luther as in Vandross. "Oh," I said. "Oh." Note to Star Wars Man. Sometimes even I get sick of my prattle.

All Greek to Me

Before I actually entered the world of haute couture and hot gossip, writing the society page of *The Irish Times* would have been way up there on my list of all-time favourite jobs.

The brief, I imagined, was a one-way-ticket to a ligger's paradise; go to absolutely every flash party book launch, awards ceremony and premiere. Drink champagne. Ask smiling socialite where she bought her frock. Eat exotic canapé. Flirt with A-list movie star as he tries unsuccessfully to introduce me to class A drugs. Drink more champagne.

It was only a two-week trial but I had long-term plans. I reckoned nobody would be able to resist my witty exchanges with the cream of Irish society and my cruel, yet clever, put-downs of the nation's wannabes. Celebrities would court me all the while fearing the power of my pen. I could exist happily on a diet of smoked salmon, fine wine and mini-sausage rolls. There would be long nights and early mornings in the VIP section of Renard's nightclub all in the name of research. Powerful if unattractive politicians would feed me foie gras and beg me not to expose them. All this, and as much Cristal as I could stomach, would be mine.

But the dream ended before the first glass of bubbly touched my freshly glossed lips. My debut was a glamorous make-up promotion at Brown Thomas. Transvestite sexpot Ru Paul was the guest of honour. The problem was 'she' was the only 'celebrity' I recognised.

The champagne went flat as I surveyed the room, bursting with unidentifiable models, television presenters and someone who looked like that guy from the Power City advert.

Sweating at the thought of having no names to fill what was supposed to be the main piece in my first society report, I sidled up to a fellow journalist who kindly pointed out a few people. But they all looked the same to me.

What's more, the same people seemed to turn up at every soiree I was asked to cover: businessmen, stylists, actors, property developers and 'It girls' whose names I could never remember. I barely lasted the two weeks in my new job, and canapés have never tasted the same.

With no regrets I moved humbly back into the realm of general reportage, occasionally covering the odd celebrity wedding of stars so famous I couldn't fail to recognise them. I had learnt my lesson. This wannabe just wasn't cut out to mix with people with double-barrelled names.

Recently, I was covering a corporate World Cup soccer event, the Ireland vs Germany match as it happens, when I spotted the squire of Slane Castle, Lord Henry Mount Charles, himself no stranger to the society pages. I was a bit low on quotes so I asked him what he thought of the match. I scribbled away as he said something about the tension of the game being bad for his heart.

Then I remembered my celebrity blind spot. Just to make sure of his identity I asked him how preparations for the Slane gig were coming along. "Great," he said. "Wonderful." I went back to the office to file my copy, making sure to include his beating heart.

At the office the next morning, the answering machine spewed forth two very disturbing messages. One was from a man who called himself Nick the Greek. "You won't know me," he said in treacle tones, "but I'm Nick the Greek. I've been a bit naughty."

You've probably guessed by now. It wasn't Lord Mount

Charles I had encountered the day before but his friend Nick, who explained that he couldn't resist leading me on. The practical joker cushioned the blow with the news that this wasn't the first time the pair had been mixed up.

This information made it no easier to listen to the next message. "Hello, this is Henry Mount Charles, could you please give me a call," said the voice.

In the event, Lord Mount Charles was extremely good-natured about my blunder. A few weeks later, I met him in person at the Independence Day celebrations at the US ambassador's residence in the Phoenix Park. He told me that Pat Kenny had once been similarly hoodwinked into believing the two were brothers which made me feel a tiny bit better but not much.

Funny how things come full circle. The other night, standing on the front step of a house in a salubrious suburb of Co. Dublin, I asked a few questions about the well-heeled folk who lived nearby. My host pointed to where he said a guy called Nick Unpronounceablegreekname resided.

Looking at the house, I was overcome with *déjà vu*. And then I remembered. More than ten years ago as a teenager with a part-time job in a catering company I served canapés to Nick and his posh friends in that very house.

And now it's payback time. To what I hope is his acute embarrassment, I can exclusively reveal that back then the man they call Nick the Greek had a photo of himself arm in arm with Chris de Burgh that took pride of place in the downstairs loo. At least I think that's who it was.

Crying for Me, Myself and Di

As usual, I left no time to pack for this short trip. And when I examined my holdall, the contents showed why packing in the dark wasn't advisable. I know there was once a brief fashion moment when black was the new black and I must have been the epitome of fashion with my ten different versions of black-skirt-and-matching-shirt combo. These days, the only positive thing I can say about my wardrobe is that whenever I get a last-minute request to cover a funeral, chances are I will be wearing suitable attire.

This time five years ago, I had no problem finding the perfect outfit in which to attend the funeral of Princess Diana. Or the live screening of same on a giant television in Brown Thomas, at least. It was no easy task trying to talk to shoppers glued to the coffin on TV about their feelings for the dead woman as I gave full vent to my own. Biro isn't tear-resistant I discovered when, back at the office, it took longer than usual to make sense of my scribblings.

I'm writing this in my brother's house in east London. Hackney, to be precise. Mo Mowlam lives at the bottom of the street. Sometimes Michael sees her pottering in her garden as he cycles to work in the morning. One of these days he says he is going to call in and offer to give her a hand with the pruning. If his plot of herbs and courgettes and runner beans out back is anything to go by, she could do worse than invite my green-fingered sibling in. I'm in London to do a story about Diana, the aftermath. Up until now, I felt I would be well qualified.

Diana's death provided the unifying JFK and Elvis moment some of us missed. Where were you when you heard she had died? Whatever your feelings about the woman, it would be a miracle if you didn't have a "Diana's dead? Yeah and I'm Prince Philip's love child" anecdote or two.

I wasn't one of those who came home from a night out, turned on *Sky News* and saw the shocking headlines about Dodi and Di. I was awoken the following morning by a phone call from my boss who told me what had happened as I struggled to sound normal through a humdinger of a hangover. It makes me feel ashamed now, but if I'd heard a friend or relation had died in a car accident I don't know if I would have cried as much as I did in the weeks that followed. I was either writing about Diana or crying about her and more often than not I engaged in a morbid kind of multi-tasking. Type. Sniff, wipe. Sniff. Wipe keyboard. Sniff some more.

At the British Embassy in Dublin, where people came in huge numbers to sign the books of condolence and lay flowers, I cried so much while trying to record events for this newspaper that Brenda from the *Gerry Ryan Show* mentioned my condition live on air. It was not, you will appreciate, one of my proudest professional moments. When I wasn't working, I was prostrate in front of the television, tissues in one hand and remote in the other hungry for more images and information that would feed my grief. I thought about it every minute. I lost sleep agonising about William and Harry and the most appropriate tone for the letters of consolation I would write. I cursed Charles and hurled abuse at Camilla. When sensible people who took the "squillions of people you don't know die, every day" approach to the tragedy reproached me, I railed against their inhumanity. "You don't understand," I sobbed. "I knew her. I felt her pain."

I knew her? I felt her pain? It embarrasses me now more than I can say. Especially when wandering around Kensington Gardens, looking up at the palace windows, gawping with the other tourists at her dresses on display – Diana was a woman who knew the value of brightly coloured clothing – and walking the path that five years ago was knee-deep in bouquets. It was then I realised my feelings at the time had been as superficial as the sequins on her evening gowns. Because instead of the churning in my stomach that dogged me when she died, I felt . . . well, the truth is I felt nothing. The memory of her passing had no meaning at all. Psychologists had a lot to say about the outbreak of mass hysteria triggered by the death of this fairytale princess. In hindsight and after much soul searching, my tuppence worth is maybe we weren't actually crying for Diana, we were crying for every mad, bad, sad event that ever happened in our lives.

I know now, I was crying because for those crazy days I had convinced myself it was socially acceptable to wander around bleary eyed, mourning a woman whom I had about as much in common with as Mother Teresa, whose death occurred around the same time. I realise now that I wasn't actually being sad for Diana Spencer. Not at all. I was wearing the black that can make you feel invisible and having the time of my life simply being sad.

Striking a Chord

'Tis the Saturday before Christmas, and all through my flat, there is tinsel and fairy lights and other festive tat. The laundry basket is overflowing with socks and with smalls, in the hope that St Nicholas puts a wash on when he calls.

Some people do the yule thing with originality, creativity and aplomb. Right this minute, their houses smell of mulled wine, gingerbread men and cinnamon sticks. The hall is so packed with holly, jealous neighbours say it's a health hazard, and every surface in the house groans under the weight of poinsettias.

Christmas tree decorations are not just decorations. There is a theme. The wise visitor will not enquire about the distinct lack of shiny baubles or silvery stuff hanging from the branches. So 1970s apparently. A few ornaments handcrafted by Balinese maidens and a star they picked up on holidays in Rome does the job quite nicely, thank you.

The children of these Christmas experts look like they have walked straight off the set of *Mary Poppins*. All scrubbed and tubbed and adequately fed, they frolic around looking adorable and forcing mince pies with brandy butter on everyone. At this very second, they are sitting in front of a roaring log fire fashioning their own crackers from recycled cardboard before opening Day 21 of the limited edition Advent calendar to coo over the intricate etching hidden behind the window.

Don't mind me. I am only bitter that while they made lists and planned themes, I reluctantly rummaged through a box marked 'Decorations (Halloween/Christmas)' and opted for cheap odds and ends that don't match. There is white tinsel around the picture frame and gold tinsel around the telly, while a host of silver angels are in full flight above the kitchen door. And flickering flashing lights are draped along the curtain rail. Hector Gray chic, I like to call it.

I do have an Advent calendar though. The fact that its theme is Bob the Builder Does Christmas should not detract from that fact. Plus, there are little chocolate people and industrial machines behind each window. And how many of you professional yuletide folk can say that? Not putting a huge amount of effort into the aesthetic element of the season leaves time for more important things. Mand came over for one of our regular guitar sessions. The boyfriend was dispatched to the off licence on cider duty and was laughed right back again when he returned with only one bottle.

Songwriting is thirsty work, and only when we had six litres of the stuff in the fridge and the Christmas lights on full flashing mode did we feel sure we could be properly creative. Mand and I have high hopes for our latest composition but to be honest I am disillusioned with my slow progress on the musical front.

This is how it is supposed to work: having bought a guitar, you discover that you are in fact Eric Clapton in a dress. You put pen to paper and realise that the lyrical genius of John Lennon has dodged Mark Chapman's bullets and flown through space, time and 'Strawberry Fields' to be passed on to you. You open your mouth and pitch-perfect honeysuckle oozes from your lips. A passer-by reaches into his pocket and thrusts a handful of coins at your feet. "Compared to you," he whispers reverentially, "that Eva Cassidy bird was a crow." Back to reality with a tuneless twang. I have been learning the guitar for a year now. I know

'Elephants Always Display Great Big Ears' because it is an easy way to remember the strings. I know the F chord is so called because it is so effin difficult to master. Bah I say, and Humbug.

So, this Christmas I will mainly be struggling with music books with such dishonest titles as *It's Easy to Play Guitar* when I am not watching *It's A Wonderful Life* for the zillionth time or munching chocolate Advent tractors. One thing I will definitely do on Christmas Eve is return to that perfect poem by Clements Clarke Moore. The author of ''Twas The Night Before Christmas' was embarrassed that this work was his most celebrated when for much of his life he had toiled over Greek literature and in-depth biblical studies.

I doubt he would be too pleased either that it has been hijacked by just about everyone. There's a student version ('Twas the Night Before the Finals and all through the College), a *Star Trek* version ('Twas the Night Before Christmas and all through the Ship) and even a Ground Zero take ('Twas the Night Before Christmas and Ground Zero lay still) on that definitive Christmas work.

Someone far too sentimental for their own good once said Christmas is not just a date on the calendar, it is a feeling in your heart. And even if he didn't like to admit it, Mr Clarke Moore knew better than anyone how to tap into that feeling. So whether you are sipping mulled wine under freshly cut mistletoe or laughing at your hopelessly inadequate decor, Merry Christmas to all and to all, a good night.

Toast Mistress

What would you say is the number one fear of people in the United States? Terrorist attacks? Osama Bin Laden? An invasion of freeloading Irish politicians? Actually, it's none of the above. According to an American company, the greatest fear of people in the land of the free is the fear of public speaking. This company claims that most Americans would rather die than speak to a large group of people. Sounds perfectly rational to me.

Unaccustomed as I am, I recently had reason to speak in front of a scary amount of academic types when I was one of the judges for the Merville lay seminars in UCD. Each year six PhD students present their research projects in the fields of pharmacology, chemistry and biochemistry to a group of lay people. They have to clarify the complex, demystify the mysterious and generally speak in plain English, which is harder than you might imagine for your average science boffin.

They did brilliantly. I and the other judges – author Dermot Bolger, singer Mary Coughlan and bank executive Ronan White – were sated with knowledge as we retired to the judging room. The students told us about research into coronary disease, free radicals, the spread of breast cancer, growing kidney cells and chiral drugs in a way we would be able to explain later, almost without fault, to our nearest and dearest.

After an amicable discussion we picked a winner and then it was time for me, as chairman of the judges, to make a speech – in front of hundreds of people. In the presence of Pat Kenny and the Minister for Education and Science, Noel Dempsey. The terror of this moment had kept me awake the previous night when I had turned, as we so often do in times of crisis, to the internet.

"Fear of Public Speaking: Eliminated Immediately. Guaranteed for Life." Yes, please. "Many people's fear of public speaking can be traced back to something like an incident at school . . ." Oh dear. It all comes flooding back. Fourth year. Sion Hill, Blackrock. A debating competition.

I have written five foolscap pages of perfect prose on the subject of why people were really better off living in the tenement buildings of Sean O'Casey's time. I have printed it all out in capitals onto multicoloured cue cards. I am standing in an almost empty classroom practising my speech ten minutes before the debate is to start. I know my speech off by heart. I say to my friends, Tanya and Martina, that I don't need the cue cards. They try to convince me to at least bring the cards up to the podium but I shrug them off. "Cue cards are for losers," I say, and dump the notes in the bin.

A battalion of Simon Hart shoes echo brightly off the cold floor of the concert hall. Looks like the whole school is here. They are in for a treat.

My name is called. I stand. I walk to the top of the room. I am perfectly calm. I open my mouth and instead of five foolscap pages of perfect prose this is what comes out. "Sean O'Casey said . . . he said . . . about tenements . . . O'Casey . . ." The entire school is looking at me. I can do this. I can.

"Tenements . . . tall buildings with damp walls." It is no good. I am dying.

Tanya and Martina are torn between throwing me sympathetic looks and collapsing into hysterical laughter. They manage both. I think of the cue cards in the bin. I can't remember any of it. My eyes are welling up now, my face is burning, my hands are damp, my throat is sore. The head mistress with whom I enjoy a hate/hate relationship stands up and quietens those who are still sniggering. She says she is sure my speech would have been "deeply impressive" had things gone to plan. And I can tell she means it.

Back at the altar of the internet, I read on: ". . . and so an irrational fear is born. Attaching emotions to situations is one of the primary ways that humans learn. Sometimes we just get the wiring wrong."

Makes sense, tell me more. "We teach your conscious mind to connect different positive feelings to the thought of appearing in public . . . like learning to ride a bike." Fine. Where do I sign? "The investment costs less than a round-trip business fare . . . $985."

Excuse me?

It is showtime at the Merville lay seminars in UCD. I stand up. I am shaky and a little red-faced but I read my speech. I read it straight from the A4 page. People laugh in the right places. I relax. And in a few relatively painless minutes it's over and I am sipping a glass of white wine.

And so in memory of that great orator St Patrick, I offer the following piece of advice on public speaking completely free of charge: never, ever, bin your cue cards. Thank you and goodnight.

Brain Drain

When the BBC ran the *Test the Nation* IQ test a year ago, the poor people of Derry came bottom in this barometer of brainiacs. I don't know how local celebrities Dana or Phil Coulter felt about it, but being dubbed the dumbest folk in Great Britain and Northern Ireland obviously galvanised the Foyleside intelligentsia because when the test was run again a couple of weeks ago, Derry people shot to the top with an average IQ of 107. Now that's what I call a cerebral comeback.

Interestingly, Northern Ireland scored higher than any other region polled, which just goes to show a healthy intelligence quotient doesn't necessarily mean heightened problem-solving ability. But that's small comfort to all of us who failed to scale the dizzy intellectual heights we thought possible before sitting down to do the test.

I, for one, was quietly confident of emerging as the person who wore the intelligence trousers in our house. It's not like I am actually a member of Mensa but, you know, I could be if I wanted to. The same way that if I actually wanted to play chess I could learn. It just so happens that I prefer a nice uncomplicated game of draughts of an evening, that's all.

So even as I sharpened my purposely purchased pencils, I told my boyfriend not to worry, that it was only an IQ test and it didn't mean anything. Emotional quotient is so much more important I told him with as much magnanimity as I could muster. I will still share my life with you even when – I mean if – it turns out that my brain is a more efficient machine than yours.

When I'd finished this pep talk he just smiled enigmatically in the manner of one who knew something I didn't. Which, of course, he did. Quite a few things, as it turned out. Namely how to add, subtract and make sense of fractions. As I feared, the maths section let me down badly although I still don't understand what the square root of anything, a question which can be worked out on a calculator, has got to do with intelligence.

I flew through the language and memory categories, barely putting a foot wrong, but when they started asking things like if Mary paid X for a tin of sardines and Y for a jar of honey then how much would it cost to feed an average family in Ballymorebrainy, my mind short-circuited. I even managed to get a question wrong which just required adding up five simple numbers. I could feel my IQ dropping with each unfathomable question. I had begun the test feeling that I was intellectually compatible with the presenter Anne Robinson, but now she was starting to get on my nerves.

He, of course, broke out in grins when asked to add two sixths and one third of a litre, while I got a carton of milk from the fridge and made an intelligent guess. Intelligent but wrong, as it turned out. Like all the rest of my mathematical guesses.

We had done the BBC's relationship test earlier in the year and achieved exactly the same (very high since you ask) score, which we judged as a glowing testament to our compatibility as a couple. But as I looked at him mentally working out the speed of a tractor full of haystacks travelling down the M50 or something equally irrelevant, the urge to call him speccy-four-eyes and rip up his answer sheet far outweighed any romantic feelings I harboured at that moment.

Bizarrely, we got exactly the same score in the end which, depending on which way you look at it, means we are as intelligent, or as stupid, as each other. I am not going to reveal exactly how intelligent/stupid that makes us for professional reasons. That night his 17-year-old brother rang. His score was 10 points higher than ours. My sister rang. She beat us by 24 points. "It's only an IQ test," she said kindly, "it doesn't mean anything."

It took a few days to get over the shock that Mensa probably wouldn't be beating down the door to get me to sign up. And a few days more to accept that, on paper at least, I wasn't actually brainier than him.

In hindsight, downing a bottle of red wine as we did during the test probably wasn't the cleverest idea and, according to experts, I am well within my rights to blame alcohol for my disappointing score. I should also add, in our defence, that we were eating a Chinese takeaway when we took the test. You can't, I have discovered to my cost, concentrate on maths puzzles and prawn crackers at the same time. Which some people might say is only logical. But then what would I know?

Smell the Roses

With two hours to go before the family wedding, I was wandering around Covent Garden in London trying to find a handbag and a shawl. My hair was done in an upstyle, admittedly there was a bit more up than there was style in my bouffant, but I knew it would be fine. I mean it wasn't me that was getting married. Not this time.

"It's, um, Oriental," said my mother, gazing at my head. "You don't like it do you?" I asked her. "I don't like it," she agreed. Frustrated, I gave up on the search for a dainty handbag and bought a more practical straw basket in a sale, that I thought would go nicely with the pink chiffon wrap I had found. "You can't wear that," she said, pointing at the basket which was decorated with straw melons and pineapples. "It's grand," I sulked, catching sight of my reflection in a shop window. One hour to go and my Oriental bouffant was already starting to lose its bouff.

Some are born girls and the rest have girliness thrust upon them. Ladies' Day at the races. Charity Balls. Weddings. These words are like music to the ears of born girls. It'll give us an excuse to dress up, they say. The rest of us, the fakes, we mumble in agreement but secretly wouldn't mind if we never had to dress up again in our lives.

Born girls come into this world knowing millions of mysterious things. Like how to apply fake tan. Or how to blend eye make-up. They know that black doesn't go with navy and that, most of the time, it pays to play just a little bit hard to get.

Grooming is an old-fashioned word but they know exactly what it means. They save for months to get the perfect pair of shoes to match the perfect skirt, which they always send to the dry cleaners and never throw in a hot wash by mistake.

Born girls wear matching underwear in case they get lucky. Or at least so they can look good in an *ER* scenario. Occasionally us interlopers manage to camouflage ourselves, and I like to think that sometimes you wouldn't know the difference between us. But look closer. By our unplucked eyebrows you will know us. That and our unravelled hems.

For an ungirly journalist, the Rose of Tralee festival, where I spent three days last month, is not the best place to hang out. They were like princesses most of them, not a hair or accessory out of place. But they weren't all perfect. At one point, there was a vicious rumour going around that one of the Roses had turned up to an engagement in a creased linen suit. (Fake girls think it's OK if linen creases but real ones know there is no excuse). There was really no hope for her after that.

The part I liked best was during rehearsals when the Roses would wear their off-duty gear and they looked almost normal. But even then they had a way of making a sloppy tracksuit look sophisticated. Something to do with having matching lipstick and runners, I think.

At one of these rehearsals I met an acquaintance whom I hadn't seen for a couple of years. I was delighted to see this friendly face until he spoke. "Ah, Róisín," he said, "I didn't recognise you, you've put on weight." I was interviewing Ulster or Texas at the time. I tried to explain this observation away. "Er, actually what happened was since the last time I saw you, I did put on weight but I am now in the process of losing that weight. So actually in the past six months I have lost weight." (What I was doing justifying myself to him like this I still don't know.) "No," he says, pressing his point home, "you've put on loads of weight, I would barely have known it was you." Right so. Grand. See you for a drink later.

I was mortified. The Rose I was interviewing at the time, Toronto maybe or Queensland, she turns to me and says I shouldn't worry. Guys are just too honest for their own good. "Actually," she adds, "I prefer it when my boyfriend tells me the truth even if sometimes the truth is hard to hear."

The implication of the encounter bears down on me. If I was a proper girl this wouldn't have happened. If I was a proper girl, I would have been so traumatised at the prospect of not fitting into the right-shaped clothes that I would have made sure it never came to this. I diet, but I don't diet hard enough or else I wouldn't be standing here while a Rose of Tralee contestant looks down at me with sympathetic eyes. I need to shave my legs. She is probably wearing matching underwear. In that moment, I surprised myself with the realisation that I wouldn't have it any other way.

The Artless Dodger

Once upon a time I had an accountant. She was a friendly woman who knew cunning things about tax-free allowances and P60s and adding up and taking away.

She prised my fingers from my ears and my head from the sand, and made me send her all kinds of bills and receipts so that I could get myself out of a nasty situation that had developed with the Revenue Commissioners.

I should have lived happily ever after, but somehow I got it into my head that this accountancy lark didn't look too taxing after all. She tried to keep a straight face as I informed her that I would sort out any outstanding financial issues myself. I can't say she didn't warn me, because of course she did. I distinctly remember one particular phone conversation in which she said that, while I had paid the tax people a hefty whack for my time as a self-employed freelance journalist, there was still a period that was unaccounted for.

When she told me the matter wasn't going to go away, however fervently I prayed it would, I thanked her most sincerely for her advice and promptly forgot all about it.

Occasionally the issue would surface in my mind, manifesting itself in a nagging feeling, the kind you get when you can't remember if you left your ceramic hair-straighteners on. Months passed. Years even. And eventually I managed to convince myself that nobody in the tax office was interested in me or the itsy-bitsy matter of my unpaid debt. Every time I heard about those Ansbacher people evading millions with off-shore accounts, I had a mini-celebration in my head. My logic was impeccable. As long as the tax people were busy chasing those dodgy millionaire business-types they wouldn't possibly have time to take any interest in little old forgetful me.

Amazingly, though, it turns out they have a whole load of people working for them whose exact job title is Officer In Charge Of Chasing So-Called Forgetful Types Who Think They Are In No Danger Of Ever Being Chased. Or something equally catchy. Around 18 months ago they started hounding my ex-husband for the money, because at the time of the debt – my debt – we were being assessed under his PPS number.

At this point let me sympathise with people who get melty-head syndrome when things such as PPS or P60 or P-whateveryouarehavingyourself are mentioned. I will try to make this explanation of my financial affairs as basic as possible for all of our sakes.

It's no surprise that my past caught up with me, but even in this era of spam and chain mail, there can be no less welcome e-mail than one I received at this trying time. "Em, excuse me, but could you sort out your tax affairs and get these people off my back? Hope life is treating you well. Yours etc., Ex-Husband." Not good at all.

The mortification roused me to action. I spent three or four days on the phone trying to find someone in Tax World who would listen to me and understand that Ex-Husband wasn't really to blame and begging them to please let me pay back the money in instalments over the next year-and-a-half.

We made a deal. I paid them some cash up front and then they sent me instalment forms which I could use to send them a tax offering every month. My head had been on the block, and this represented a reprieve of sorts. So what did I do? That's right. I lovingly stored the instalment forms in a folder marked 'Tax Thingy' and promptly forgot about them.

They tell me this is the time of year when sensible people start sorting out their annual tax affairs, and that's why I am relating my salutary tale. But I have to admit I do feel a bit like one of those sports people who has taken drugs and then, having been caught rapid, gets all evangelical about the dangers of said drugs. The Cathal Lombard Effect, I think it's called.

Having said that, I would still like to appeal to anyone with skeletons in their tax closet to pick up the phone and dial the Revenue. You might be surprised to learn that they don't bite. Well, I don't think they do, but it's probably best to phone them rather than arrange a face-to-face meeting just in case.

You see all my life I thought tax was something only grown-ups had to worry about. Turns out I am grown up. I got another load of e-mails from Ex-Husband this week. He'd been threatened with court action all because of me.

"Ex-Wife, Please pay this before they send me to jail, Yours Faithfully, Ex Husband." The lady in the tax office was very understanding. And the cheque, I swear, is in the post.

Bully for Me

I had just put a €2 coin into the supermarket trolley. It was stuck there in a slot designed for €1 coins. I was standing there waiting, I don't know, for a trolley technician to appear when I saw her. "Hello," she smiled. "I put the wrong coin in," I replied. Like I needed to say that. Like she needed to know.

I hadn't seen her in years. We stood there, her handsome husband, their beautiful little boy and we two acquaintances from another time. My stomach squirmed as snippets of our briefly connected lives came back to me. She was a friend of a friend in primary school. We hung around together for a while and when I went to Irish college she came too. I'd been to this Irish college a couple of years in a row so I knew the *scéal*. I was a noisy regular, a reigning Swingball champion. She was quiet and intelligent and she was new.

Naturally she presumed that as a friend, or even a friend of her friend, I'd be looking out for her. Helping her fit into a strange place. It was probably one of the reasons she chose that particular Irish college. She thought that knowing someone like me would make life easier. She was wrong.

I don't think I have thought of it once since then. But here, beside the trolleys, I couldn't help but remember. I was not a good friend. Worse, I was a bully. I made her life in Irish college miserable. I made her open, friendly face twist into a worried frown. I wondered how she could be so nice to me now, so friendly. I smiled back and asked about her little boy but inside I felt sick.

Later, I rang a friend to tell her. I knew she'd had an experience with a former tormentor recently and that she would understand. What happened was that she saw this woman walking down the street and every nasty thing that person had ever done to her in school came flooding back. She had to cross the road to avoid her. She was a grown woman but in the presence of this person she felt like a defenceless child.

She told me not to be too hard on myself. It was hard though because, in truth, I knew the girl in the supermarket was not the only person I had been unkind to around that time. That night I was too sorry to sleep much. I'm sorry now.

Trying to understand, I looked back and realised the kind of pain I caused that girl had been doled out to me in the past – but the abused becoming the abuser seemed too neat an explanation.

All those abusive friendships where I spent my time trying to please and being punished when I got it wrong don't tell the full story. And anyway, I had been serially mistreating my little brother way before that. I'll never know how he grew up to forgive me but I'll always be grateful that he did.

I think some people must be born with a bullying gene. You see them in your work. In your home. Out socially. People without the bullying gene find it hard to cope. They don't know how to react to bullies. Reformed or potential bullies know what to do when it happens to them but mostly it doesn't happen because the wise bully stays away from them, preferring softer targets. Like the woman in the supermarket back when she was a girl.

I keep hearing this ad on the radio, an announcer asking: "Are you being bullied?" "Do you know someone who is being bullied?" Funny thing is, I bristle madly with the injustice of it now. When another friend of mine, an adult man, was being bullied recently, I ranted and raged and wanted to take the matter into my own hands. At his request I didn't. When I see his bully, also an adult man, I can taste his cowardice, his arrogance and his ignorance as though it were my own. I want to shake him. Show him the damage he is doing, mostly to himself. But I don't. Somehow I can't.

All I can do is look back and, in looking back, try to understand. I am wearing white ankle socks with red pom-poms, too-tight red canvas slip-on shoes, a bright-blue polyester ra-ra skirt and a matching top. I had begged my mother to buy this outfit from Penney's for our school big day out. I am standing on sloping grass on the grounds of a castle, proud as anything in my pom-poms. Everyone else is wearing jeans and T-shirts.

People I thought were my friends are laughing at me and my outfit. I pretend not to notice and I laugh to myself, as though I've just made my own hilarious private joke. I am alone. I don't fit this slot. And, not for the first time, I don't know what to do.

Brood Awakening

I was in Mount Temple School in Dublin recently giving a talk to transition-year students. Much as I enjoy talking to students, my stomach always sinks slightly before these gigs when I think back to exactly how interested I was when people came to give talks in my school.

My aim back then was to have as much fun as possible at the visitor's expense, no matter how many interesting things they might have had to say. In fact, the more interesting their stories, the more likely I was to misbehave. I remember giggling moronically through a school talk by the late, great actor Ray McAnally, who had fascinating things to say about starring in a Hollywood blockbuster. A jumped-up journalist with a milk stain on her jacket would have been devoured alive.

Visiting Mount Temple made me wish I had grown up on the northside, so my mother could have sent me there. It's a multi-denominational school with no uniform code and a less pronounced 'them and us' attitude when it comes to pupils and teachers. The relaxed atmosphere doesn't suit everyone, but I know it would have suited me. Famously, Mount Temple is where a guy called Larry pinned up a notice on the school board for people to form a band, which led to Feedback – an early version of a certain musical combo called U2 – taking shape in the school music room. As I shared scones with a few of the staff, I was told that Adam Clayton's music teacher despaired of trying to teach him to read sheet music. Funny, the things you learn when you go back to school.

The reason I mention Mount Temple is because four of the students who gathered in the library were nursing babies. Not real babies you understand. Baby dolls with computer chips embedded to make them behave like real babies. They may as well be real. These faux-babies cry when they need changing or feeding or attention and don't stop until their guardians perform the appropriate task. It leads to the cutest scenes around the school. Such as two 15-year-old boys concentrating hard as they change the nappies of their charges.

Not everyone is as committed. Some got so sick of the crying that they left the babies outside in the car all night. But there is no escape from the all-knowing computer chip which diligently registers any doll-related abuse.

The babies are provided by the health board. They are designed to encourage students to abstain from unprotected sex in order to avoid accidentally ending up parents before their time. It hadn't worked with two of the young women I spoke to. They call their babies Amy and Jamie. They love them. They don't want to give them back. So that plan has backfired.

Anyway, I was looking at these girls with their little brown babies, and for probably the 50th time that week I asked myself whether I wanted one of those. I'm at that age where one thinks about these things. And there are plenty of reasons why the answer should be yes.

Reason number one: I am sartorially prepared. I wouldn't have to buy any maternity clothes because I already seem to have quite a lot of items on my clothes rail that fall into that category. In work today, I am wearing tracksuit bottoms masquerading as trousers and a top that sports a smock-like frontal area. Pregnant Colleague (PC) informs me these would do quite nicely should I get myself up the Damien.

Reason number two. I am physically prepared. Initially I

was a bit worried about the fact that I already have a bit of a belly – which is kind of like saying Ray Burke took a bit of a bribe – and that pregnancy would render this area elephantine. But, helpfully, PC pointed out that in fact the baby could nestle comfortably into the bulge and hide there for at least four months before anybody noticed there was something different about me.

Reason number three: Everybody else is doing it. Well, everybody except my friend and I, who spend a lot of time talking about trying to do it, but not much else. Meanwhile, people are getting pregnant all over the place. Congratulations to them and all that, but pregnancy-related peer pressure is a bit of burden. What if we can't? What if we don't want to? What? You're having another one?

Reason number four: I've finally accepted the fact that we won't be perfect parents. What has been holding us back is that we might say or do something that will ruin any new being's life. I asked a relatively new parent about this. "What if we mess up," I said. "You definitely will, to some degree," he replied. But he managed to convince me that when the child grew up, it would have developed the capacity to undo any of the damage we have done.

It seems I've no excuses left. Perhaps it's time I started on the folic acid. I think what I'll do first, though, is ring the health board and see if they have any of those other babies left.

All by Myself

When I went recently to a remote part of west Cork for a week, I expected to return at one with myself and the world in general.

I thought I'd be floating home on a tide of well-being, the kind that swells after serious self-nurturing and creative expression. Silly, silly me. I ended the seven days pretty much sick of the sight of myself and in the clutches of the biggest, baddest hangover this side of Skibbereen.

Nothing beats time spent alone in a rural retreat, the sea and mountains so close you can touch them, the sky an ever-changing oil painting. There is time to reflect. Time to write. Time to turn into even more of a slob than usual, not bothering to get dressed some days, and one memorable day not even getting out of bed except to use the bathroom. But I digress.

In the past I sat through two ten-day silent Vipassana retreats, rising at 4 a.m. to meditate. The difference with those spiritual holidays is that your activities are tightly scheduled, so you know what you are supposed to be doing every second. There are people serving you vegetarian feasts at meal-times, so not a minute is wasted thinking about what or when to eat. There are no diversions such as television or books or bottles of wine. You can't sneak out every five minutes to have conversations with friends about what they plan to have for lunch, just to avoid the real task at hand. With someone else in charge of my time – me – the rules were a little more ambiguous. That is, there weren't any rules. Not really.

My first mistake was not making a list before doing my week's shopping in Cork city centre. I had only 20 minutes before catching the bus to my remote destination and ran around like a contestant on *Supermarket Sweep*, grabbing random items – pink Cava, boil-in-the-bag salmon, Pot Noodle – as though the world was about to end. It meant that by day three I had run out of appropriate supplies and was forced to seek help from Mary, who was in charge of the magnificent house I was staying in. She kindly picked me up and drove me into Schull, which, it turns out, has the best convenience store in the whole of Ireland. They stock varieties of organic rice cakes I didn't even know existed. Their wine selection was impressive too. Which brings me to my second mistake.

Before departing Dublin I had asked a friend how many bottles of wine he thought I should pack to get the creative juices flowing. "Well," he pondered, "as it's you, I'd say one a day and three extra just in case." I was mortally offended. This was a week for clear thinking and clean writing, not getting sloshed and maudlin' and wandering around in my pyjamas, feeling sorry for myself. Although, in the end, I confess a teensy bit of my time was spent doing exactly that. OK, a hefty chunk. Oh OK, maybe half my time there was spent in this mode.

There were breakthrough moments even so, thanks to my understanding that in the sticks no-one can hear you scream. Following a fraught mobile phone conversation with the ex-husband wherein he told me a few home truths about the end of our relationship, I cracked open another bottle and found myself engaging in a spot of primal scream therapy. I hadn't let go like that since the day he told me he was going to leave. This was when the middle-of-nowhere nature of my location really came into its own. I screamed at the dark clouds. I yelled at the valley. I roared at the still waters.

Naturally I felt better after unleashing all that rage, at least until later when I spotted a rogue Post-it note stuck to the door alerting me to the fact that someone had called while I'd been in mid-primal episode. Oops.

When you are alone for a week in four-channel land, strange things happen. You start to think it's OK to have a drink at noon. You start to nod sagely at the contributors to *Liveline*. You look forward to the jaunty theme tune of *The Afternoon Show*. You sing sad songs loudly and have conversations with yourself, such as the following. Me: "Isn't that hilarious that some of that laundered IRA money was found in a box of Daz." Me: "Oh my God! That IS hilarious. It's washing powder and the money is going to be LAUNDERED. Oh my God!" Scintillating stuff.

After a week alone with only Joe Duffy, *The Afternoon Show* crew and their psychic dog-healer-type person for company, I was thoroughly sick and tired of me. I was irritated by my all-consuming need to make up for the lack of company with constant grazing on yoghurt-covered rice cakes. I was sick of the way I woke in the middle of the night at the slightest noise, convinced that someone with evil intentions was lurking outside the bedroom window.

On the up side, I somehow managed to get all the work that I was trying to do done. On the down side, I need another week to recover. How does it go again? All by myself. Don't wanna be. Anymore.

Musical Youth

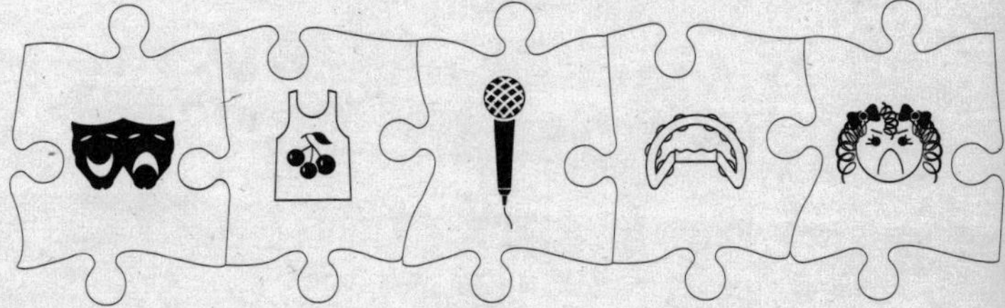

Three Chords and My Youth

She was Sugar, I was Honey. The very first day we went busking was in the summer of 1988 when it seemed as though the entire city was celebrating one thousand years of Dublin. Wandering down O'Connell Street, we stumbled on the Millennium Busking Competition, already in full swing.

Using the relentless charm that was our trademark, we convinced the organisers to let us enter despite our late arrival. I was wearing a polka-dot dress and a tambourine. She was a goddess with a guitar. We only knew three songs.

After our performance, we wandered around town, stopping to sing our limited repertoire wherever it might be profitable. I can see us now, singing our hearts out to the crowd of face-painted strangers who pressed around us on Grafton Street. I could have sworn I saw Larry Mullen throwing us a few quid. We used our busking money for McDonald's chicken sandwiches, bowls of chips from the Coffee Inn on South Anne Street and pints of black velvet. It's years since I've had cider mixed with Guinness. I wonder would it taste the same?

Later on, she went to the Clarence bar on the quays. It was different then. Shabby but with a charm that you don't find in Dublin hotels any more. I went home. We had given the organisers my home number so one of us had to wait by the phone. Realistically, we hadn't a chance. The buskers who played before us were gorgeous boys, with Beach Boy voices and smiles we couldn't resist. We christened them the Cutie Beauties and decided we wouldn't really mind if they beat us with their harmonies and their songs of cigarettes and whiskey and wild, wild women.

But when the phone rang, a man's voice told me we had won. He wanted us to do a turn in the Olympic Ballroom that night where we would pick up our prize – a voucher entitling the bearer to spend what, for us, was a small fortune in a well-known music shop. I made him repeat it three times. And then I rang the Clarence. They had old-fashioned wooden phone booths in the lobby. We screamed at each other for a few minutes in disbelief before I hopped on the bus back into town.

Our win merited a paragraph in *Hot Press*, although our collective cleavage was of more interest to the reporter than our version of 'Ticket to Ride'. To further increase our profile, we went into *The Irish Times* one day and gave the photographers on duty an impromptu performance and, no, it never crossed my mind that I might end up working alongside them. Understandably, they laughed a lot and took pictures of us that never appeared.

We fared better with the *Evening Herald*, which published a half-page interview accompanied by a huge photo. There were smaller pictures of Sinead O'Connor and the Hothouse Flowers, also former buskers, in the spread. Sugar and Honey, the article suggested, might just be the next big thing. We went further afield. In London, we busked in the corridors of the underground, where our voices bounced off the walls and carried on up the escalators. For those gigs, we needed only one song as the commuters passed by in a hurry sometimes stopping to chuck coins at our feet.

We blagged pizza from street vendors and made friends with a man dressed in a sheet who ate raw chicken and thought he was God. In London, if you had no money and nowhere to stay, something would always turn up. If you suspected you were being kidnapped, you just waited for the right moment and made your escape. If the digs you found smelt of curry powder and there was someone's dead grandmother in the sitting room, you quietly packed your black bin liner and sneaked out the front door.

If you placed all your casino chips on number 17 in a tribute to Mandy Rice Davies of Profumo Scandal fame, the roulette wheel came good and you had enough funds to last you the rest of the month. I haven't seen Sugar for a while and I don't know when I will again. But the memories stay precious. We could do anything we wanted, be anyone we wanted to be. There were no rules. And we laughed at people who viewed life in terms of what was acceptable and what was not. There were times, lots of times, when we should have been very scared. But we never were. And I miss that. It was like the thrill of potholing when I was 13. Slithering down a crevice somewhere in The Burren, crawling for several kilometres not knowing if you would get stuck, eventually emerging through another hole covered from head to toe in orange muck. You wouldn't catch me climbing into a hole in the ground now – I would feel trapped where I once felt free. Once upon a time, that kind of danger was exhilarating. Once upon a time, we were Sugar and Honey. And, for the record, we rocked.

Help! I Need Somebody

Well I was just 17, you know what I mean, when I decided that if I did nothing else significant in my life I would one day meet and marry Paul McCartney. I never felt able to compete with Linda, what with her vegetarian sausages and rock photography, but if Jane Asher, of cakes and *Crossroads* fame, had managed to woo him once then surely I would be in with a chance. Just as I thought my time had come, Heather Mills, with her winning looks and Adopt-A-Minefield campaign, whisked him up the aisle again. I could not compete.

But I'm not bitter. In May my favourite musician of all time will be performing in Dublin and while our wedding may have been put on the long finger, Operation Meet-A-Beatle is in full swing.

In a recurring dream, which persisted well into my twenties, Paul McCartney would call and try to persuade me to sneak out of my bedroom so that I could help him write songs. "I'm nothing without you, luv," he would whisper mournfully, a Liverpudlian Heathcliff at my window.

"You're like John minus the mean jibes about me not being the arty one." "Oh you are silly, Paul," I'd reply before climbing down to where he waited, guitar slung across his back just like in one of those grainy black and white shots of the band during the Hamburg days. Paul and I would then make, er, beautiful music together until the alarm went off for school.

Abbey Road, *Revolver*, *The White Album*. I played them loud and proud in my bedroom, returning to Morrissey whenever I needed music as fuel for my teenage angst. A black and white poster of the Fab Four in full Beatle dress was Blu-tacked onto the wardrobe. Paul's face was the last thing I saw before my eyes closed so in hindsight it was inevitable he would creep into my dreams.

In waking hours, I sought out the next best thing and became a groupie to a Beatles tribute band. They were called The Beatless and they played in pubs all over Dublin. Some nights, if you closed your eyes tightly, you could have been in The Cavern in Liverpool where it all began. Those were sweet and sweaty nights trying to make eye contact with the band during 'Love Me Do' while making sure you didn't miss last orders at the bar. "Aaaaaghghghghgh," we screamed our Pernod and blacks sloshing madly in our half-pint glasses. "Aaaaaaaghgghgh!"

The band featured a Lennon and McCartney hybrid in the form of lead singer Nigel from Wolverhampton. He had the adorable puppy-dog looks of Paul combined with the acerbic wit and unpredictable temperament of Lennon. It was a dangerous combination. I fell madly in love.

Unfortunately, Nigel/Paul had a penchant for models, although he did become a sometime boyfriend of my best friend for a while. Undeterred, I was a regular in the front row mouthing all the words to 'Oh! Darling', 'Things We Said Today', 'I'm A Loser' (no, the irony is not lost on me) and 'Ticket to Ride'. Sometimes we went back to parties in the band's flat where I would invariably make a fool of myself. One particularly memorable morning I awoke damp and disoriented in the bath. Rock, you could say, and roll.

Just last year, I was sent to report on the marriage of Paul and Heather in Castle Leslie. The couple came out to speak to the media and I swear Paul looked at me with what I like to call meaning. It is, of course, equally possible that he just had something in his left eye.

For security reasons I can't reveal too much detail, but Operation Meet-A-Beatle is not proving as straightforward as the other carefully planned celebrity encounters of my youth. With Morrissey, it was simply a matter of turning up at the Shelbourne Hotel and following him onto the tour bus. With Nick Heyward of Haircut 100, we wandered around London and asked friendly policemen where he lived. Somehow I suspect this one might be more difficult, if only because I have to get past Heather.

In desperation, I tried the old stalking-as-official business chestnut, casually suggesting to my boss that perhaps she might consider little old me for the job of interviewing McCartney. Somehow I think she suspected my interest was not strictly professional. The breathless Glenn Close in *Fatal Attraction*-style delivery of my request may have given the game away.

I still have faith, though. You have to when your teenage dreams come so tantalisingly close. The thing is, you are older now, the posters are torn and tattered and the CDs stacked in alphabetical order. Norah Jones beside James. Eva Cassidy next to Coldplay. Keeping hold of your dignity, making sure you don't look like a fool, is important these days. And yet, just once more, you want to wake up to the sound of music. Let it be.

Simply the Vest

'Nothing Rhymed'. 'Clair'. 'Alone Again (Naturally)'. 'We Will'. 'Matrimony'. I listed these songs to a friend recently in a discussion about our all-time favourite music. She looked at me blankly. "You know," I said, "Gilbert O'Sullivan." "Right," she said, "I didn't know you liked opera." "*O'*Sullivan," I said, "not *and* Sullivan." "Oh," she said, "tell me more."

I thought everyone knew about Gilbert. I've been listening to him since I was little, him and Barry Manilow, another much-maligned songwriter introduced to me by my mother. Manilow used to have a weekly show on Friday night and, as a treat, I'd be allowed stay up and watch. For some reason we had the sitting room to ourselves those nights, other members of the family not being quite as enamoured with the big-nosed one as we were.

You didn't get to see Gilbert on television though. He was everywhere in the early 1970s but, by the time I discovered him, he wasn't likely to turn up on *Top of the Pops*. All I had were some dusty cassette tapes which I played until his lovely voice singing his wacky lyrics – he actually has a song called 'Ooh Wakka Doo Wakka Day' – grew thin. By that stage, I knew every lyric of every song and I loved him almost as much as I loved Paul McCartney.

As a teenager, when I wanted to get even more depressed than I already was, I would turn the lights off and The Smiths up, but I'd always make sure I had at least one listen to 'Alone Again (Naturally)'. This song, which holds some kind of record for radio play in the US, starts off with Gilbert singing that he wants to climb the nearest tower and jump off. It's a song about wanting to end it all, about bereavement, about lost love, and the jaunty little tune makes it even more melancholy.

'Alone Again' describes grief better than anything else I have ever heard. Near the end of the song, there are lyrics about the death of a father and the reaction of his widow. "And at 65 years old/my mother, God rest her soul/couldn't understand why the only man she had ever loved had been taken/leaving her to start with a heart so badly broken/despite encouragement from me, no words were ever spoken/and when she passed away I cried and cried all day/Alone again, naturally."

I met Gilbert once – it must be more than ten years ago, I think – when he performed in a sort of retrospective of his life. My mother and I sat in a box at the theatre and queued up for ages afterwards until we were shown into a little room back stage. I remember his hair, all big and fluffy, and he didn't say much, but he signed a book of his songs that I'd bought. It's still a prized possession.

Gilbert never tried to be cool. Some less charitable people would say he couldn't have been cool if he tried. When he started out, he wore outfits inspired by his heroes, Charlie Chaplin and Buster Keaton, grey flannel trousers, braces and an old man's cap. He never lived down his Bisto Kid days. Later he started wearing preppy American jumpers with a big red G emblazoned on the front.

Long before Live Aid, before it was cool to care about starving Africans, Gilbert was wrestling with his conscience in lyrics. "When I'm drinking my Bonaparte Shandy, eating more than enough apple pies/Will I glance at my screen and see real human beings starve to death right in front of my eyes?"

He wrote songs about babysitting, and if 'Alone Again' makes me cry, the whistled intro to 'Clair' is pure joy.

There is some classic Gilbert trivia on the sleeve notes of his new CD. His favourite tipple is strong Assam tea but only out of a china cup, never from a mug. He has never drunk beer or hard liquor but he does like good red and white wines. He doesn't trust electric kettles and always makes them boil for longer than set. Rock and Roll.

He loves a good pun does Gilbert, and that's why when I walked into a record shop and saw he had a new 'best of' album out called *The Berry Vest* I wasn't surprised. The cover features the kind of vest your granddad might wear with a bunch of cherries on the front. A berry vest, if you will.

Best of all, Gilbert O'Sullivan, originally Raymond O'Sullivan, is Irish. I don't know if he has been given the freedom of a city, or if there's a statue of him somewhere, or whether there's a plaque on the house in Waterford where he lived until he was seven years old before moving to England, but there should be. Do yourself a favour. If you half remember him, if you loved him once or if, like my friend, you've never heard of him, go out now and buy *The Berry Vest* of Gilbert O'Sullivan. You'll wonder where he's been all your life.

My Well-Spent Youth

There was this girl a year below me at school who, for a while, I wanted to be. She was a Billy Barry kid. She had a natural blonde bob. She had been cast in one of the lead roles in a production of *Bugsy Malone* at the Olympia Theatre. Onstage her name was Tallulah, but really it was Karen.

I watched her from afar, as she rose through the Dublin musical scene, landing roles in Cinderella and other pantos. While the rest of us had regular Christmases, she would be immersed in a world of rehearsals and dressing rooms, flesh-coloured tights and Twink. "Snot fair," I muttered a lot around this time. "Just snot fair."

When our school did a production of *The Sound of Music*, I had my eye on the role of the governess Maria, but knew deep down that the part belonged to her. Sure enough, after the producer had whittled it down to me and Karen, her name was posted up and I got cast as one of the nuns.

It wasn't long before she got a part in *Grange Hill*. I know! *Grange Hill*. Any thoughts I had harboured of becoming her best friend and getting her cast-off tights and sparkly make-up were dashed, and she was off to London to become rich and famous and possibly marry Tucker Jenkins. It was too much to bear.

It was around this time I joined DYT – Dublin Youth Theatre. I knew I was too old for *Grange Hill* but I still thought I could be an actress, even if I'd never get to hang out with Twink. My older brother and sister had been in

DYT and I remember going to the Project theatre to watch one of their plays and into the Norseman afterwards for Coke. I didn't know why, but I knew I wanted to be part of that world.

DYT was – and still is – located in a crumbly old house on Gardiner Street and for a few years of my life it was the most exciting place to be. There were no Karens, but the place was full of interesting people who loved drama but hadn't found a real outlet for it until they joined.

The talent in the place was breathtaking. But I didn't feel jealous – just glad to be a part of it. It was the best reason to get out of bed on a Saturday morning.

And then there were the boys. I had at least five unrequited crushes during my time in DYT. There was one boy, I'll call him John, who everyone fancied not just because he was gorgeous, but because he seemed oblivious to our attentions as he sat in a corner stroking a cat and breaking hearts all around him. After the end of every production there were parties back in the house and you might declare your love for a fellow DYTer, only to be told by said person that he was already going out with someone who had a neck as graceful as a swan. Bit too much information maybe, but you got the message and agreed that, of course, it would be better to stay friends.

There was acting, too, in between all this hormonally charged activity. The highlight for me was a production of *The Plough and The Stars*, which was ingeniously set in the DYT house, a tenement just like those Casey wrote about.

The play began in the house and then cast and audience moved out into the streets around it, which had been transformed to look like 1916 Dublin. I was a Salvation Army woman, preaching God's word as the audience passed by on their way to Tony's pub, where the bar scenes were taking place.

My younger sister, Katie, was in the audience when I wore a blue crushed-velvet evening dress and movie star make-up in a production of Tennessee Williams' *This Property is Condemned.* I had to walk along railway tracks eating a banana. Katie later joined DYT, too.

In keeping with the fruit theme, I also appeared in a production we devised ourselves, in which I had to wear awful-looking leggings and a basket of fruit on my head. Enda Walsh, who went on to write *Disco Pigs* and do brilliant theatrical things in Cork, had one of the main roles in the play.

I never quite made the cut as an actress myself, but plenty of this country's best actors and directors have come through DYT. Veronica Coburn is one of them, and tonight her company, Barabbas, is hosting a fundraising gala where proceeds from their production of *A Midsummer Night's Dream* at Dublin's Project will be donated to DYT.

I never did hear what became of Karen, but I figured out who I was and, more importantly, who I wasn't, in that house on Gardiner Street. And that's what I call a really worthy cause.

Strumming My Pain

You could call me the Incredible Sulk. You wouldn't like me when I'm angry. Oh, to look at that photo, all hands on head and diamante love chain, you might imagine I was a jolly person to be with. And sometimes I am. But when I lose it, I lose it, if you know what I mean.

That nursery rhyme about the girl with the curl who when she was good she was very, very good and when she was bad she was horrid? That just about sums it up. The other week, for example, I was expecting a gang of people around for a buffet-style dinner. I had loaded up with batons of bread and cheese and salami and olives from the French market in the Docklands. The prices the French stallholders were charging must have had them laughing all the way to le bank. All I can say is their goose would have been well and truly stuffed had they tried it with the good denizens of the Dordogne.

Alors. I cycled happily away with three bags swinging from each handlebar. By the time I got home I was panicking a bit. Three hours to go before seven people arrived for food. I was planning to do some class of a thing with aubergine and goat's cheese because someone I knew had been to a restaurant and enjoyed it for their starter and it sounded easy when she explained how to do it over the phone. But I was a bit frazzled. I needed help.

Upstairs, my co-host was sanding a door. I could hear the steady rhythm of sandpaper and sighs. I asked him, trying to keep my voice steady, how long he would be. "Half an hour," he said. Half an hour later he was on another door, wiping dried plaster from it.

A number of things had become a priority for me. Tidying a place that was in tatters. Washing salad leaves. Doing creative things with slices of aubergine and extra virgin olive oil. All of this seemed important. Wiping plaster from doors did not.

I'm not going to lie to you. What followed wasn't pretty. It reminded me of the worst kind of childhood tantrums. Those long choking sobs that felt good for a while, as long as you were in control and not so good when you couldn't stop even if you wanted to. My co-host, wisely, had escaped to clear a gutter or something. Given my state of mind I had no choice but to cancel.

If you ever find yourself in a similar position, feel free to steal my choice of cancellation text message. It goes something like this: "Sorry for the short notice, don't feel well, can't do dinner tonight xx."

It was true. I didn't feel well. I couldn't do dinner tonight. I should have been relieved but all I felt when I looked at the kitchen full of food was rage. And then I picked up my guitar.

I've written before about my long relationship with that instrument. About my basic knowledge of chords and lack of discipline when it comes to practise. I know how to play about three songs, two of which I wrote myself. If there isn't G, A, D and, at a push, E minor, involved, forget it.

Despite my lack of prowess, strumming seems to calm me down. For this and other reasons, I am delighted that Ireland is about to host, for the first time, its very own guitar festival run by 24-year-old Alec O'Leary. Alec believes the guitar is much misunderstood. Some people (guilty as charged) seem to think of it as accompaniment and forget that as a solo instrument it takes some beating. At a party the other day, I watched a man position his guitar so it rested on his lap. He plucked the most beautiful music from it that no words, no lyrics were necessary. It was as complex as Chopin and every bit as inspiring.

The highlight of the festival is a master class by John Williams, one of the world's greatest classical guitarists. You had to audition to take part in the actual class but there are still tickets available to watch the master and pupils at work. There are concerts and classes, workshops and seminars. I was given a two-hour lesson myself recently. Stretched stiff little fingers over my first bar chord. Learned how to be more creative, to take a break from the chords, to experiment more freely with different sounds.

So if you ever find yourself in a similar position, feel free to steal my choice of reverse cancellation text message. It goes something like this: "I know I am an eejit and it's short notice but if you still want to come to dinner, please do." So they did. Music soothed this savage beast. Roll on the guitar festival.

Carry On Singing

It's easy to become blasé about the rights we are afforded in a democracy, rights that are denied so many people in the world. The right to free speech. The right to vote. The right to murder 'Don't Cry For Me Argentina' while reading the lyrics from a screen and being heckled by your friends. The right to karaoke is truly a fundamental one, so have pity on the people of Vietnam.

In Hanoi, the Ministry of Culture and Information has just drafted legislation to close down the hugely popular karaoke parlours that are dotted around that country. "Eighty per cent of karaoke bars in Vietnam harbour negative phenomena that could affect our culture in the long run," Le Anh Tuyen, director of the ministry's legal department, said this month. "Police have discovered that many karaoke parlours actually serve as brothels, or as intermediaries for call girls." And then the clincher: "Many songs do not have pleasant lyrics."

You would wonder from this whether officials are as bothered by prostitution as they are by the likes of Christina Aguilera's 'Dirty', the lyrics of which could quite reasonably be described as unpleasant. As one local karaoke impresario pointed out, if prostitution really is the problem, surely they should get rid of massage parlours, not karaoke parlours. Or they should shut down those venues which are providing microphones with callgirls on the side.

It got me thinking about how much we take karaoke – the lovely literal translation is empty orchestra – for granted.

There are some people, I am told, who have never done karaoke at all. I myself have enjoyed karaoke in a variety of places. In the early hours of the morning in New York's East Village and in the Kremlin – the gay bar in Belfast as opposed to the Moscow landmark. I've sung my heart out in a grotty bar in Portrush, Co. Antrim, and in the Windjammer, a tiny pub off Pearse Street in Dublin where the art form of karaoke is given the respect it deserves.

Once, in a dedicated karaoke club in Winston Salem, North Carolina, I scored so highly on the clapometer that I was asked up to do the finale of 'Summer Lovin'' with the owner playing Travolta to my Newton John. To this day, it's the highlight of my karaoke career, apart from the time I won a karaoke competition with my version of Ronan Keating's *When You S(h)ay Nothing At All.* "Itshamazing how you canshee right through ma heart." Gets them every time.

The reason karaoke became so popular in Asian countries is that audiences there tend to listen respectfully when someone has gone to the trouble of giving them a tune. We, on the other hand, are far less confident about exposing ourselves in front of crowds that are considerably less tolerant of substandard warbling. But while Vietnamese fans are being stifled, closet fans here have been thrown a lifeline. It's called Karaoke Box and it's well worth singing about. I heard about it from my sister, who was walking past a new restaurant in Dublin the other day and saw Karaoke Box written discreetly on the sign. She rang me straightaway. "Could this mean?" I asked. "Maybe," she replied. "I'll be there in ten," I said.

Ten minutes later we walked into the Japanese restaurant and were disappointed to find no sign of a karaoke stage or so much as a microphone. The waitress approached, and when we asked whether they did karaoke, she led us downstairs to the private karaoke booths. That's right, karaoke fans, booths which you can hire by the hour, a place to sing privately, to your heart's content.

I rounded up the troops. Brother, sister, sister-in-law, sister's friends. For two hours that evening we entertained ourselves with songs from every decade. We paid homage to everyone from The White Stripes to The Carpenters, Sinead O'Connor to Johnny Cash. My own personal highlight was discovering that I do a passable version of Lulu's 'To Sir With Love', while the brother impressed with 'A Boy Named Sue'.

It wasn't all plain singing. With just a lone fan whirring in the corner, the booths get unbearably stuffy and some nerves were frazzled. As the temperature rose, I confess I got a bit too attached to the microphone, causing the sister to remark I was more karaoke Nazi than Queen and the brother to swear he was never going karaokeing with either of us again. But not being from Vietnam, we don't have to fight for our right to fight in a private karaoke parlour. And for that we should always be grateful.

No More Working for a Week or Two

My Best-Laid Plans

I took a month off recently. Four whole weeks. I had plans. Big, fat juicy plans. This is what I said to myself at the beginning of my stay-at-home holiday. And at the time I meant every single word: "I will start The Novel. I will clear out my wardrobe. Old friends will come around for impromptu dinners sourced from shiny new cookbooks. They will be served dishes dreamt up by Nigella, but effortlessly prepared and presented and personalised by me. Afternoons will be spent browsing in bookshops and, in the evenings, there will be bracing and romantic walks up mountains and across beaches.

"Ah, yes. Four rejuvenating weeks during which I will learn to love brown rice, porridge and rice cakes and possibly learn how to drive. Rising at 6 a.m., I will watch the birds swoop over the Liffey and maybe write a few poems about their early morning ritual. I will go to the Millennium Wing of the National Gallery and ponder the power of art. I will go to Tower Records and buy a complete collection of The Smiths and The Beatles and a foolproof book on playing the guitar. I will stop being a three-chord wonder and apply myself. I will write another song. I will go to the theatre or the opera and not leave furtively at half-time.

"I will not smoke, I will not smoke, I will not smoke. I will knock on the door of the house in Sandymount. The one built in place of our family home which, after my mother sold it, had been knocked down by the new owners.

I will ask whoever answers the door if they will let me go out to the back garden for a while.

"I will not go on pointless shopping trips buying an umbrella because it has a cute baby-face print or buying stuff without trying it on. If I fail in this last resolution, I will not leave the unsuitable items with their tags still on, crumpled at the bottom of my wardrobe. I will clear out the wardrobe. I will."

This is what I actually did over my four-week sojourn. On an average day, I rose at lunchtime to watch reruns of *Dawson's Creek* and *Murder She Wrote* with my sister. Sometimes I watched *Fifteen to One*. A couple of times I turned on the computer and sat looking at the screen waiting for The Novel to write itself. No joy. I looked enviously at the book-launch invitation for Joe O'Connor's magnificent book *Star of the Sea* and considered ringing him for a few tips. But *Richard and Judy* started, and I forgot.

I booked a driving lesson. And then cancelled. I wasn't feeling well. The guitar stayed in the corner and The Beatles stayed in Tower Records. Nobody came for dinner. But then I didn't ask anyone. Jamie Oliver, volume one, and Delia remain the sole occupants of the cookbook shelf. I cut out a few recipes from the *Observer Food Magazine* and bought the ingredients. Now there are wilted packets of rosemary, thyme, lemongrass and rocket at the bottom of my fridge.

I made sandwiches every day for my boyfriend to take with him to work. I bought him a lunchbox. "Very fifties housewife," my sister said, and I took it as a compliment. I discovered a site on the internet where you can play card games such as Spades and Hearts with people from all over the world. I met a Canadian girl online who told me about her cyber romance with a guy from Ballymoney. She had just returned from her first and last visit to his home in the bible belt of Northern Ireland. "I still like him," she said. "I just didn't like where he lived."

A couple of times I played cards with complete strangers until 6 a.m. and so got to see the birds swooping over the river, but I was too tired to appreciate their grace and couldn't think of any decent rhymes to go with Liffey except "it smells a bit squiffy".

I got into a routine. My days began to resemble that of Will Freeman, the main character in Nick Hornby's *About a Boy*. He's a shallow, selfish idler who divides his days into half-hour "units" of time. Having a bath is one unit; watch-ing *Countdown* is one unit. Reading the paper is two units. Will wonders how people with jobs get the time to do anything. Dossing, if done correctly, is not as easy as it looks.

I ate porridge once but decided I would never like rice cakes unless they started making a pizza-flavoured version. I babysat for my sister's three children. I was beaten by nine-year-old Fionn at chess and watched *The Princess Bride* when the children went to bed. One day, I cleared out my wardrobe. Six bulging bin liners later, I felt like I had climbed Everest. It took me three days to recover.

"Life is what happens while you're busy making other plans," said John Lennon. I plan not to make any more plans. It's the only way I'll ever get anything done.

I Wanna Be Old

I have only been in Palm Springs for two hours but already I'm thinking of selling up and taking early retirement to live in a trailer near the desert. On the way over to the internet cafe, I took a break from shopping and sat down on a bench beside a bronze sculpture of, as I live and breathe, Lucille Ball. I passed Frank Sinatra's old house, thought I saw Bing Crosby and celebrated by buying a pair of earrings shaped like Betty Boo.

While sunbathing by the hotel pool, I discovered that, if I positioned my lounger strategically, I could see snow on the mountains even as I burned.

On top of all that, I've been pedicured and manicured by a six-foot tall Chinese man who confided with pride that nails "is not my real job, sugar – in real life I am a Karaoke queen". When I told him I was from Ireland, he snipped expertly at my cuticles and said, "In Orange County, I know it well."

The walls of the internet cafe are covered with paintings of naked adolescent boys by a man named, I kid you not, Randy Bailey. The only other diners at the moment are three septuagenarians ladies who lunch. They remind me, in a good way, of *The Golden Girls*, all raucous laughter, knuckle-dusting rings and shiny brooches shaped like poodles. Currently they are trying to work out how much they owe for their meal while the coffee-shop assistant makes a corned beef salad roll, no mayo, hold the onion, for a white-haired man the girls say is the spitting image of Burt Lancaster in his prime.

"Your sandwich was six dollars and 95 cents, sweetie, you do the math," laughs the one with the pointy sunglasses. "But, honey, I only had tap water and you had a Snapple," snaps her friend.

The one who has obviously spent decades diffusing these kinds of situations, makes a joke about them both being tighter than her husband's underwear as she hitches up her fawn velour pants, flashes a toothy smile at Burt and makes a beeline for the unisex toilet. The other two don't laugh. And that's when I notice all three women are wearing exactly the same brand of white runners.

In case you think I am just here on some frivolous people-watching exercise on the west coast of America, eaves-dropping on older people in places like Cappuccino.com, then let me say . . . so what if I am? The sun is shining, the fountains are trickling, the golfers are golfing and I am feeling more relaxed than I have felt in a long time despite having bought yet another pair of shoes before actually – here's a new idea – walking in them first.

At least the pain is bearable knowing my toes look nice.

I would recommend this place to everyone, especially wheelchair users, elderly people and those who favour the sedentary style of holiday. The age profile around Frank Sinatra's old stomping ground makes it clear why he went around singing "you make me feel so young" all day.

Every time you say to yourself, I have never seen anyone that old wearing a baseball cap turned backwards, you see someone even older tottering down the street in the same improbable headgear.

And wheelchair accessibility is *de rigueur* everywhere from the trendiest restaurants to budget hotels. Once you get over the novelty – let's face it, proper wheelchair access is still a lofty aspiration at home – you get a kick out of the system that suits everyone and discriminates against no one.

There are signs on the pavement banning skateboarding and rollerblading, and I wouldn't be surprised if local authorities introduced a speed limit for pedestrians. Basically, what with the heat and the gorgeous mountain scenery and everything, nobody here seems in a rush to get anywhere and so far that has suited me just fine.

I am even more sloth like than usual after the Journey From Hell that precipitated my arrival in Palm Springs. A delay caused by a mysterious technical fault in Dublin meant I missed the connection to Los Angeles in London and so was switched to another airline for a later flight.

Except there was a light smattering of snow in Heathrow which naturally meant that plane was delayed for seven hours while the wings were de-iced because, and I bet you never knew this, there are only two de-icing machines in Heathrow and when the captain said "believe me ladies and gentlemen I am just as frustrated as you" I doubted it very much.

So we get to Los Angeles at midnight, and I have missed my flight to Palm Springs, and British Airways have lost my luggage and by the time I reach my destination the next day, I reckon I have aged at least five years.

Still, once I get here I potter around with a huge smile on my face thinking how easily I could settle down in Palm Springs, despite the blisters on my feet and the fact that I have nothing to wear to this evening's black-tie ball.

And when I go shopping for clothes and toiletries to replace my missing stuff, it seems perfectly natural that I put white runners and a baseball cap at the top of my list.

A New York Story

The first time I took Manhattan, I was recently married with a rucksack on my back, and the place scared me half to death. I remember walking out of our hotel, a budget, art-deco dive, my skin prickling with fear at the sight of my first skyscrapers, jumping when I bumped into a man who I imagined was about to do unsavoury things to us for a few dollars more. He didn't of course. He just shrugged and continued walking towards the subway. We got as far as a fast-food joint before I had to turn around, leaning against walls for support on the briefly terrifying walk back to the hotel.

We weren't supposed to be in a hotel. We were supposed to be staying in the studio flat of a friend of my brother's friend. But there had been a mix-up and, fresh from the plane, we ended up in an Irish bar in the East Village called The Scratcher with no place to stay. Somehow, even scared and homeless, we felt safe in this East Village bolt hole between Second Avenue and Bowery, with its fairy lights on the windows, stubby candles melting on tables and the small, smiling barman who came from Dublin. His name was Mark, he said handing us two gratis, welcome-to-America, sorry-for-your-troubles, beers.

With the beers arrived a cordless phone, a phone book and encouraging glances while we rang every cut-price hotel in New York. When we found our digs, there were more, congratulatory, take-it-easy, relax-now, sure-it's-all-sorted beers and advice as to how we would find the place. The Scratcher became a haunt for that brief holiday.

We rode the lift to the top of the Twin Towers, trawled Macy's until we argued and ate hotdogs on the street. With Mark and his welcoming banter as a touchstone, I quickly learnt to love the city, not to be scared witless by it.

The second time, I was recently single and could be found meandering Greenwich Village with purpose, but without anywhere to really go. On one bitterly cold night, I went to see *The Blair Witch Project* and stayed, frozen with fear on my seat until everyone had left. Like a homing pigeon, I headed for The Scratcher and propped myself up at the long wooden bar while Mark polished glasses and told me that in his other life he was a singer-songwriter. Later a tall, dark stranger on his way back from a party took the stool next to me and we drank Jack and Coke all night, occasionally exchanging loaded small talk until they kicked us, gently, out.

The barman was still there when I returned another year with my boyfriend. It was early and the place was empty. We drank a glass of Guinness, said goodbye to Mark and ventured out, touring the pubs of the village and ending up in a private karaoke booth at 4 a.m. singing 'We Are The Champions'.

We downed cocktails in Times Square and, feet hurting from my bargain-basement shoes, I walked back to our hotel in my boyfriend's new size nines. Another trip saw us walk hand in hand up the ramp to see the still-smoking ruins of those towers. On that visit I felt more at home in New York City than ever before and I cut loose the Scratcher-style apron strings that I'd clutched to so fiercely on previous visits. Instead of it being the end destination, the bar became a much-loved stop on my too-irregular tours of magical, mysterious Manhattan. Normally the last place I want to be on holiday is in an Oirish bar, but I'd recommend The Scratcher over all the rest as a first stop for the greenest New York novices.

More than any suite of rooms on Park Avenue, I'll always

think of The Scratcher as my Irish embassy, with Mark, and the other staff, the laid-back ambassadors.

Things have moved on since my last visit. I turned on *The Late Late Show* last year to see someone who looked exactly like barman Mark singing about a girl called Suzanne. It was that Mark – Mark Geary. A guy who left Dublin in the early 1990s with all the rest clutching a Green Card and a one-way ticket. Mark Geary who had $100 in his pocket and a heart full of dreams. Barman Mark, making it at home. I felt oddly proud.

And so, when I saw him in Vicar Street, at the launch of the Lisdoonvarna Festival, I went up to him and gave him a hug. Despite the transient nature of our acquaintance, he smiled and said, “I wondered where you’d got to.”

I listened to his album, *33 1/3 Grand Street*, the next day and was struck by the lyrics on one song: “God doesn’t know me/or answer my calls/he don’t know me from Adam/or Eve at all.” I felt like that once, on a cold New York night and I found shelter in The Scratcher. Sláinte, Mark. Stay lucky.

A Muddy Good Time

He had badgered me for weeks about the secret location but all I would tell him was that we were going on a dirty weekend. At the airport, his eyes scanned the monitors hopefully as we approached and then passed the check-in desks for Paris, Venice and Milan. "Amsterdam?" he enquired before he took in the fact that we had stopped right beside the desk marked Swansea. "Oh," he said. "Grand."

A weekend in the Welsh seaside city of Swansea might not be the average person's idea of a summer holiday, but with the house and the decorating and the ongoing haemorrhaging of money from our bank accounts, that is the way it had worked out.

It wasn't what we might have hoped for – a fortnight in Tuscany, say, or a villa in the south of France. And it certainly wasn't a month in Argentina, where my younger brother Michael is skipping off on his honeymoon after he gets married to the lovely Rukhsana in London today.

Not having any holidays planned makes you realise that we have become a nation as obsessed by other people's holidays as we are by the weather. Myself and the boyfriend have been fielding the questions since the end of May. "Will you be getting away anywhere this year?" "Where are you going on your holidays?" "Have you been away yet?" No. Nowhere. And no. For a while there I considered sticking a sign on my forehead – something like: no holidays for me this year, but thanks very much for not asking.

But here we were anyway, off to Swansea in a plane with

propellers and a red dragon painted on the side. To Swansea, home of Catherine Zeta Jones and a local seaweed delicacy called laver bread. As I said, I promised it was a dirty weekend and I don't renege on my promises. The penny dropped for him as we drove into the Llanelli's Wildfowl and Wetlands Trust where the second annual Welsh Mud Festival was taking place. I don't know what I expected but it certainly wasn't chocolate fondue with marshmallow dips. We stayed long enough to feed the astonishing variety of birds that make their homes on the wetlands and watch a man making a mud hut. We missed the 'welly wanging' event, unfortunately. Or maybe it wasn't that unfortunate. We'll never know.

After a walk on one of Gower's gorgeous golden beaches and a tour of a castle, we went back to the city for the evening. There's a place in Swansea called Wind Street which dates back to medieval times and was one of the only streets in the city left standing after the blitz. Due to its antiquity, its high number of young ladies in belly tops and the pervasive stink of aftershave, we dubbed it Temple Bar-On-Sea. We only got half way up the street before we were assailed by two women in *Carry On Nursing* outfits collecting money for charity.

We ducked into a Spanish restaurant called La Brasseria, across the road from Morgan's Hotel, where Zeta Jones has a room named after her, for respite. "Your table, itsa number eight," said the enigmatic waiter before leaving us alone and menuless. We waited five minutes before we noticed that there seemed to be a lot of activity down at the delicatessen counter. When we went there we were told to choose what we wanted from the array of raw fish, meat and vegetables. Upstairs there was another deli counter with an even more bewildering selection.

If it wasn't for the waiter who noticed our confusion –

well it's hard to decide what to eat when you are eyeball to eyeball with the raw ingredients – we might still be standing there now. He took us in hand and recommended that we share a fish called sewin which is found in Welsh rivers. "Believe me," he said, "it's divine."

The fish was brought whole to our table, covered in the rock salt in which it had been baked. It was filleted in front of us, and heaped in a huge pile on our plates. "It's divine," I said, shoving great mouthfuls of the stuff into me. We decided we could paint the sitting room next month and ordered champagne. Later we got chatting to the owner, who told us that Catherine Zeta Jones, only he called her Catherine, was in with her husband last week. "But Catherine, she was a regular here before she wazza famous," he said. I'll give her one thing, the woman has taste. In food anyway.

The couple are known as 'the Douglases' round Swansea way, or so the man from Action Bikes told us when we enquired about cycling to nearby Mumbles, Zeta Jones's home village. The air was crackling with seaside activity, we had fresh sardines for dinner on a veranda overlooking the lighthouse and cycled past the ancient ice-cream parlour along a winding coastal path until darkness fell.

Later, as we pushed our plastic buckets of two-pence pieces through the slot machines and tamed towering ice-creams on Mumbles pier, I decided that I would definitely be back. All things considered, that weekend in Wales was probably the best summer holiday we never had.

The Life of Siddhartha

Asian pop music blares from speakers hidden in the branches of a coconut tree and a bullock lopes past, bells tinkling from his bowed head. Women pump water into pink plastic buckets while men squat and spit at the side of the road. A cockerel noisily greets the sun as it rises over the sacred mountain of Arunachala, spreading a buttery glow over its slopes. Cock-a-doodle-doo! By my first morning in India, I feel oddly at home.

My brother Brian has been asking me to visit since he first moved here in 1995. Siddhartha, I mean. I have to remember to call him Siddhartha here in this land where people named David or Donna by their parents back in England or the US answer only to the names given them by their Indian gurus. Siddhartha came home once from his travels and insisted we all stop calling him Brian. He relented when we shortened Siddhartha to Sid. People who have known him for years in India seem to love it when I forget the name given to him by his late guru and call him by the name my mother gave him instead. He, on the other hand, isn't quite so impressed.

Thanks to Siddhartha, I had a softer landing than I anticipated. Never being one to luxuriate in that pre-travel period, I had grown less enthusiastic about the trip as the date on my plane ticket drew nearer. The more people told me how jealous they were of my upcoming adventure, the more I worried that the plane would crash. The more those who had already been there said it could change my life, the more I fretted about the food.

Shortly before I left, a marketing friend took me along to the making of a television ad for one of her clients, a travel agent. When the director called action, the boy in a hospital bed stared goggle-eyed at a female doctor who was not wearing her uniform but a pair of swimming togs. The idea was that the doctor was looking forward to her holiday so much that in her mind she was already sipping sangria on the beach. I tried to picture myself in a sari but could only see me struggling to use the squatting toilets Siddhartha had told me about. "And we don't use toilet paper here" he had added to my horror.

After one of many sleepless nights I decided to express my concerns to Siddhartha. He e-mailed me back immediately to say Mother India would take care of everything, that she was waiting patiently for me with tenderness and with love. It was at this point that I seriously considered trading in my ticket for a fortnight package holiday in Torremolinos.

But when you resist, persist, as the Westerners out here are fond of saying. From the moment Siddhartha met me with a garland of sweet-smelling jasmine at Chennai airport and bundled me into a taxi for the four-hour journey to his apartment, the foreboding I hadn't been able to shake disappeared.

And now here I am in the pilgrimage town of Tiruvannamalai, dressing up for the ashram in a salwar kameez (a rather fetching billowing trouser and long shirt combination). I'm dodging the sadhus (wizened men with matted hair in orange robes) and their outstretched hands. I'm giving out to the drivers of the rickety auto-rickshaws when they charge too much or take a wrong turn.

I'm taking chai in the afternoon sun and listening to the stories of inner transformation as told by fresh-faced Germans to an old woman who has heard it all before.

I'm celebrating Pongal (the Indian new year) in the back garden of a 16-year-old girl called Viji. Watching as she makes sweet rice in a pot, timing it perfectly so that it bubbles over just when the sun begins to rise.

But it's not all sweet rice and spirituality. The dreadful music which begins at around 5 a.m. from the two temples near where I am staying is a winter-time custom to wake anyone who might be tempted to have a lie-in during these cold – by Indian standards – mornings. And when I am not burying my head in a pillow I am slathering myself with mosquito lotion but still manage to get bitten all over. And then of course I scratch the bites on my arms and somehow my face becomes infected and nasty boils erupt on the tip of my nose.

The homoeopath I visit wears thick glasses and asks a series of bizarre questions while, behind a tatty curtain, a boy, who can be no more than 14, waits for instructions on which potion to mix. "Are you an optimistic person," he asks me. "Do you lose your temper easily?" And then, an easy one: "How old are you?" I tell him. "Tsk, tsk," he says, "not your physical age, your emotional age." "Right now," I say, "I feel around 12." He nods soberly and the boy gives me a small plastic bottle of clear liquid which I am to shake exactly six times each night before taking six drops in three teaspoons of water before bedtime. After two days, I am looking normal again. Mother India, taking care. You just have to believe it.

Buddha and Sister

I have sneaked out to write this halfway through a ten-day retreat in Bodhgaya, the village in Bihar State where the Buddha got enlightened while he meditated under the famous Bodhi Tree. The guide books tend to warn tourists that Bihar is a lawless land where kidnappings, murder and corruption are commonplace. The Buddha's auspicious awakening, it might not unfairly be concluded, was the best thing ever to happen in Bihar. That was 2,600 years ago.

By rights, I should be writing this from Goa. Last week I told you how we had tossed a coin and how the brother lost the toss and how that meant the pair of us were supposed to hop on the motorbike, and point it towards the west coast. But the brother's heart was calling him here, so it turns out I won't be needing my swimming togs after all.

Getting to Bodhgaya from our base in Tiruvannamalai, in southern India, was probably the most uncomfortable 60 hours of my life. First of all, while he took the bike to the train station at Chennai, I had to share a taxi with his most recent ex-girlfriend, the one who left him to begin a relationship with a woman, the one who also happens to be a teacher on the retreat. It wasn't the most relaxed four-hour taxi ride, you'll understand.

To his credit, the brother had tried to make my life easier by booking the second-best class on the train. Three less fortunate members of our party were stuck in sleeper class with a family of six children, including two sets of twins under the age of four, who occupied hammocks that were hung across their berths. In the nights there were always at least two children roaring the carriage down, while in the mornings mysterious damp patches materialised on their rucksacks. Fresh from another ten-day Buddhist retreat, the intrepid three remained incredibly good-natured throughout. Weirdos.

Up in second class, we were sharing sleeping quarters with two Indian families who – unusually in my experience of the incredibly sweet-natured Indian people – didn't seem to understand the word 'share'. They sprawled all over the seats at meal times and turned them into beds whenever they felt like it, leaving me and the brother to wander homeless through the train.

I don't know which was worse – a man coming to sit on my berth to stare at me and make comments about my weight – "So big," he marvelled, "so fat" – or the 55-hour train journey being delayed by four hours due to some women on the tracks protesting at the kidnapping of their railway-employee husbands.

Perhaps it was sleep deprivation, or an intense resistance to the upcoming retreat, but, by now, I had stopped surrendering to the unpredictable ways of India. This was a problem because, as the brother keeps repeating like a mantra, surrendering is the only way to survive an adventure here.

When we arrived in Bodhgaya and walked into the place which was to be our home before the retreat started, something in this traveller snapped. Maybe it was the stained sheets on the bed at the Rainbow Guesthouse, or the buzzing mosquitoes, or the cobwebs in the corners, or the smell of damp in the air.

During dinner, I couldn't speak, couldn't eat and sat fiddling, like an escapee from a lunatic asylum, with the buttons on my cardigan. The kindness of my travelling companions, their concerned looks or gestures, meant nothing. It's shaming now to think of the way I had to be bundled into a jeep and brought to what I am assured was the finest hotel in Bihar State, where I spent the average backpacker's budget for three weeks in India on a bottle of beer, a hot bath and breakfast in bed.

And now? Ah now. The retreat, in total silence, is taking place across the road from this internet café in a Thai monastery. My bed is a straw mattress outside on a terrace where I sleep fitfully beside 20 other women under a large pink mosquito net. I wake at five every morning in the freezing cold and spend the day in sitting, walking, standing or eating meditation. I detest at least ten of my hundred fellow retreatants, think I will die if I eat another spoonful of rice, and wonder how I am surviving on one tenth of my calorific intake at home.

But at last this agitated traveller knows peace. Peace at night time when the roof of the temple twinkles red, gold, green and blue and there is a perfect crescent moon in the sky. Peace three times a day, when the monastery bells are rung, and the families of stray dogs who live here howl a strangely melodic canine chorus. Peace when dinner is served and it's a metal mug of hibiscus tea and a small green apple. Maybe the Buddha and his teachings were the best things to have come out of Bihar in 2,600 years. And what precious, transforming things they are.

In My Black Nude

I read an article during our so-called summer about the proliferation of wetsuits on the beaches, lakes and rivers of this island. Apparently wearing togs is so ten years ago. At the time the article appeared, I couldn't think of anything worse than wandering around an Irish beach in what a friend calls "the black nude". But times change. People change. Invites arrive for surfing weekends and suddenly you are in Bundoran voluntarily changing into your very own black nude. Life is hilarious like that.

I made a few initial mistakes when planning the week-end. Three to be precise. If you suspect you might suffer from wetsuit nervosa it's best not to bring your super-fit boyfriend, your surfing-experienced brother and your nymph-like sister-in-law along. You are just not going to look good beside these people, even if you did starve yourself for three days before the trip. And refraining from eating the batter off your batter burger is not technically starving yourself anyway. I think the word you are looking for is delusional.

They say everyone suffers from a spot of wetsuit nervosa, but this is patently untrue. Cameron Diaz didn't look too worried about the size of her thighs when I spotted her catching some waves in a magazine recently, and Cian Egan of Westlife always looks pretty relaxed in his. It seems that for some people donning a wetsuit is, if not exactly slipping into something more comfortable, then at least slipping into something that won't make others confuse them with a type of sea mammal. I am not one of those people.

Before I elaborate on the extreme sport known as Getting Into A Wetsuit, I would like to say a few words in favour of holidaying in Bundoran. It gets a bad rap, this seaside town, but we all had a grand time. On the Friday night we saw two great bands, either of which would make the wannabes on the *X-Factor* quiver in their trainers.

Innuendo may have a slightly dodgy name but the cute threesome have their own brilliant brand of that Busted/McFly-style music going on. Maybe they should change their name to McBusted. Down in the Bootleggers bar we boogied to Box T, a big hulk of a man who can play the electric guitar with his teeth. Need I say more?

It wasn't all fun. The boyfriend was harassed and not in a good way by a woman in one pub and I was poked in the back repeatedly by two blokes in another. On the plus side, the place is so full of Dublin people lured here by the promise of living in a real-life surfing town that there is a cool mix of the local and the blow-in. The town also boasts an exceptional restaurant called La Sabbia where you get whole sea bass or a generous plateful of melt-in-the-mouth calamari for a price not found elsewhere in Rip-Off Ireland. Here endeth the Bord Fáilte advert.

Back to the changing rooms at the Donegal Adventure Centre, where your correspondent was growing sweatier by the minute. I'm sure you will understand my decision to get changed into the wetsuit in a locked toilet cubicle as opposed to the open-plan changing room where I could hear the other beginner surfer chicks struggling into theirs.

"Hey, look, it's easier to get it on when you are in the shower," I heard one of them say. Well thanks for sharing, but the ordeal was humiliating enough without adding water to the equation.

But it was a surfing weekend, and water had to be added eventually. Keeping my knee-length waterproof jacket on over my wetsuit to delay the mortification, I lumbered out to meet the others. I gave boyfriend a sneak preview when no one was looking and asked him to try and say something kind. "You look, er, buoyant" was all he could come up with. I retorted by informing him that some men get even more mortified about their wetsuits, and that quite a few strategically stuffed socks have been employed by surfer dudes over the years. That wiped the smile off his face.

Off we went to Tullan Strand, where I wore the jacket right up to the water's edge. Somehow I forgot my embarrassment in the ocean where we spent hours being tossed around, our foam boards tied to our ankles and the dreaded wetsuits keeping us warm. The brother, sister-in-law and boyfriend all managed to surf standing up, however briefly, and with the help of the authentic-looking surfing instructors even I managed to catch a few waves, albeit lying horizontal on the board. The fact that I would be prepared to endure Wetsuit Hell again to go surfing in the Atlantic ocean says an awful lot. Buoyant? There are worse things they could say.

Power to the People

The sky is a brilliant blue and decorated with just the faintest wisps of candy floss cloud. In Dublin's St Stephen's Green this scene might look peculiar – a slightly dishevelled looking woman sitting cross-legged on a hill, tapping her thoughts into a laptop. But this is Central Park and nobody even looks in her direction. A bird lands, looking for crumbs from her cream cheese bagel, and that's about as much attention as she warrants on this sunny Manhattan morning.

She always ends up here on her last day in the city. She imagines bumping into Yoko, out for a stroll with Sean or returning home to the Dakota building for a nap. She wonders what she would say to her. Or whether she would say anything at all. She leaves the hill to sit on one of the nearby benches paid for by people whose names are etched on brass plaques. Under the cool shade of trees, she eavesdrops on conversations that replicate themselves over and over until it seems like everyone is reading from the same script.

Such a shame. It's so emotional. Can't believe we are here. And then a man is saying to a woman, "Honey, you know he was young when he was shot." And she is saying back to him, "But how young, honey? What age was he when he died?" And he is working it out. He thinks Paul and Ringo must be about 60 now, so if John was shot in 1980, that would have made him, well it would have made him . . . " but before he can complete the sentence, a hippie rolling a cigarette speaks without looking up and says, "John? He was 40 when he died."

The couple smile shyly at him and this gives the long-haired man all the encouragement he needs. "Funny thing," he says, "at the beginning of that year John always said that life begins at 40." The couple are not sure what to do with this information so they walk away, and the last we see of them, the man is shaking his head sadly. "All the good ones," he tells the woman. "The ones who made a difference. All shot. Bobby, Jack, Malcolm, John."

We are all here, in this part of the park, for a reason. Some are just resting in between their jogs or their dog walking or their rollerblading excursions. The fact that they are sitting beside the black and white 'Imagine' mural honouring Lennon is of little or no consequence. These people could be anywhere. Others are on a daily pilgrimage. They've come here for years, correcting the factual errors made by tourists. Throwing out tantalising morsels of Lennon-related trivia, titbits which suggest that maybe the hippie guy really did hang out with the Beatle guy, but you don't want to ask and he doesn't really want to tell. The rest of this constantly changing crew – excitable Japanese girls, well-spoken Englishmen, people with Jehovah's Witness name tags – just want a little piece of John to take back with them to wherever they came from in the world.

It's so peaceful here, so quiet. The only sounds are from a jazz trumpet coming somewhere from the east, the wind rustling the trees and the occasional honking horn of a cab. A sign asks politely that visitors don't make too much noise because this is a place for quiet recreation. The request is respected. There is a magical quality to the silence. We sit listening to the same conversations filter through as though hearing them for the first time.

And then Gary and Lisa arrive with their dog Mary Jane.

They have a binful of fresh rose petals of every colour which they dump onto the ground. Lisa throws the dog a bone and then starts sorting through the petals they have collected from florists in the neighbourhood. Gary wants mostly yellow ones today, so that's what Lisa picks out from the multicoloured debris in the trash cans. Gary has been creating petal peace signs on the mural on and off for around ten years. It has been a daily event for the past 12 months. Not because of the war in Iraq, necessarily, but then that sort of became the reason.

A crowd gathers to watch him work. "Welcome to New York," he tells them as he lays out petals on the ground and sprinkles them with water. "Welcome to the jungle." One woman wants to know why he does it. It's simple. "John was about peace," he tells her and all he is trying to do is finish what John started. "I need more yellow, Lisa," he says as the sign begins to take shape.

Lisa can't stay long today. When she is finished sorting the petals she has to go and sell the empty bottles she collects to make money. The couple have been living on the streets, beside the river mostly, for a few years. "It's not so bad," she says. People are kind and when the really cold weather comes they go to Florida. Last night they were sitting on these very benches and someone came around with sacks of food for them and Mary Jane. It's not so bad. Not on a day like this when the sun beats down and the peace petals shimmer. Strawberry Fields. Forever.

What Are We Like?

I am eating dim sum in Bangkok when I realise what it is that has been niggling at me during this brief trip. Since our arrival, the locals have been tripping over themselves to be of service. Without exception, staff smile and hold eye contact and make you feel at home.

A fellow traveller who gets lost is almost accosted by people anxious to help. It niggles away at me. No race of people can be that nice. There must be some agenda. I add hoisin sauce to my pancake and silently curse my cynicism. I know full well there is no agenda. I am just confused by a style of welcome too often denied visitors at home.

Thailand has its problems. Our tour guide told us you could get arrested if you speak ill of the royal family in public for example. So nobody does. And the problems surrounding the sex industry warrant another article on their own. But as a tourist roaming the streets, I feel safe and warm and welcomed even amid the chaos of this oriental city.

Our lunch host, Daranee, a Thai woman born and bred in New York who has moved to the country of her parents, asks me why I am so surprised. "What are people like in your country?" she enquires.

It's a good question. Back in Dublin I take a taxi from St Stephen's Green. The driver starts talking. "Anyway," he says, "I was just laughing at something before you got in." He says this conspiratorially, as though continuing a conversation we were having earlier. "A girl got into a taxi at the Gresham Hotel," he says, "and the driver, a coloured, was playing with himself." He uses actions at this point, in case I don't quite understand.

"The poor girl," he continues. "Shocking isn't it?" I fall silent for a while. I know exactly what this man wants to hear. Agreement that this island would be a better place if the likes of him were banned from driving taxis. Instead, I ask why he had felt the need to mention the man's skin tone when relating the alleged incident.

He sighs and says because in all his years driving a taxi, "blacks are the only ones who refuse to pay". I ask him what that has got to do with the story he told. "Well they're all like that, you know, they are coming into this country and taking stuff away from us and it's disgusting."

And you think you should be telling me this?

"I'm entitled to my opinion," he says.

I just wondered would you have told that story to a black person were they sitting in the back of this cab?

"I don't talk to black people. I don't like them."

"What about Samantha Mumba? Or Paul McGrath?"

"I don't like black people."

"You are entitled to your opinions but I am entitled not to have to listen."

"I will shut my mouth in the future."

"It's probably best."

"€8.90 please."

"Keep the change."

Don't get me wrong, I love Dublin warts and all, but Daranee's question got me thinking. What are we like? On a Saturday night a young librarian pushes his bike down Grafton Street, our Bond Street or Fifth Avenue when you think about it, and is beaten unconscious in a lane. The same night a woman has tufts of her hair pulled out in another attack. I am coming out of a concert on Dame Street and a man is chasing after a woman who is running away from him. "I am going to kill you, bitch," he shouts. And on she runs in her high heels. For her life.

As sure as summer follows spring, the next few months will bring stories of the rental cars of German or French families being vandalised and the contents fleeced.

Much more trivially, being ripped off in a cafe is no welcome either. In Lisbon I can buy a cup of coffee in a china cup for 40 cents. Or in Rome, with a view of ancient ruins thrown in, I'll pay €1 for my cappuccino. In my local sandwich bar, I buy a black coffee in a paper cup for €1.75. Céad míle fáilte, y'all.

Back in the office a real welcome with no strings attached, the kind I've been craving since leaving Bangkok, is wrapped up in an anonymous letter. A £20 sterling note flutters out of the old-fashioned envelope. It is from someone who read about my pilfered Trocaire box a few weeks ago and decided to send me this money instead of placing her usual bet on the Grand National. There is no name. Just "from a 78-year-old widow who gave up chocolate for Lent". I hope somebody buys you a big, fat Easter egg tomorrow, whoever you are.

Home Truths

Home Sweet Home

I can't go home, not really. They knocked it down, you see. After my mother sold the family home, the new owners demolished our white house on Sandymount Green, where the door was always on the latch and you had to shout over the voices of the inhabitants if you wanted to be heard.

The new house is painted a depressing shade of not-quite-brown-not-quite-green. A sign to the right of the door reads Plastic Surgeon. Ladies enquire about having their faces lifted on the site where I grew up, and that speaks volumes about the way Sandymount village in Dublin has evolved.

Every time I go back there, which is often, I have an irrational urge to knock on the door of our house – or at least the house they built where it once stood – and ask them politely why they demolished our higgledy-piggedly home but kept our garden shed standing.

If I crane my head over our/their back garden wall from the Methodist church next door, I can see it, the last physical reminder of a family who once needed that space for bits of bikes or tins of emulsion.

Back then, the sign beside the door read Inglenook. Even though the house never looked like the kind that should have a name, Inglenook, carved in wood, fitted perfectly. My mother and father bought the house 40 years ago after falling in love with the two-bedroom former schoolhouse facing the triangular area of grass, conker trees and flowers. He was from Bath Avenue in Irishtown, she was an east-ender from London.

Five years ago, my mother sold the house, having just made the final mortgage payment on the original loan of £1,900. How it could take 35 years to pay off a mortgage of that size I don't know, but I believe there were a few near misses with the bailiff along the way. Four boys in one bedroom. Four girls in the other. But where did you sleep, I ask my mother now? "Sometimes upstairs, sometimes downstairs," she says with a smile.

Dinner was 6 p.m. sharp and our presence at the long wooden kitchen table was non-negotiable. All ten of us, later nine, sat down to dinner every evening and told stories about our day. There was lots to tell because, back then, Sandymount had several playgrounds, only some of which have survived.

We had obstacle courses in the back garden and a tyre swing on the apple tree. In the land around Park Avenue and Windermere, both now home to apartment blocks, we climbed orchard walls and gathered blackberries. Scoring apples and berries on the same day was a good result as Mother would make an apple and blackberry tart for afters.

Some days, a sister or brother might say let's go to "the tins", the wasteland near Beach Road that has now been landscaped, and we would spend the afternoon making huts from cardboard and corrugated iron.

The best playground of all was Sandymount Strand. Around the corner from Inglenook, a barefoot stroll up Newgrove Avenue, a daredevil race across Strand Road and then down the stone steps in a tumble of buckets and spades and towels. Messing about in the 'little cockle lake' and when we were older the 'big cockle lake'. Catching shrimp and crabs and sometimes – if you stood on them very carefully and didn't make a sound – tiny plaice.

We didn't want to go home so Mother brought the Sunday dinner down to the strand, all carefully wrapped in tinfoil. I have a mental photograph of that day. The sun is shining, the roast potatoes steaming and there's a leg of chicken in my sandy hand.

When our father died, the younger members of the family didn't go out to the cemetery at Deansgrange but were looked after by the Borzas, an Italian family three doors down who ran a chipper.

Back then, you could sit in the shop at formica tables and be served by Mrs Borza, who wore gold hoop earrings and a tight bun in her hair. But that day we huddled in their back sitting room as the family served up anything we wanted. So I discovered funerals smell like chips and, at eight years of age, that was fine by me.

At Christmas time, we put on shows in Inglenook for the nuns at Lakelands convent on Gilford Road where I went, grudgingly it has to be said, to primary school. Mother would adapt a pantomime for us to perform. One year it was *Puss in Boots*. I was a princess with two lines: "Father, I'm bored" and "Father, I'm still bored."

I went back to Lakelands the other week and found Mary Price, who taught me in infants, now the principal, the nuns having left some time ago. She was holding a summer school for children with dyslexia. I remember her warm and smiling, singing 'A Frog Went A-Courting He Did Go' in the classroom when I was three. I laughed but I don't think she was joking when she told me this year's sixth class went out to celebrate their 'graduation' in the Italian restaurant on the green.

Mrs Daly in sixth class encouraged me to write and, after leaving school and waitressing in London, I began my journalism career back in Sandymount at the local paper, *NewsFour*. My first 'scoop' was an interview with the Hothouse Flowers, after I ran into them by accident at the cashpoint machine. The paper was run by Community

Services, a CE project which my mother helped start more than 20 years ago.

Today, I sit in the Green and the memories of the scrapes I got into seem to whisper through the grass. There was the day I got my head stuck in the railings and the fire brigade had to come and cut me out; the day I burnt my leg after falling on to a plastic milk bottle that was melting in a backyard bonfire; the night I fell headfirst on the pavement during a game of chasing, got a cartoon bump and a doctor from St Vincent's asked if I knew what day it was.

You would never think it these days but Sandymount, where everyone used to know everyone else, used to be a bit of a ghost town. There wasn't much apart from the two pubs, McAuliffe's chemist, a post office, Mapother's newsagent, Miss Roddy's sweet shop and Bracken's grocery store where the Spar on the corner is now.

Today, you are lucky to find a parking space and the village is packed with people and places to go.

So many changes and yet strolling around, you can still hold on to and taste the things that have stayed the same.

The men standing outside Ryan's pub in the sunshine, putting the world to rights. Bruno and Angela Borza still serving the finest chips in Dublin. My dad's brothers and sisters still living in the area. *NewsFour* is still one of those thriving but threatened CE projects that, in addition to being a useful resource for locals, helps the people who work there in so many important ways.

I dream of living here again, in this perfect mixture of bustle and seaside solitude, modernity and quirky character. For economic reasons – this is D4 remember – I doubt I ever will.

But I keep finding reasons to come back. I'm a northsider now, but I'll cross the Liffey for that perfect cod and chips.

I do my banking on Sandymount Road. I'm still a member of the video store.

I even shop in the supermarket and remember a time when it was called H. Williams and the introduction of tortilla chips to the shelves constituted serious culinary news.

These days my mother and I go for lunch in the Italian restaurant, sip lattes in the smart coffee shops, browse in the boutiques or just sit in the Green and watch the youngest of her grandchildren play where she used to watch us. Indian incense and dream catchers are sold where Miss Roddy used to dole out the penny sweets and pink cake.

I can't go home in Sandymount, but I will always feel at home. Memories, like certain garden sheds, are built to last.

Why Location Matters

Everybody who bought their house or apartment back when owning your own home wasn't such a big deal is moving on up the property ladder. One friend bought beside a Dublin canal, another in Co. Wicklow. Both kept their first home to rent out and the income on that will help with the mortgage repayments on the new place. It feels like I'm being left behind, so one night I decide to ring a man who knows about these things.

"Yes," he says, after a quick bout of mental arithmetic, "it's eminently feasible." Magic words. You can tell he says them a lot. Suddenly I am knee-deep in brochures and I go to sleep dreaming about prospective second homes.

I have ten appointments to look at houses not by the canal or down the country but in places I have never been before. I tell one taxi driver that I am looking around East Wall and he sighs and says, "Listen, love, that's only Sheriff Street with a different name." I ask him to bring me to a house in Harold's Cross but he isn't too pushed about that area either. "See that pub," he tells me, "a man was shot there the other week."

In the end I love the ramshackle house that would need a lot of work but despite the shooting incident, Harold's Cross turns out to be just like Ranelagh or Rathmines or Sandymount or Donnybrook or Ringsend – all areas I can see myself settling down in but all way out of my financial league.

Still, I count myself very lucky that I have one home, and

two houses begins to sound a little greedy when I think of friends struggling wildly to finance their first home. But I am like a woman possessed, looking over the fence at the Jones's new gas barbecue convinced I'd better get one too or run the risk of being the odd one out at the next coffee morning.

I think I have been living in an apartment for too long. You never know your neighbours and if you make too much noise they don't leave a note or anything. They tell the caretaker and he then has to leave a note highlighting the rule you broke in yellow pen. I used to love that anonymity, but when a friend was telling me about the woman who lives beside her and the kids on the next road, I realised it was years since I felt part of any kind of community. "There are still people who look out for each other," she tells me. You tend to forget such things in apartment-land.

A house it is then. I want to see if I can grow herbs in a garden and I want an upstairs and a downstairs and a room of one's own. I become more realistic, restricting my internet property searches to Inchicore and North Strand and Phibsboro and East Wall, deciding, after some thought, that the Sheriff Street remark was mean spirited.

My brother lives in East Wall, I tell everyone who looks askance at me when I mention I am looking there. It's an up-and-coming area, I say, putting on my best estate agent's voice.

Walking back from an unsuccessful house hunt along the quays, we pass the regular crowd of drinkers beside the Custom House, with their cans and their chat and their toddling children. It is freezing and I want to ask them about the babies in the prams, whether they should be out here in this weather. I hear myself saying it in my head but I can't say the words out loud.

So I walk down the road to Store Street Garda Station to

ask them about the children and the policeman on duty is matter-of-fact. "We can't do anything," he says, "we see children with blue feet and we can't take them off the drug addict who is holding them because there is nowhere for the child to go." He says this a few times because he can see I am not really taking it in.

"Babies with blue feet," he says. He thought I was going to complain about the drinkers because their cans and their carousing are not the right image for Dublin. What would the tourists think? That's what annoys most people.

He'll send a car past the drinkers for me, but there isn't really anything he can do. I feel like Billy Bragg when he sang about being a victim of geography.

The places I want to set up home and garden in, I can't afford. And deep down I know the reason I want to live in those places is because when you are there, the chances of seeing or hearing about babies with blue feet are very slim. In fact, living in the more expensive locations you could almost forget there was such a thing. And that kind of forgetting doesn't come cheap.

Time to Settle Down?

Barbie's pregnancy has raised all sorts of problematic issues. Is Ken the father, for kick off? And, if you don't mind me asking, Mr Mattel, is she planning to get married? Will she do a Posh Spice and regain her figure straight after the birth? How on earth will she pay for childcare? And, I know it's a little early, but has she got the baby's name down for the local Multi-D? I really think we should be told.

It's a destructive habit of mine but when I'm supposed to be sorting out important matters, I tend to immerse myself in irrelevancies. The reproductive activities of a plastic plaything should not be high on my list of things to make me go hmmmm at the moment, but I'll try anything to avoid tackling the move.

I worked it out last night, in-between bouts of mentally designing Barbie's maternity wear, that I have moved house 15 times already since I left home at the age of 19. That's 15 lots of cardboard boxes, removal vans, broken plates, new front doors, neighbours and last-minute light bulbs. Fifteen lots of nice to meet you, what's that noise, it's only the wind/a cat/next door's TV and I wish they'd turn the music down. Maybe we should turn the music down. You get the picture.

They say moving and divorce are the most traumatic events in a person's life. Well, I've tried both and I'd take the courts every time. Of course, I've made a list. I've made lots of them but don't ask me where they are. I've been re-reading *Winnie the Pooh* and I think he had the right idea, simply living for the joy of honey and lazy afternoons. I don't recall him writing lists. Bothersome, weasely things.

Suddenly watching home makeover programmes is not a pleasantly diverting experience; it's homework. These programmes are forcing me to look into my heart and figure out where I stand on wicker. Am I a minimalist when it comes to interior design? Or would I prefer a home draped with multicoloured ethnic fabrics imported from Bombay? Suddenly having Laurence Llewelyn-Bowen in to make such decisions for me doesn't seem like such an appalling idea.

While we are preparing to move, everyone else we know is also bustling with activity. People getting married. People having babies. House warmings. Christenings. Engagements. Disengagements. Emigrations. It's enough to make you want to bypass this frenetic, no-time-to-smell-the-coffee part of the human life cycle and just skip forward to the bit where our children, correction our happy, successful, well-adjusted children, have bought us a holiday in the south of France just for being good parents. We are sipping Chablis a sun-washed terrace and congratulating ourselves on a life well lived.

In the sunset of our lives, there will be no need to worry about extensions collapsing or dodgy bathroom tiling or which colour would work best in the hall. In the sunset of our lives, we can read Agatha Christie novels and eat Mr Kipling cakes ad nauseam without caring a fig for what people think.

But that kind of forward thinking is just wishing your life away and, in truth, all I want to do is wish the next few months away. More specifically, I want to wish into oblivion all the clutter that has accumulated around my person through 15 – fifteen – house moves. How did I come to own all this stuff? An Amiga computer, so ancient I would be embarrassed to bring it to a charity shop. A bagel slicer (who makes these things?). Two broken irons. One broken ironing board. Suitcases of clothes I'll never wear. Boxes of candlesticks I'll never use. Horrible crystal glasses ("I can't throw them away, they are crystal," I remember reasoning). A plastic bag full of miniature items liberated from hotel bathrooms. I mean, you just never know when you might need a dinky sewing kit or cute little shoe buffer. Well, do you?

Somebody once bought me a book called '*New Leaf, New Life: how to do everything and still have time for yourself*'. I never got around to reading it. Obviously. But when I open the broom cupboard and 15 moves worth of possessions tumbled out, I wish I had.

It's not the thought of moving these things to the new place that is irritating me, it's the thought of moving them again and again and again. We drove around there the other day. The board outside said 'Sale Agreed'. It seemed so final. And then it occurred to me that what I actually want is to settle down. I want this house to be the last one in which I deposit all my bits and pieces. For better. Or for worse.

Handymaniac

I have a steamer in one hand and a scraper in the other when a man who looks like a Mormon, but is actually a representative of a well-known takeaway pizza outfit, rings the doorbell. He is Canadian. He doesn't tell me this straight away but after I cough up €40 in exchange for a handful of pizza vouchers we discuss the matter at length. "I'm Canadian, I haven't quite got the lay of the land yet," he says. "Fascinating. Tell me more," I reply.

We chat for a while about the difference between Canada and the United States before moving on to the quality of his competitors' pizza-toppings. It really is amazing what passes for an anchovy these days and don't get me started on all that plastic pepperoni. He assures me his toppings are unrivalled and I go back inside wondering – as if I don't already know – how much damage a 12-inch with extra cheese might do to my healthy-eating plan.

My co-steamer is not impressed. "You just paid €40 to get out of doing a bit of work," he accuses, looking as intimidating as you can while brandishing a large yellow sponge and wiping wallpaper from your hair. "You would have bought shoe polish off him. Or stale bread," he says. I adopt a wounded look and, still clutching the scraper for appearances sake, offer to make the workers a nice cup of tea. "More skiving," I hear him mutter as the smell of burning martyr fills the air. But I am too busy boiling the kettle in what passes as our kitchen to respond.

Everyone said it would be thrilling. Starting from scratch.

Your own blank canvas. He certainly thinks so. Even though we are supposed to be on holidays, he sets the alarm for eight each morning and pushes me out of the bed. I say bed but it's actually a mattress on the floor so at least I don't have far to fall. We bought a house as far as I recall, so how come we only live in two rooms? It's like camping but without the option of a home to go to when the novelty of roughing it wears off.

He hates camping, but inexplicably, he thrives on this. He folds his specially designated work clothes in a neat pile at night while I rummage through the black plastic bag wardrobe in the morning and put on whatever comes to hand. That's how I managed to get vinegar and water mix – the man in the hardware store, his new best friend, swears it works wonders on stubborn wallpaper – on my brand new skirt. He sighs the sigh of a contented man and fantasies about doing renovations for a living.

At 1 p.m., on the nose, he says, "Right, time for dinner." "Time for lunch," I say, correcting him. "No," he smirks, adjusting his jeans which are riding down in a worrying manner, "it's dinner-time." He goes to see how his brother is getting on with the sitting room while I wonder when exactly my boyfriend turned into Handy Andy and how I could have possibly missed the signs.

We sit on crates, upholstered with scraps of musty carpet. I suggest going for, um, dinner in the smart new coffee bar which has opened down the road.

He takes a bite of his doorstep-sized hang sangwich and slurps his tea and says, "This will do grand," as he flicks through *The Sun.* What feels like ten minutes later he says, "Back to work then. No rest for the wicked." I suddenly remember an urgent deadline at the office and am out of there quicker than you can say four-be-four.

I don't go to the office, of course. I go to my sister's

house which has proper facilities. She is at work so I make beans on toast and sit on her well-stuffed sofa. I file my toenails and then paint them a colour called Princess In Pink. I free my mind of the tyranny of home improvements and think philosophical thoughts about *Big Brother*'s latest victims. I tackle important but not too taxing issues, such as why does Nush smoke if she is such a yoga fiend and what possessed Cameron to balance that apple on his head?

It is 6.30 p.m. before he knocks on the door, all freshly scrubbed and sweet smelling and looking not at all like a builder. He says work is progressing nicely and paints a picture of a time when it might be possible to invite people over for dinner. He pours me a glass of wine and I feel hopeful about the house for the first time all day. Then he goes and spoils it all by grabbing the remote control. "Great," he says as I bury my head in a cushion, "we're just in time for *Changing Rooms*."

Restoration Drama

We took a hammer and a chisel to the walls and found ourselves with a relationship, I mean a living room that resembled the worst hit parts of central Baghdad. I knew the rubble and the dust and the exposed brick would eventually be banished by fresh plaster expertly applied by a long-lost cousin who has come to save the day. But I don't think we'll find the kind of bonding formula we need down at the DIY superstore.

Never mind the house, our romance has been gutted since we started this 'project'. For weeks I couldn't accept that we are not supposed to have a social life anymore, not while he was driven by a work ethic that would impress Ian Paisley. I wanted everything done, NOW! with as little effort from me as possible. He spent every spare hour trying to make this happen and still, inexplicably, I was not satisfied.

Instead of working as a team, we seemed to be going in different directions, like Dr Doolittle's Pushmepullyou. A friend who found herself in a similar situation phoned for advice and I heard my voice wise and calm telling her the kind of things I should be telling myself. In desperation, I sought out the self-help section of the bookshop. All the titles seem so 1987. *Don't Sweat The Small Stuff. The Little Book of Letting Go. Why Me, Why This, Why Now?* And, *Who Moved My Cheese?* (Excuse me?) Sadly the one I wanted – *Help! I Think I Am Going To Kill My Boyfriend If He Doesn't Stop Running Around Like A Headless, If Handy, Chicken* – was out of stock.

I ducked out of the dustiest duties to go to a party where I met a couple who were married for more than 40 years. Fascinated, given my predicament, I asked them what their secret was. "Communication," she said. "Understanding," he said. I made appropriate "aren't you great" noises to intimate how incredible they were, silently hating them both.

Some days are worse than others. The other night he demolished the bedroom wall saying the plaster was loose and there was nothing else to be done. What annoyed me more than the devastation was the fact that he was so obviously enjoying the process. Now it's not the best idea to get hysterical when you are trying to convince the neighbours that living beside us will be a breeze. But I managed it quite spectacularly that evening.

E-mail helps, of course. A cold clinical list of Things To Do and a reminder of the amount of money left to do it with can keep things moving when all communication has broken down.

The rows are whispered so the harsh words don't filter through the ceilings and walls of the kind people who are letting us stay until the house is ready to properly inhabit. Everything we need to live is carried from house to house in half a dozen Bags for Life. Our bags are for life although we increasingly look at each other in ways that suggest we are not quite as sure about us.

Still, rows are healthy aren't they? They clear the air, and we need an industrial humidifier to see through the fog that has settled in our house.

Some days we are not even sure which bit of the house, which job, which bill we are rowing about. We hang on grimly to the argument because it seems more familiar than anything else right now. That we are in conflict seems to be the only thing we can agree on. In these stormy seas, it is the raft to which we cling.

When the long-lost cousin arrived and said Demolition Man had actually done the right thing by smashing up parts of our home, the taste of humble pie mingled with the grit already lodged in my throat. I got stuck in with the chisel and hammer, watching with satisfaction as huge clumps of plaster crashed onto the carpet. Underneath, the mortar was coarse and unlovely yet it held the bricks together. They may have wobbled slightly in places but for the most part they still held fast.

The cold war continued until the morning we sweated for half-an-hour trying to squeeze a large sofa through a small door. Like everything else, it looked hopeless, until he noticed the sofa legs could be screwed off and I suggested we turn it upside down. The sofa slid easily through and our spontaneous, self-congratulatory laughter seeped into the parts the humidifier had failed to reach. Wordlessly and with smiling eyes we acknowledged that when push me comes to pull you, we can work together, albeit pushing and pulling at each other all the way.

The living room looks like we might have a few undeclared weapons in the basement but in our hearts we know we've got ourselves a bunker. Even if sometimes we forget exactly where it is.

Those Who Can't, Shop

All those years I spent longing to be a grown-up, I never understood that being adult meant standing in Shower City debating the merits of a square-shaped toilet over its curvier, less expensive, cousin. Or, in the same establishment, being patronised by a sales assistant when it emerged I didn't know that certain models of power shower required a pump and that these pumps add hundreds of euro to the cost.

Another thing they don't teach you in Home Economics is that a set of taps for a sink can cost up to a grand. Talk about throwing good money down the drain.

I've taken to not opening my bank statements on the basis of what I don't know can't keep me awake and in cold sweats for much of the night. The Visa man rang the other day to politely enquire when I planned to make that minimum payment. Panic set in. "Sorry," I said, "I can't hear you, you're breaking up, beep, beep, beep." "You are on a landline," he pointed out in a patient but unamused tone.

"So many tiles, so little time." "Multicoloured Indian slate on the kitchen floor," the assistant suggested. I presumed we would get a discount because some of the tiles were chipped. "They are supposed to be like that, it's a natural material," sniffed the assistant who had sussed us for the renovation virgins we are. Naturally, I bought four boxes.

Apart from a few excursions to Tiles-R-Us, we have so far escaped morphing into one of those glum couples in the aisles of B&Q, which in my limited experience stands for

Bickering and Quarrelling, or swooning over curtain fabric in Hickey's. As a result, work on the house is progressing rather more slowly than we'd hoped. For my part I tried to distract myself with shopping expeditions until I couldn't hide the bags any more and he became suspicious.

When forced to assess the financial damage, I was horrified to discover how much of the 'doing-up-the-house kitty I had frittered away and how little I had to show for my frittering. Much too late, what remains has been transferred to his account. Of course, I kept a little back for emergencies of the cosmetic kind.

The first step is to acknowledge you have a problem, and I see it as a positive development that I've been thinking about what I would ask ex-*Big Brother* contestant turned TV presenter Anna Nolan if I appeared on her new life-transforming programme *Ask Anna.*

So far Anna has cured people of their fear of dogs, helped women become cabaret artists and coaxed a shy man out of his shell. I was in Marks & Spencer buying a shirt similar to three others I own after splurging on earrings I won't wear when I mentally composed the letter: "Dear Anna, I spend money I don't have on things I don't want/need. Help!"

With a fortunate sort of spendthrift serendipity, I just received an e-mail about another TV show aimed at people just like me. The fact that *Show Me The Money* is a blatant RTÉ rip-off of the BBC's *Your Money Or Your Life* should not deter those of us up to our Grecian-style mosaic borders in debt. Financial expert Eddie Hobbs does an audit of participants to unearth their most heinous spending crimes. Eddie, I suspect, would not be impressed by my tendency to over-tip taxi drivers as a reward for them not talking. Never mind my habit of stuffing notes into pockets or grocery bags instead of into my wallet.

How I long for Eddie to "optimise my income and

lifestyle choices" and perhaps pay off my Visa bill while he's at it. Of course, I would have to confess about that auction we went to the other week, the modern kind that sells everything from grotesque disco balls to state-of-the-art microwave ovens. How my arms had to be pinned down to stop me from bidding for a mini-television, a cappuccino maker and a pressure cooker, none of which we actually needed, needless to say.

As soon as the co-homeowner's back was turned, I splurged €20 on a set of knives that, as it turned out, couldn't cut butter. But the auctioneer, an irresistible combination of David Brent and Alfie Moon, had described them so well – "The butcher's choice ladies and gentlemen, these are quality items, I kid you not, unbeatable value etc etc..." – that I couldn't resist.

The upshot is that I've been reigned in. The ATM card confiscated. The Visa under lock and key. The nearest I get to retail therapy is browsing through colour cards, wondering if one pink wall and three white ones would work in the bedroom. And how badly said colours would clash with the disco ball.

Tick Tock, Drip Drop

Suddenly, all the girls I knew at school are pushing prams, decorating nurseries with fluffy white clouds or displaying their neat bumps with pride at ante-natal classes. For a while there everyone was busy getting married. Now they are all busy getting pregnant. Or thinking very hard about it anyway.

I bumped into Sally-Anne in town on Saturday afternoon. As though having a baby wasn't enough of an accomplishment, she had also managed to accessorize her outfit perfectly with two-month-old Jacob's babygro. He was dozing off, and she was off for a well-earned glass of wine. I watched her walk away, with a funny, squirming feeling in my stomach.

The squirming started up again when someone told me they bumped into Tanya coming out of Holles Street. She has a few days to go, but I didn't even know she was pregnant. There are some people you think you will never lose sight of. She was one of them. Now I don't even have her telephone number to call and say all the things I would like to say, to tell her how thrilled and excited I am for her. Of course I could find the number. But that's not the point. I should already have it.

I remember in our teens us talking about the baby issue. I was typically fuzzy while she spoke about how she would like to have children but only in her early thirties after she had travelled and sussed out what she wanted to do for a living. She did both and now she has a few days to go before another chapter begins. I always envied her that ability to follow through, to make things happen in sequence, the way they should.

I did things the wrong way around. I got married when everyone else was happy to have a boyfriend. I got divorced when everyone else was walking down the aisle. And now everyone is having babies, and my stomach squirms as though it's trying to tell me something that I'm sure I should already know.

If this squirming, wriggling feeling is actually the tick, tick, tick of the legendary biological timepiece, then I can't hear it over the biblical style floods that have raged in our house for a week. If it wasn't for the increasingly depressing plumbing situation – funny, none of that was mentioned in the estate agent's description of our house – I might have had time to think things through properly. Time to isolate exactly what it is that this mini-baby boom is making me feel. But I've spent most of the week waiting at home for plumbers who never come and wondering how so many water-related mechanisms can go so horribly wrong all at the same time.

The drains outside were blocked and spewing soapy water from the washing machine all through the yard. The water from the taps in the sink was refusing to go down the plughole. The pipes underneath the sink were either leaking or congested with a greasy substance peppered with ground coffee.

The toilet wouldn't flush. Water spilled from the bottom of the dishwasher. And the valves on the leaky radiators needed replacing.

Through all this we huddled on the battered green sofa as though it were a life raft and distracted ourselves with musings on the colour of the dining-room walls. Croquet it's called, chosen at the last minute because someone told us green was a good colour to eat in. We've got tins of pashmina for the bedroom walls but the decorating has been halted by the plumbing emergency to which we can see no end. I poured Drain Fairy down the sink only for it to trickle back out from under the kitchen cupboards. It's been that kind of day.

Through all this, I tried to imagine what it would be like to cope with such domestic disasters and look after a child at the same time. I tried to imagine it, but all I could see was chaos. On balance, having a baby is probably too hefty a life event to consider simply because that's what most of your peer group are currently occupied with. But I can understand how a person could start to feel left behind. How a person could start questioning herself, questioning himself closely on the very issues they always had a firm position on before. Do I want to have children? Do I even want to have one child? And if the answer doesn't flow out immediately, like so much water from a tap, a person might start to feel like there was something wrong.

Surely it couldn't be normal to feel so ambivalent about such an important issue. All of this goes through my head as I mop up the floor for the fortieth time, settling down on the sofa, waiting patiently for a plumber who never comes. Drip, drip, drip. Tick, tick, tick. I'm still waiting.

Mellow Yellow

It took ten months, but finally one room in the house is completely and utterly finished. It's called the Yellow Room on account of the pale buttery walls and the beautiful bunch of daffodils blooming on the windowsill. The carpet is the colour of porridge oats, and the lampshade is a cream, mirror-encrusted dangly number picked up in New Delhi, which, believe me, is a far more tasteful item than it sounds. The yellow room is a restful oasis in our dust bowl of a home. And I did none of it myself.

Thank goodness for DIY fairies. A brother with a paintbrush. A mother with an eye for just the right shade of mellow yellow. A carpet man (unrelated) who got in and out in a few hours. How many people does it take to put up a multi-tiered lampshade? One. And, that's right, it wasn't me.

Despite my lack of involvement in its creation, I spend most of my time in the Yellow Room. It was designed as a calm workspace, but I find myself doing everything here, simply because, at the moment, it's the most pleasant place to be.

I treat the room with all the reverence of a temple. Shoes, even white sequined slippers, are left outside. The Yellow Room is where I listen to the brilliant new Juliet Turner album on the stereo and Ray D'Arcy on my lovely new Roberts Radio.

There is hardly any furniture, which means you can prostrate yourself on plump cushions and relax properly. I am thinking of moving the lone wicker sofa somewhere else and making it totally furniture-free. It's where I come to practise the guitar, to write and to read. And it's where I light vanilla incense and sit down to meditate.

Ooops. I was wondering how long I could last without mentioning the M word. Since returning from India, I have been in serious danger of alienating friends and family with all this hippie spiritual talk. For example, I started off this column fully intending it to be an update on the still unfinished state of my house. There's a wheelbarrow in my sitting room, what's a girl to do, that kind of thing. Three paragraphs in, and somehow I've gone diverted to matters of the spirit again. I wouldn't mind, but people have started to talk.

Over an all-day-breakfast the other day in Sherie's, my local caff, the best male friend was sharing some personal stuff. So I rummaged around in my brand new bag of ancient wisdom and plucked out a few classic pieces of Eastern philosophical advice. Advice for which I genuinely thought he would be grateful.

He listened with a slightly pained expression for a while before he cracked. "Stop it at once," said he, waving a sausage around in an aggrieved manner. "It's like going to lunch with one of those desk calendars. Thanks and all," he said, "but I have one of those thought-for-the-day yokes at home, and no harm to you Mrs Ghandi Lama or whatever you are calling yourself this weather, but it makes more sense than you do."

I laughed so hard an old woman eating liver and onions nearly had an accident with her offal. But I got his point. I have become a bit evangelical. Forgotten the part where the Buddha says you should hold all things lightly. I've lost sight of the joy. I can't see the wisdom for the cheese, so to speak.

In desperation I rang the best female friend demanding she tell me something ludicrous about my life at the moment, something that even I couldn't interpret in a spiritual way.

"Well, there is the dressing gown," she said. "What dressing gown?" I asked. "That dressing gown," she replied with a smirk so wide I could hear it.

It turned out she was referring to the dressing gown the boyfriend was wearing in the Yellow Room when she came to visit the other day, the one he had wrapped around him like a monk's robe while we listened to a few soothing mantras on the CD. "What was wrong with it," I asked her. "Well if you don't know, then you really do need to lighten up," she said, cackling down the phone in an alarming manner.

I went up to the Yellow Room to investigate. And there it was. A forgotten Christmas present from the mother-in-law-to-may-be. Lying directly underneath the Indian lampshade, scrunched into a ball on the porridge oats carpet. It is furry and it is lilac. It has white polar bears on it. And snowflakes. And stars. The boyfriend has had the thing around him like a shawl while meditating for two weeks and he never even noticed how ridiculous he looked. And, perhaps more worryingly, neither did I.

So that's it. Normal service is to be resumed. No more talk of dharma or of karma, in public anyway. In private, he'll keep wearing the polar-bear dressing gown, and I won't laugh when he does. There has to be a spiritual message there somewhere.

Huffing and Puffing

There is a biting wind blowing through the house. It's the kind you can't keep out with a door snake. I look at the houses of friends. So solid. So secure. And I wonder. Does the same wind ever blow through their homes, and do they worry, like I sometimes do, that the wind will one day blow the house down?

I don't know how he puts up with me. He is either an angel come to save me from myself or a masochist in search of a permanent thrill. I look at friends and I wonder whether everything is really as perfect as it seems with their chocolate box relationships and, if it isn't, would they tell me, because I need to know. Maybe we can whisper it to each other, just very occasionally, and tell each other it's okay if sometimes things are not perfectly perfect. If sometimes it's awful. If sometimes we want to run away and hide and be on our own for ever, or at least until such time as that bloody wind dies down.

The last time I felt like this, the last time before now, we were down the country in the middle of nowhere. I had the map. We were driving to put a bet on the Grand National. I don't know where it came from, that chill wind, because the sun was shining down and if anyone had passed us they'd have thought all was right with the world. But suddenly I was red-faced and fuming and the map was flung out of the window. I watched it fluttering down a country lane, managing to smile at the thought of a map getting lost. "If we don't have a map, is it possible that we can still know where we are going?" I asked him this at the time, but he didn't reply because it was a silly question and anyway, he'd had enough of me for one day. When we got to a place where there were pubs and people we put a bet on. We lost. Still, we smiled and that night lit candles to set along the side of a bath. Calmly came another day.

I met a woman a few years ago who out of nowhere started telling me about her husband and the cosy house they had. At least, she had thought it was cosy at the time. I stood there, embarrassed, not wanting to know, but not wanting to hurt her feelings by telling her to stop. She told me everyone else knew a gale was blowing through her house, but that she, wrapped up warm and smug in a cloak of self-satisfaction, couldn't feel it. When the day came and he left and she learnt about the woman he was in love with, her cosy house came tumbling down around her. She shivered as she spoke. I think of her when the wind blows.

Is everything all right? Yes, fantastic, you say. But, of course, often it is not. You have been with the same person for 10 years, for 15 years, or even for 10 months, and you might be a bit bored. The way she cuts the crusts off her sandwiches could drive you demented. The way he doesn't answer when you ask him a question has you wrecked in the head. Sometimes you might want to shake her. Sometimes you might want to rage at him. And actually there is another girl who gives you butterflies in the stomach, the way that she used to. Sometimes you dream of running off to a place with white sands and no ties, but then you remember you have to go buy a pint of milk and something for the dinner. When someone asks if everything is all right, it's not very often you really tell the truth.

And maybe that kind of honesty is the way forward. A way to look with more realistic eyes at the structure of important bonds. I've been thinking about how these chilly times are just as important as the ones where we feel that warm glow in the pit of our stomachs. If we try, we might see that it all fits together somehow. I am trying. I am trying very hard.

Most of the time, trying feels worthwhile. Using love as a foundation, hoping for the best. But when the wind blows, it feels as though the house is being torn down brick by brick. You remember a story from the Bible and all you can do is pray that this house isn't built on sand. That's the kind of detail you won't find in any title deeds. There is a biting wind blowing through the house. Is there such a thing as a permanent draft excluder? And if it exists, do I want one? Yes. And no.

Green-Eyed Monster

My friend has just bought a house in Co. Wicklow and, hard as I try, it's proving impossible not to make comparisons with my own humble abode.

It's true that I opted for city living, a terraced palace within walking distance of work, but then no-one bothered to tell me it was possible to buy a house within my budget that boasted a back garden with an actual stream running through it. It goes without saying I am thrilled to bits for my friend. Thrilled, I tell you.

I wouldn't mind but my Status Anxiety had already reached crisis levels after another friend had a hot tub (a hot tub!) installed in her back yard. Now Mr Lord of the Manor has gone one better with a natural water feature that would have Diarmuid Gavin drawing up plans for gazebos and all sorts. Is it just me or is Diarmuid oddly fanciable in those television ads for recycling? Just me then. Oh well.

Anyway, my friend is planning to get decking installed down by the babbling brook. He is going to string fairy lights through the trees. I ooh and aaah and go home and glower at my L-shaped patch of back yard. It would take a lot more than a few fairy lights, I mutter accusingly at the concrete.

If his incredible back garden wasn't enough of a slap in the face to us poor Town Mice, his master bedroom boasts a skylight, a bed fashioned from reclaimed wood and an en suite bathroom with a corner bath/jacuzzi. His kitchen/dining room is of Nigella proportions and it is home to one of those massive American fridges often seen in the homes of rappers on MTV's *Cribs*. There is an island in the kitchen. An island! He has so much space in his new pad that he can afford to use one of the bedrooms as a home for all his Star Wars toys. I know it's only Wicklow but it feels like a galaxy far, far away.

If I am jealous, and let's face it I am a tad jealous, it's mainly because after just a few weeks his house already seems to contain everything that a fully-functioning home needs. I am talking about things like proper dining room chairs as opposed to family cast-offs prone to break under guests during dinner parties. I am talking about shelves, a whole wall of them, so that one's extensive book collection isn't collecting dust on the floor. I am talking about artworks and scented candles and sumptuous sofas you never want to get out of except to take another sip of mulled wine. Needless to say he makes excellent mulled wine at the drop of a clove and keeps his brandy in a minimalist decanter.

I am talking about tableware. He and his girlfriend invited us to dinner the other day and I couldn't help but notice the elegant china vegetable dishes with lids on which meant the carrots and savoy cabbage kept warm while we ate our delicious pork in apple and wholegrain mustard sauce. I didn't even know such serving dishes existed. We only just got a milk jug the other week and it felt like a major purchase, while he already has a huge steel drawer filled entirely with cooking implements. He has a compost bin. And he has tongs. And not just any old tongs.

I would be even more jealous if it wasn't for the fact that having first-hand experience of my green-eyed nature my friend has already made me a very generous offer that I would just like to set down in detail here just in case he tries to back out of it later on. Essentially, I have been elected Chief House Minder so that, whenever he goes on holidays or business trips, the boyfriend and I can high tail it down to the sticks and pretend we own the place for the duration. We can sit by the stream, we can open and close the big fridge, we can put stuff in the compost bin and generally act like proper adults and not like people who, a year and a half after moving in to our own house, are still sitting on beanbags. State-of-the-art beanbags imported from Germany, but beanbags nonetheless.

The basic message here is always make sure you have at least a few friends who live above your means and don't mind you commandeering their houses occasionally. I know another Wicklow-based couple with a sitting room so big it could fit a three-piece-suite and a pool table which, apart from their wonderfully good company, always made their home an attractive destination.

Displaying a worrying set of priorities they got rid of the pool table when they had their baby, but they still have what I consider to be the best bath in Ireland. Unlike my own bath, which has to be topped up with kettles of hot water and even then is too shallow to give any real pleasure. Theirs, meanwhile, is deep enough and long enough to ensure hours of bathing heaven. Even writing about their terrific tub makes me want to hop on the train and go down to see it. I mean them. Honest.

Away With the Fairies

There was a fairy on the top of the tree. She was like no fairy I'd ever seen. Her legs were long and dangly, her face was as round as a full moon. If Mary Quant had fashioned fairies, she'd have made one like her with a tight haircut, heavily made-up eyes and a rosebud mouth. On Christmas morning, that mouth would be smudged with chocolate and we used to laugh because we knew that when we were asleep she had flown down and eaten one of the chocolate Santa Clauses hanging from the tree. She left its foil wrapper dangling from a sparkly thread. Naughty fairy .

I don't know where she is now. She disappeared along with the cheap baubles and other trinkets we would unwrap each year from the decorations box. Sometimes the remains of a bauble would be found smashed into smithereens at the bottom. You wouldn't believe those lovely things had come from such dangerous looking dust.

We got our first proper Christmas tree this year. I bought it after much deliberation on Camden Street, struggled home with it in a taxi, screwed it onto the stand and put it in the corner. I was delighted to find pine needles all over the carpet even though they'd told me as a sales ploy it was non-shedding. But you can't have Christmas without moaning about having to hoover up pine needles afterwards. It wouldn't be right.

I thought for ages about our decorating theme. I didn't know whether to go for the minimalist look, white feathers maybe, or go all decadent with pink velvet bows all over the tree like the kind I saw in a magazine. But then suddenly as if by magic the tree was heaving. Candy canes. Crackers. Tinsel. Wooden figurines. Angels. Chocolate decorations. Love heart baubles. Two sets of different coloured lights.

I do feel a bit guilty about the lights. Apparently it's a big decorating faux pas not to use the same colours on your tree. But it was worth it when I turned them on. I know this time of year is supposed to be about children, but we can't be the only adults who lie down in the dark and watch the lights flickering on the Christmas tree. It is too perfect looking. I know I won't want to take it down.

I took a different approach with the hall. A friend gave me a huge bare branch from her garden on which I hung baubles and strung tiny white lights. I put bunches of holly underneath the branch so it looks like it is growing out of a bush. It's the kind of thing you might see in a magazine that features pink velvet bows on Christmas trees. I am ridiculously pleased with myself.

Christmas past. The Borzas from three doors down would come bearing gifts of freshly cooked fish and chips that they hadn't sold before closing time on Christmas Eve. A pillow case at the end of the bed waiting to be filled. Nine of us in paper hats around the table. Nobody allowed to start the present-opening ceremony until all the Christmas dinner washing up had been done. Our mother sitting by the tree ready to give out the presents with the youngest like a little elf on the floor beside her. Each present presented individually. To Peter, with love from Róisín. To Michael, Happy Christmas, love Eddie. You had to wait until one present was given and opened before the next one came around. It lasted until around 6 p.m. when there'd be teetering towers of turkey sandwiches and sneaky handfuls of smoked salmon which tasted much better back when it was only an annual event. Then board games and *Only Fools and Horses* and bedtime coming with the flat feeling that it was all over until next year.

Christmas present. I've finally stopped wanting everything to be the same as it used to be, which is something of a relief, not least for my mother. Our family house, with the front window decorated like something from a fairytale, is gone and now everybody has their own houses and is busy creating traditions that their own children will remember one day. Lobster bisque on Christmas Eve for some of us because we don't live near Borza's any more. Tennis on Christmas morning because one of us lives across the road from a court. The Forty Foot swim for those who are brave enough. Hot toddies on the shore for those of us who are not.

We got our first Christmas tree this year. We borrowed a beautiful fairy with a sparkly red dress and wings from a brother who is off to snowy Canada for Christmas. She is one of those designer fairies who doesn't even have a face, never mind a rosebud mouth in which you'd think butter wouldn't melt. And I must be cured of my Christmas nostalgia because I found I didn't mind that her lack of facial features meant she wouldn't be able to see the chocolate decorations, never mind eat them. I hung a few anyway half-wistful, half-hopeful, because you never know when Fairy Quant might come to call.

Snag Lists of Life

Messy jewellery box. Squeaking floorboards. Dents in plaster. Broken handbag. Don't mind me – I'm just making an irritation list. Grubby air vent. Out-of-shape tights. You see, I went to hear one of those motivational speakers the other night. Empty sock drawer. Wine stain on wall.

We sat rapt as he explained how to make an irritation list. "Here's the deal," he said. "You just go around your home or your office or your garden, or anywhere really, and make a list of things that are bothering you." Soot coming through chimney. Scratches on wooden floors. "And then you make a plan to reduce the list over the coming weeks. Ideally, you would eliminate two irritations a week." Desk like a bombsite. Books scattered on the floor. This may take some time.

I've started with the house. Marks of unknown origin on carpet. It seemed as good a place as any. Limited space to do yoga. On the plus side, we finally had sofas delivered this week. Two blue-leather sofas. Two items crossed off the irritation list. But even though we don't have to sit on beanbags anymore, they brought with them a whole new set of irritations. Worried blue leather is tacky. No coffee table in sitting room. No pictures on walls.

With the room looking more like a proper lounge area, we started to notice things that we didn't notice before. Spiderweb on ceiling that looks uncannily like old man's armpit hair. Fly caught in web. Spider. It's a bit of a nightmare.

I don't think I will ever finish this list. I mean, the bedrooms alone would take a few weeks. No wardrobes. No bookshelves. Broken mirror. Hot press has no handles. I haven't even gone near the bathroom yet. Manky shower curtain. Excess of miniature hotel shampoo bottles and sewing kits. Broken waterproof radio.

And don't get me started on the back yard. No fabulous decking. Unrendered walls. No herb garden. Or my CD collection. No complete box set of The Beatles. No complete box set of The Smiths. No complete box set of Gilbert O'Sullivan. Actually, scratch that last one. Just found it hiding behind my Burt Bacharach collection. Phew.

They say don't sweat the small stuff. But it's the small stuff that can grind you down. Then again, if it really bothered me that much, surely I'd do something about it. No photographs in albums. Or even pay someone else to do it. Make-up box in a state.

Brought to the ultimate extreme, this concept could mean you make a snag list of your entire life. Boyfriend who makes spreadsheets to keep track of social events and football matches. Also thinks Meatloaf and Status Quo at Slane represents the ultimate gig. Also whistles through teeth sometimes. Can't wear high heels properly. Me. Not him. He can wear heels a little too well. Add that to list.

Once you start this racket, it's hard to know when to stop. Blunt scissors. Fringe a mess because cut it myself. See scissors. You could just keep going forever, spending your life cataloguing your shortcomings. Younger sister has cooler clothes than me. Also hair. And the shortcomings of the world in general. Famine in Africa. Michael Jackson's nose. Where would it all end? Basically it wouldn't. Sombrero on clothes rail. Day-old sweet-and-sour stir-fry in wok. Dingy floor tiles. Moulting rug. Moulting poncho. Not enough storage. Not enough storage. Not enough storage.

I wonder how long it would take to make a list of things

that we are truly happy with. Sun shining through blinds on the first day of spring. Things we would never want to change. Holding hands late at night on Dún Laoghaire pier. Stuff you wouldn't cross off any list. Fifteen-year-old in Tintin jumper clicking his heels with joy like Gene Kelly in *Singin' In The Rain.* I wonder how long it would take to catalogue those parts of life you'd never want to eliminate. Mandela and Geldof saying Make Poverty History. A game of table tennis on O'Connell Street. A bit of homemade bread and freshly-pounded pesto. A bit of good news on the phone.

I'm supposed to hang my Irritation List on the wall and work at reducing the number of items on it. Washing up not done. Dinner not made. Debts not paid. But how is that going to work? For every three irritations I cross off, I'll have three more waiting in the wings. Suitcase from last week not unpacked. Sunglasses lost. Passport not found. So here's the deal. I've made a decision. I'm just putting one item on my irritation list. Irritation Lists. Now all I have to do is cross it off.

Chore Wars

It's imperative that life's endless chores are divided fairly. We all have distinct roles in a relationship. You make sure I never have to take out a bin and I'll make sure you never have to iron a shirt.

If the regime operates smoothly, both parties will be satisfied that the other is pulling their weight. If it doesn't, particularly in these double-income days, there will be rows. Doors may be slammed. Resentments may simmer.

At first glance, it may appear that the division of labour in our house is grossly inequitable. But only at first glance. Sure, he does the washing, the vacuuming, the cleaning, the bread baking, the squidgy-chocolate-double-cream-covered-cake making and most other household jobs. But then he is very good at them. And that counts for a lot.

I, meanwhile, am the cook. I draw the line at baking, but I prepare an excellent dinner most evenings and occasionally do hot breakfasts at weekends. I will, on request, also rustle up a variety of sandwiches; Parma ham, baby spinach and vine tomato is a particular speciality at the moment. I can even do clever things with the exotic-looking vegetables that are delivered to the door. Pot Noodle I don't.

The other chores in my remit are not as easy to define. They cannot be judged by running a finger along the top of the telly for dust. If being resident cook weren't taxing enough, I am also the social secretary of our relationship. The ents officer of our little union. There are a lot of hidden duties in this role. Vast amounts of networking and paperwork. Serious, time-consuming research. Scanning magazines and newspapers for pleasant outings and interesting diversions. Booking restaurants. Buying cinema tickets. It really is all go.

Lately, I'd been feeling a little taken advantage of in this department. During a spare second in my busy schedule, I began to get agitated about the imbalance. I couldn't remember the last time he had initiated a night or even an afternoon out. Obviously, I don't count the trip to the furniture megastore, which was totally his idea. And suggesting we go to the recycling centre together doesn't count either.

Although I have been known to at least attempt to work around the house, efficiently throwing the vacuum cleaner around the hall every so often, I realised that, except for a period when he was trying to impress me when we met five years ago, he has been happy to sit back and let me organise our social life.

The more I thought about it the more I was aggrieved. By the time he got home from work, and I laid a steaming plate of silky tricolour fusilli carbonara in front of him, I Wanted To Talk.

It started off gently enough, with me suggesting that perhaps once a month he could arrange a date for us. "It needn't cost any money," I told him. "We could go for a walk or a cycle or a game of snooker. I don't care," I told him, "as long as the suggestion comes from you."

It wasn't long before this sensible adult conversation turned into a full-blown row. I think this was because I wanted him to come up on the spot with ten potential activities, at least seven of which were so thoughtful that they illustrated the sincerity and depth of his feelings for me. In the event he said I was completely overreacting. It wasn't pretty.

A few days later – at my suggestion, naturally – we found

ourselves on a romantic walk in a lovely seaside setting. It was perfect. Lapping water. Pale moon. The masts of ships looking ghostly in the docks.

We walked for a while in comfortable silence, but – and this may, I am willing to concede, be something of a personality defect – I wanted more. I wanted comments about the stars. Comments about love. Sweet nothings in my ear to make me feel adored.

After a few minutes he said, "I'm tired; let's go home." I didn't go home. I went to a nightclub and drank vodka and cranberry juice and thought, this will show him.

It showed him nothing. The subject wasn't mentioned again. I went away for the weekend with my mother and forgot all about it. When I came home, it was to what looked like a new house. Almost every item of domestic annoyance I had put on my domestic Irritation List had been fixed.

There was a new shower curtain. A newly organised jewellery box. The clothes rails and chest of drawers that had been cluttering up the study had been moved to another room. There was a new space for yoga. There were a variety of recently purchased candles.

Forget sweet nothings, when I came home: there were sweet somethings almost everywhere you looked. Almost everywhere. When I checked I saw that our pet spider was still lurking daintily in a cobweb on the sitting-room ceiling. You can't have it all, I suppose, but sometimes it can feel as if you do.

Night Nurse

He is sick, and in the grips of a snuffling, rasping, hacking cough that should elicit sympathy, but merely manages to irritate beyond belief. He's the soldiering-on type. The ah-well-I'll-work-through-it-and-even-though-I-don't-rest-or-look-after-myself-hopefully-it-will-go-away type. The type who after a few weeks I begin to suspect is rasping, snuffling and hacking in a deliberate ploy to drive me mad.

When I look into his watery eyes, I don't feel pity. I feel like covering him in two duvets and chaining him – there is nothing kinky about it, believe me – to the bed.

Like many people, when I am sick I don't need to be persuaded to take up semi-permanent residence upstairs. The bed where I now sit writing becomes my castle. I call him for supplies from my mobile phone, even if he is only downstairs in the kitchen. I demand 24-hour Lemsip service and regular temperature checks. "Feel my forehead, isn't it hotter than it was half an hour ago? And do you think I might have pleurisy? And can you please Google it right now and check what the symptoms are? And how long I have to live?" It's what you do, with more or less drama, depending on your personality, when you are sick. But not this brave soldier.

Rather uncharitably, I suspected he was actually trying to make himself worse when I caught him walking on the stone tiles and wooden floors in our house with no shoes on, which is the one thing guaranteed to bring on a cold in me. When I tell him the folly of this action, he claims to have a different 'heating system' to me and says that he doesn't take in cold through his feet. I gently insist that he doesn't go to work. He snuffles and rasps and hacks, and takes one of those fizzy vitamin C drinks which he has decided are imbued with miraculous healing properties. I spy our sharpest knife glinting in the dishwasher he is emptying. I have to leave the room.

Then we have a day off. As usual, he is up at 7 a.m., rheumy eyes searching for something to do in the house. A surface to wipe. A cupboard to clear out. I am still in bed. I call him up for a chat. After a while, he plods upstairs and sits on the bed. There is something on his mind. It takes a while, but finally I extract the reason for his discontentment.

It turns out he is bitterly disappointed that despite his obvious and ongoing sickness, I have yet to suggest offering to fix him a vitamin C drink or a cup of Lemsip. I haven't brought him breakfast in bed. Or even once put a hand to his forehead. And I can't argue, because he is right. When I am sick and want attention, I am so vocal about it even the neighbours know the nature of my ailment. He, meanwhile, is the grin-and-bear-it-and-hope-someone-notices type. Unfortunately, the excruciating noise he has been making has blinded me to the fact that I should be doing my bit to help. He sighs a long sigh and makes a barely audible snuffle/hack/rasp combination.

In fairness to me, this is the exact point when I spring into action. Before you can say "I give him three days to live, Mrs Ingle", he is tucked up under two duvets, with instructions not to lift his head until woken by the slightest of hunger pains. I go downstairs and I do something I haven't done in what feels like years – I voluntarily engage with some housework.

Intermittently humming 'A Spoonful of Sugar' from *Mary Poppins* and 'A Woman's Work' from *Calamity Jane*,

I transform the house. More specifically, the laundry situation in our house. "It's just the day for the drying, so it is, indeed, isn't that right?" as the mother of the sick boy upstairs would say. In a few hours the clothes are billowing away on the line and every inch of every radiator is covered. It's amazing, given that I detest it so much, that I am actually exceptionally good at this housework lark.

After his washing is done, I turn my attention to his lunch. In minutes I have rustled up a light repast of poppy seed bread topped with melted sheep's cheese with just a hint of fresh basil and sun-blushed tomato. I mix his miraculous vitamin C drinks and I whip up a Lemsip. I carry it all upstairs and watch him eat, and discuss his symptoms in minute detail. I notice his cough is more a dry wheeze now, and wearing my nurse's hat I decide this is a very good sign.

The next morning, when he has got some colour back in his cheeks, we marvel at how far a little TLC can go. That's when I start to realise I am not in the full bloom of health myself. All that running in and out of the house with armfuls of washing may have taken its toll. Rasp, snuffle, hack. Dribble, sniffle, moan. I'd call him for assistance, but, feeling much better, he has skipped off to the driving range. He seems to have forgotten his mobile phone.

I'm an Open Book

A severe storage crisis meant that, for almost a year, my book collection was banished to the floor of the spare room. After a while, the books began to whisper to each other in that sniffy way books do when they feel neglected. A well-read Marian Keyes started to tease an as-yet-unread Leo Tolstoy. A volume of Sylvia Plath whinged about the Jackie Collins bonkbuster resting haphazardly on her spine.

As a much-loved Lewis Carroll exploded with laughter, a Roddy Doyle, a John Connolly and a Joseph O'Connor had a terse conversation about each other's success in the book charts. And, in the dustiest corner, a handful of soccer and snooker tomes bemoaned the lack of like-minded souls on the floor.

It was only when their whispering started to bother the neighbours that we gave in and ordered some built-in shelves. From a distance it all looked deeply impressive. Hundreds of books standing to attention as if waiting for that random moment when they would be plucked for reading once more. Tall and small, fat and thin, sombre and whimsical. I stood in front of them and felt an unexpected sense of achievement at what represented almost 30 years of reading life. Suddenly I was ten again, making a tent from my bed sheets and aiming a dim torch at the precious pages. Turning them slowly, silently, sleepily, swimming in another time and space.

The shelves meant my reading life was now an open book. From *When We Were Very Young* through *National Velvet* to *The Curious Incident of the Dog in the Night-time*, they were spread out for the first time in neat rows before me. When I reached out and touched them they felt more than familiar. They felt like friends.

Sadly, after they had been up on the shelves for a few weeks, I started to become a bit sniffy about them myself. The first negative emotion I experienced was disappointment that I didn't own half as many books as I thought I did. Before we stacked the books I confidently predicted the shelves couldn't possibly hold them all. I imagined there would still be little leaning towers of literature all over the floor, a testament to my book-loving ways. As it turned out, there was at least one empty shelf, which the proud owner of the soccer annuals quickly filled up with board games, ruining the learned library look I was going for.

The next crisis came when I started to look more closely at the books I had accumulated. Fair enough, the four – four! – Jeffrey Archer novels had nothing to do with me, but I couldn't work out how I ended up with quite so many books on self-improvement. This reality became even more depressing after a quick tally of all the things I should have been able to do had I only read them properly. These included but were not limited to: buying a used car, driving a used car, understanding men, understanding women, speaking Serbo-Croat, speaking Polish, destressing my life, decluttering my life, convincing someone to marry and not leave me, losing weight, gaining self-esteem, being an excellent lover and being an even more excellent housewife. Guidelines on the fabulous person I could have been almost filled a shelf.

Other people's books can tell a lot about a person. With my life in books so beautifully arranged, the question was what they said about me. If the busy self-help section wasn't bad enough, at least three of the most prominent shelves were packed with the kind of colourful paperbacks that litter the bedrooms of teenage girls. Should I throw them out and replace them? And with what? With books I have no intention of reading but would like people to think I had, of course. *War and Peace. Ulysses.* Those two should do the trick.

As I scanned the shelves I grew less exhilarated and more frustrated. Why did I have so many Agatha Christie thrillers? What possessed me to hand over money for the likes of Brendan O'Carroll's *The Mammy*? Naturally, there were many books I was proud to own, but I discovered there were far too many that brought out the literary snob in me. A snob that hadn't existed before we got the bookshelves made. A snob I didn't like.

Because, when I thought about it, there was a good reason why Adrian Mole, Brendan O'Carroll, *Silas Marner*, The Royle Family, Ruth Rendell, Agatha Christie, Ross O'Carroll-Kelly, Charlotte Brontë and Morag Prunty were all happily hanging out on the one shelf. A good reason why CS Lewis, Jackie Collins, Roald Dahl, Iain Banks, AA Milne and Noel Streatfield have been, at various times, among my very best book friends.

The books collected and stored over the years speak volumes about their owners. They are the diary we never got around to filling, the autobiography waiting to be written. We might wish all the books on our shelves had Booker-winning potential, but weeding out the ones that don't make us look good, the ones that make us cringe, is nothing short of book cheating. Because they are us, for better or worse, back when we swam in another time and space.

Ave Maria

I have a cleaner. I know, I know. There are only two adults in the house. And no children. How much mess is it possible for two people to make? But it's not about the mess, exactly; it's more a problem with the distribution of labour.

I don't do any, and, as a result, I suspected my boyfriend had been considering mutiny. I was under pressure to find a solution that didn't involve getting my hands dirty. A friend suggested throwing money at the problem. And now Maria comes to our house once a week.

Being a son of Iris, my bleach-obsessed mother-in-law-in-waiting, and John, my vacuuming-friendly father-in-law-in-waiting, it's no surprise that my boyfriend is more genetically disposed than I am to domestic duties. When I asked my mother to explain why I never developed natural housekeeping tendencies, she said I was too busy making mud pies in the back garden to pay attention when she was giving lessons in ironing, folding and hanging clothes.

The upshot is that the bulk – and by bulk I suppose I mean 100 per cent – of the labour in our house has always been done by my boyfriend. He didn't actually threaten to strike, but I could tell by the way he'd been clattering around the kitchen and wielding the vacuum cleaner aggressively that he'd had enough of this Cinderfella role.

The e-mail from my friend, who lives alone but has had someone cleaning his apartment for ages, was timely. His cleaner was looking for more clients; did we know anyone who would be interested? Did we what? A few days later, I arranged to meet Maria on Talbot Street – which, incidentally, is one of my favourite shopping areas in Dublin. You can buy things there that you could never have imagined. That day, for example, I bought a Turby Towel, which you put on your head after you've washed your hair. It's a godsend for people like me who can never quite get their towels to stay on their heads after a shower. It was a bargain, too, at only €1.95.

So after I'd bought something I didn't know I needed I met the cleaner I knew I needed but felt a bit embarrassed about. We chatted about our backgrounds for a while; then Maria, who is from Romania, asked whether I had children. It was the first hint that she was going to try to clean up more than one aspect of my life. "Is terrible," she said when she learned that I am childless. She looked me up and down with a look that clearly said: "And you so old."

Maria has limited English, so there were a few comfortable silences as we walked towards the bus stop. During one of them I thought it best to tell her that I wasn't sure I had all the equipment she might need to clean the house. She suggested we head for a supermarket. That's when Maria came into her own. I'd suggest that J Cloths might be good for, I don't know, dusting or something, and she'd tut-tut and swap them for what she insisted was a superior brand of cloth, which looked exactly the same to me. She'd also point knowingly at Cillit Bang while I'd wonder aloud if all those chemicals weren't a bit dangerous. Maria just looked at me pityingly and shoved it into the basket. I never knew cleaning required such a strange and multicoloured array of products. I'd spent our weekly karaoke budget already, and we hadn't even gone into the mop-and-bucket shop.

After buying a state-of-the art mop and bucket we got the bus to my house. Maria tackled the kitchen and bathroom with gusto while I got on with some work. By the time my boyfriend came home, she was still hard at it, and I could see he was feeling a little bit left out. "Do you think she'll do everything?" he sighed, the yearning in his voice suggesting Maria might be charitable and leave him with a room to vacuum or some crumbs to wipe. But Maria is so thorough that it looks as if he is going to have to find other ways to amuse himself in his spare time. I've taken to leaving brochures for massage courses around the house. I can only hope.

I didn't enjoy watching Maria work, but part of me felt I might learn something. I certainly did. Cleaning a kitchen means wiping tiles and taking everything out of the fridge and the cupboards. Dust, contrary to what I have always believed, is the same as dirt and needs to be removed. From everything. Unfortunately, I could only watch for a little while, as we had a soiree to attend. Feeling pleased with myself in some new gear, I passed Maria in the hall. "Not like that," she said, appalled. "You are not going to a party like that." It took me ten minutes to convince her that my dress was meant to be creased. She was still shaking her head in dismay when I waltzed out of the door. I have a feeling she's going to be very good for me.

Acknowledgements

Several years ago journalist Peter Murtagh gave me a break when I was on work experience and he was editor of *The Sunday Tribune*. I am still extremely grateful for that early opportunity. Thanks are also due to ace photographer Kim Haughton who got me the work experience in the first place. Cheers, Kimbo!

I value the support of all those who work with me in *The Irish Times*, especially everyone on the *Magazine* – those clever people who correct my mistakes and are responsible for the titles of the columns. I thank, in particular, Shane Hegarty who phoned me up and asked me to do the first bunch of columns, and Patsey Murphy, editor of the *Magazine*, for constant encouragement and lots of laughs.

To my brothers and sisters and their significant others: Sarah Ingle and Willo Roe, Eddie Ingle and Katy O'Kennedy, Brian Ingle, Rachael Ingle and Paul Burgess, Peter Ingle and Aoife Walsh, Michael Ingle and my very patient yoga teacher, Rukhsana Kauser. I am grateful to all my family for their friendship and support, especially Rach and Bri.

Honorary family mention goes to our youngest sibling, the stunning and stylish Karaoke Queen Katie 'Howdya like me now?' Ingle for her constant constructive criticism, hip urban lingo and fashion advice. Thanks for everything, Katie.

And to the Ingles: the next generation. Love to Fionn, Bláithín, Mella and Rossa Ruadh who have provided plenty of inspiration and fun over the years. Love to Peter and Niel Ingle, the always entertaining Winston Salem posse. Love and kisses to my fairy godchild Hannah 'Hollywood Baby' Burgess and her little sister Emma. Kisses to the latest little Ingle whose name was not available as this book was going to print.

To my other family, the Hobson clan of Portadown, Co. Armagh, especially Stefan, Ethan, Nanny Sarah and my lovely, if bleach-obsessed, mother-in-law-in-waiting Iris Hobson. I know I'm not the daughter-in-law of your dreams but thanks for always making me so welcome.

To Roddy O'Sullivan and Ali Power – thanks for friendship and sound advice. Love to old friends Tanya Lalor and Martina Griffith. When are we meeting up, Ritas? Thanks to Marie-Therese, for the good-times and the mad-times – especially the mad times.

Respect to all the founding members of the yet to be inaugurated and in some ways mythical Noodle Writers Club: Yummy Mummy, Questions and Answers Babe and Portu Gal. To Quentin Fottrell (and Jewel!) for help with the name of this book. To Fionnuala McCarthy, who has come a long way, baby. And to Mladen Popovic for all the happy memories, because I know we both have so many of those.

To Faith O'Grady from the Lisa Richards Agency – thanks for helping out this slow learner. And to Hodder Headline Ireland: Ciara Considine, my editor – thanks for getting me to dig deeper at exactly the right time – Breda Purdue and Ciara Doorley.

Hey to Emma 'Cute as a Button' Barnett in Noa Noa for lunchtime laughs and some really cool stylings. And thanks to the management and staff of Dublin restaurants Sherie's and Ukiyo for offering both the best breakfast in town and a discreet singing space for past-it popstrels.

I thank the folk at accommodation finders Adams and Butler who got me a beautiful place to stay when I badly needed a retreat. I also sincerely thank Ray Carroll of the K Club in Co Kildare – a true gentleman.

Brian Nolan at Detail design studio in Dublin took some much appreciated snaps of my bag and slippers which found their way onto the book cover, thanks Bean! Thanks to Anú Design for creating the great cover. I'd like also to thank Kim and Mark simply for being fabulous. And Jaya and Christopher from Open Dharma for their words of wisdom in India and France. Namaste. Thanks and love to the Borza family, Miss Roddy and Sr Agnes for making Sandymount a great place in which to grow up.

Amanda 'Such a Nice Lady' Brady is not only a great friend but she's a rare talent and her wonderful illustrations can be seen throughout this book. Thanks for the magic, love you, Mand. Paul 'Livin' Each Day as if it's His Last' Howard, is another person I am lucky to call my friend. His innate goodness and huge heart are a joy to be around even if he is infuriatingly talented. Love you, Paul.

Ann Ingle deserves a paragraph on her own but I won't make her proofread it like she did the rest of this book. Many thanks are due to her for all those hours of painstaking work. The best oracle anyone could ever have, the person who knows what I am thinking before I think it myself, I am proud to call her my friend as well as my mother. I can never thank her enough for everything she has done, not just for me, but for all the family. Like the great man said, "Sometimes you can't make it on your own." Never mind a paragraph, she should have her own book. Now you just have to write it, Ann.

And finally to my gorgeous Domestic God, walking partner, Sudoko rival and personal baker St Jonny Hobson of Portadown. I don't know how you put up with it all but please never stop. I love you the most. Kisses and prostrations, Ró. xxx